PRINCIPAL WASHINGTON IN HIS PRIVATE OFFICE, TUSKEGEE INSTITUTE.

Booker T. Washington's

Own Story of His Life and Work

Including an Authoritative Sixty-four page Supplement

BY

ALBON L. HOLSEY
Member of Executive Staff Tuskegee Institute

The Original Autobiography brought up to date with a complete account of Dr. Washington's sickness and death. Containing the only photos of the funeral and burial

**Fredonia Books
Amsterdam, The Netherlands**

Booker T. Washington's Own Story of his Life and Work

by
Booker T. Washington

ISBN: 1-4101-0799-X

Copyright © 2005 by Fredonia Books

Reprinted from the 1901 edition

Fredonia Books
Amsterdam, The Netherlands
http://www.fredoniabooks.com

All rights reserved, including the right to reproduce this book, or portions thereof, in any form.

In order to make original editions of historical works available to scholars at an economical price, this facsimile of the original edition of 1901 is reproduced from the best available copy and has been digitally enhanced to improve legibility, but the text remains unaltered to retain historical authenticity.

INTRODUCTION.

I HAVE cheerfully consented to prefix a few words introductory to this autobiography. While I have encouraged its publication, not a sentence has been submitted to my examination. From my intimate acquaintance with the subject, because of my connection with the Peabody and the Slater Education Funds, I am sure the volume has such a strong claim upon the people that no commendation is needed.

The life of Booker T. Washington cannot be written. Incidents of birth, parentage, schooling, early struggles, later triumphs, may be detailed with accuracy, but the life has been so incorporated, transfused, into such a multitude of other lives,—broadening views, exalting ideals, molding character,—that no human being can know its deep and beneficent influence, and no pen can describe it. Few living Americans have made a deeper impression on public opinion, softened or removed so many prejudices, or awakened greater hopefulness in relation to the solution of a problem, encompassed with a thousand difficulties and perplexing the minds of philanthropists and statesmen. His personality is unique, his work has been exceptional, his circle of friendships has constantly widened; his race, through his utterances and labors, has felt an upward tendency, and he himself has been an example of what worth and energy can accomplish and a stimulus to every one of both races, aspiring to a better life and to doing good for others.

It has been said with truth that the race problem requires the patient and wise co-operation of the North and the South, of the white people and the Negroes. It is encouraging to see how one true, wise, prudent, courageous man can contribute far more than many men to the comprehension and settlement of questions which perplex the highest capabilities. Great eras have often revolved around an individual; and, so, in this country, it is singular that, contrary to what pessimists have predicted, a colored man, born a slave, freed by the results of the War, is accomplishing so much toward thorough pacification and good citizenship.

While Mr. Washington has achieved wonders, in his own recognition as a leader and by his thoughtful addresses, his largest work has been the founding and the building up of the Normal and Industrial Institute, at Tuskegee, Alabama. That institution illustrates what can be accomplished under the supervision, control, and teaching of the colored people, and it stands conspicuous for industrial training, for intelligent, productive labor, for increased usefulness in agriculture and mechanics, for self-respect and self-support, and for the purification of home-life. A late Circular of the Trustees of Hampton Institute makes the startling statement that "six millions of our Negroes are now living in one-room cabins." Under such conditions morality and progress are impossible. If the estimate be approximately correct, it enforces the wisdom of Mr. Washington in his earnest crusade against "the one-room cabin", and is an honorable tribute to the revolution wrought through his students in the communities where they have settled. Every student at Tuskegee, in the proportion of the impression produced by the Principal, becomes a better husband, a better wife, a better citizen, a better man or woman. A series of useful books on the "Great Educators" has been published in England and the United States. While Washington cannot, in learning and philosophy, be ranked with Herbart, Pestalozzi, Froebel, Hopkins, Wayland, Harris, he may be truly classed among those who have wrought grandest results on mind and character.

J. L. M. CURRY.

WASHINGTON, D. C.

CONTENTS.

CHAPTER.		PAGE.
I.	BIRTH AND EARLY CHILDHOOD	13
II.	BOYHOOD IN WEST VIRGINIA	23
III.	LIFE AT HAMPTON INSTITUTE	35
IV.	HOW THE FIRST SIX YEARS AFTER GRADUATION FROM HAMPTON WERE SPENT	43
V.	THE BEGINNING OF THE WORK AT TUSKEGEE	53
VI.	THE FIRST YEAR AT TUSKEGEE	59
VII.	THE STRUGGLES AND SUCCESS OF THE WORKERS AT TUSKEGEE FROM 1882 TO 1884	67
VIII.	THE HISTORY OF TUSKEGEE FROM 1884 TO 1894	88
IX.	INVITED TO DELIVER LECTURE AT FISK UNIVERSITY	113
X.	THE SPEECH AT THE OPENING OF THE COTTON STATES' EXPOSITION	125
XI.	AN APPEAL FOR JUSTICE	159
XII.	HONORED BY HARVARD UNIVERSITY	175
XIII.	URGED FOR A CABINET POSITION	193
XIV.	THE SHAW MONUMENT SPEECH, THE VISIT OF SECRETARY JAMES WILSON, AND THE LETTER TO THE LOUISIANA CONVENTION	201

CONTENTS.

CHAPTER.		PAGE.
XV.	CUBAN EDUCATION AND THE CHICAGO PEACE JUBILEE ADDRESS	222
XVI.	THE VISIT OF PRESIDENT WILLIAM MCKINLEY TO TUSKEGEE	239
XVII.	THE TUSKEGEE NEGRO CONFERENCE	255
XVIII.	A VACATION IN EUROPE	271
XIX.	THE WEST VIRGINIA AND OTHER RECEPTIONS AFTER EUROPEAN TRIP	292
XX.	NATIONAL NEGRO BUSINESS LEAGUE	309
XXI.	THE MOVEMENT FOR A PERMANENT ENDOWMENT	335
XXII.	A DESCRIPTION OF THE WORK OF THE TUSKEGEE INSTITUTE	349
XXIII.	LOOKING BACKWARD	369

SUPPLEMENT.

XXIV.	PRINCE HENRY MEETS BOOKER T. WASHINGTON	392
XXV.	GLIMPSES FORWARD AND BACKWARD	395
XXVI.	AN APPEALING PERSONALITY DR. WASHINGTON'S STRONGEST ASSET	400
XXVII.	STATE EDUCATIONAL TOURS	407
XXVIII.	RURAL EXTENSION WORK	410
XXIX.	THE FIFTEENTH ANNIVERSARY OF THE NATIONAL NEGRO BUSINESS LEAGUE	418
XXX.	NATIONAL NEGRO HEALTH WEEK	427
XXXI.	LAST SPEAKING ENGAGEMENTS	432
XXXII.	SICKNESS AND DEATH	445
XXXIII.	THE FUNERAL	454
XXXIV.	THE TUSKEGEE ORGANIZATION AND THE TUSKEGEE SPIRIT	460

Booker T. Washington's
Own Story of His Life and Work

CHAPTER I.

BIRTH AND EARLY CHILDHOOD.

Many requests have been made of me to write something of the story of my life. Until recently I have never given much consideration to these requests, for the reason that I have never thought that I had done enough in the world to warrant anything in the way of an autobiography; and I hope that my life work, by reason of my present age, lies more in the future than in the past. My daughter, Portia, said to me, not long ago: "Papa, do you know that you have never told me much about your early life, and your children want to know more about you." Then it came upon me as never before that I ought to put something about my life in writing for the sake of my family, if for no other reason.

I will not trouble those who read these lines with any lengthy historical research concerning my ancestry, for I know nothing of my ancestry beyond my mother. My mother was a slave on a plantation near Hale's Ford, in Franklin County,

---

I am indebted to and beg to thank Mr. E. Webber for valuable assistance rendered in connection with the preparation of this publication. BOOKER T. WASHINGTON.

Virginia, and she was, as I now remember it, the cook for her owners as well as for a large part of the slaves on the plantation. The first time that I got a knowledge of the fact that my mother and I were slaves, was by being awakened by my mother early one morning, while sleeping in a bed of rags, on the clay floor of our little cabin. She was kneeling over me, fervently praying as was her custom to do, that some day she and her children might be free. The name of my mother was Jane. She, to me, will always remain the noblest embodiment of womanhood with which I have come in contact. She was wholly ignorant, as far as books were concerned, and, I presume, never had a book in her hands for two minutes at a time. But the lessons in virtue and thrift which she instilled into me during the short period of my life that she lived will never leave me. Some people blame the Negro for not being more honest, as judged by the Anglo-Saxon's standard of honesty; but I can recall many times when, after all was dark and still, in the late hours of the night, when her children had been without sufficient food during the day, my mother would awaken us, and we would find that she had gotten from somewhere something in the way of eggs or chickens and cooked the food during the night for us. These eggs and chickens were gotten without my master's permission or knowledge. Perhaps, by some code of ethics, this would be classed as stealing, but deep down in my heart I can never decide that my mother, under such circumstances, was guilty of theft. Had she acted thus as a free woman she would have been a thief, but not so, in my opinion, as a slave. After our freedom no one was stricter than my mother in teaching and observing the highest rules of integrity.

Who my father was, or is, I have never been able to learn with any degree of certainty. I only know that he was a white man.

As nearly as I can get at the facts, I was born in the year 1858 or 1859. At the time I came into the world no careful registry of births of people of my complexion was kept. My birth place was near Hale's Ford, in Franklin County, Virginia. It was about as near to Nowhere as any locality gets to be, so far as I can learn. Hale's Ford, I think, was a town with one house and a post-office, and my birth place was on a large plantation several miles distant from it.

I remember very distinctly the appearance of the cabin in which I was born and lived until freedom came. It was a small log cabin about 12x16 feet, and without windows. There was no floor, except one of dirt. There was a large opening in the center of the floor, where sweet potatoes were kept for my master's family during the winter. In this cabin my mother did the cooking, the greater part of the time, for my master's family. Our bed, or "pallet," as we called it, was made every night on the dirt floor. Our bed clothing consisted of a few rags gathered here and there.

One thing I remember more vividly than any other in connection with the days when I was a slave was my dress, or, rather, my lack of dress.

The years when the war* was in progress between the States were especially trying to the slaves, so far as clothing was concerned. The Southern white people found it extremely hard to get clothing for themselves during that war, and, of course, the slaves underwent no little suffering in this respect. The only garment that I remember receiving from my owners during the war was a "tow shirt." When I did not wear this shirt I was positively without any garment. In Virginia, the tow shirt was quite an institution during slavery. This shirt was made of the refuse flax that grew in that part of Virginia, and it was a veritable instrument of torture. It was stiff and coarse. Until it had been worn for about six weeks it made one feel as if a thousand needle points were pricking his flesh. I suppose I was about six years old when I was given one of these shirts to wear. After repeated trials the

---
*The War of the Rebellion, 1860-65.

MRS. BOOKER T. WASHINGTON.

BOOKER T. WASHINGTON I, II AND III.

torture was more than my childish flesh could endure and I gave it up in despair. To this day the sight of a new shirt revives the recollection of the tortures of my first new shirt. In the midst of my despair, in connection with this garment, my brother John, who was about two years older than I, did me a kindness which I shall never forget. He volunteered to wear my new shirt for me until it was "broken in." After he had worn it for several weeks I ventured to wear it myself, but not without pain.

Soon after my shirt experience, when the winter had grown quite cold, I received my first pair of shoes. These shoes had wooden bottoms, and the tops consisted of a coarse kind of leather. I have never felt so proud since of a pair of shoes.

As soon as I was old enough I performed what, to me, was important service, in holding the horses, and riding behind the white women of the household on their long horseback rides, which were very common in those days. At one time, while holding the horses and assisting quite a party of visiting ladies to mount their horses, I remember that, just before the visitors rode away, a tempting plate of ginger cakes was brought out and handed around to the visitors. This, I think, was the first time that I had ever seen any ginger cakes, and a very deep impression was made upon my childish mind. I remember I said to myself that if I ever could get to the point where I could eat ginger cakes as I saw those ladies eating them, the height of my ambition would be reached.

When I grew to be still larger and stronger the duty of going to the mill was intrusted to me; that is, a large sack containing three or four bushels of corn was thrown across the back of a horse and I would ride away to the mill, which was often three or four miles distant, wait at the mill until the corn was turned into meal, and then bring it home. More than once, while performing this service, the corn or meal got unevenly balanced on the back of the horse and fell off into the road, carrying me with it. This left me in a very awkward and unfortunate position. I, of course, was unable, with my small strength, to lift the corn or meal upon the horse's back, and therefore would have to wait, often for hours, until someone happened to be passing along the road strong enough to replace the burden for me.

My owner's name was Jones Burroughs, and I am quite sure he was above the average in the treatment of his slaves. That is, except in a few cases, they were not cruelly whipped. Although I was born a slave, I was too young to experience much of its hardships. The thing in connection with slavery that has left the deepest impression on me was the instance of seeing a grown man, my uncle, tied to a tree early one morning, stripped naked, and someone whipping him with a cowhide. As each blow touched his back the cry, "Pray, master! Pray, master!" came from his lips, and made an impression upon my boyish heart that I shall carry with me to my grave.

When I was still quite a child, I could hear the slaves in our "quarters" whispering in subdued tones that something unusual—the war—was about to take place, and that it meant their freedom. These whispered conferences continued, especially at night, until the war actually began.

While there was not a single slave on our plantation that could read a line, in some way we were kept informed of the progress of the war almost as accurately as the most intelligent person. The "grapevine" telegraph was in constant use. When Lee surrendered, all of the plantation people knew it, although all of them acted as if they were in ignorance of the fact that anything unusual had taken place.

Early one morning, just after the close of the war, word was sent around to the slave cabins that all the slaves must go to the "big house," the master's house; and in company with my mother and a large number of other slaves, including my sister Amanda and brother John, I went to the "big house," and stood by the side of my mother, and listened to the reading of some papers and a little speech made by the man who read the papers. This was the first public address I had ever heard, and I need not add that it was the most effective one to which it had ever been my privilege to listen. After the reading of the paper, and the speech, my mother leaned over and whispered, "Now, my children, we are free." This act was hailed with joy by all the slaves, but it threw a tremendous responsibility upon my mother, as well as upon the other slaves. A large portion of the former slaves hired themselves to their owners, while others sought new employment; but, before the beginning of the new life, most of the ex-slaves left the plantation for a few days at least, so as to get the "hang" of the new life, and to be sure that they were free. My mother's husband, my stepfather, had in some way wandered into West Virginia during the war, and had secured employment in the salt furnace near Malden, in Kanawha county. Soon after freedom was declared he sought out my mother and sent a wagon to bring her and her children to West Virginia. After many days of slow, tiresome traveling over the mountains, during which we suffered much, we finally reached Malden, and my mother and her husband were united after a long enforced separation.

The trip from Franklin county to Malden,

West Virginia, was the first one that had taken me out of the county where I was born, and, of course, it was quite an event, especially to the children of the family, although the parting from the old homestead was to my mother a very serious affair. All of our household and other goods were packed into a small wagon drawn by two horses or mules. I cannot recall how many days it took us to make this trip, but it seems to me, as I recall it now, that we were at least ten days. Of course we had to sleep in the wagon, or what was more often true, on the ground. The children walked a great portion of the distance.

One night we camped near an abandoned log cabin, and my mother decided that, instead of cooking our frugal meal in the open air, as she had been accustomed to do on the trip, she would build a fire in this cabin and we should both cook and sleep in it during the night. When we had gotten the fire well started, to the consternation of all of us, a large and frightful looking snake came down the chimney. This, of course, did away with all idea of our sheltering ourselves in the cabin for the night, and we slept out in the open air, as we had done on previous occasions.

Since I have grown to manhood it has been my privilege to pass over much of the same road traveled on this first trip to West Virginia, but my recent journeys have been made in well-appointed steam cars. At the time I first traveled through that part of Virginia and West Virginia there was no railroad, and if there had been we did not have the money to pay our fare.

At the close of the war our family consisted of my mother, step-father, my brother John and sister Amanda. My brother John is director of the mechanical department of the Tuskegee Institute, and my sister, now Mrs. Amanda Johnson, lives in Malden, West Virginia. Soon after we moved to West Virginia my mother took into our family, notwithstanding our own poverty, a young orphan boy who has always remained a part of our family. We gave him the name of James B. Washington. He, now grown to manhood, holds an important position at the Tuskegee Institute.

While I have not had the privilege of returning to the old homestead in Franklin county, Virginia, since I left there as a child immediately after the war, I have kept up more or less correspondence with members of the Burroughs family, and they seem to take the deepest interest in the progress of our work at Tuskegee.

CHAPTER II.

BOYHOOD IN WEST VIRGINIA.

We began life in West Virginia in a little shanty, and lived in it for several years. My step-father soon obtained work for my brother John and myself in the salt furnaces and coal mines, and we worked alternately in them until about the year 1871. Soon after we reached West Virginia a school teacher, Mr. William Davis, came into the community, and the colored people induced him to open a school. My step-father was not able to spare me from work, so that I could attend this school, when it was first opened, and this proved a sore disappointment to me. I remember that soon after going to Malden, West Virginia, I saw a young colored man among a large number of colored people, reading a newspaper, and this fired my ambition to learn to read as nothing had done before. I said to myself, if I could ever reach the point where I could read as this man was doing, the acme of my ambition would be reached. Although I could not attend the school, I remember that, in some way, my mother secured a book for me, and although she could not read herself, she tried in every way possible to help me to do so.

Every barrel of salt that was packed in the

mines was marked, and by watching the letters that were put on the salt barrels I soon learned to read. As time went on, after considerable persuasion on my part, my step-father consented to permit me to attend the public school half of the day, provided I would get up very early in the morning and perform as much work as possible before school time. This permission brought me great joy. By four o'clock in the morning I was up and at my work, which continued until nearly nine o'clock. The first day I entered school, it seems to me, was the happiest day that I have ever known. The first embarrassment I experienced at school was in the matter of finding a name for myself. I had always been called "Booker," and had not known that one had use for more than one name. Some of the slaves took the surnames of their owners, but after freedom there was a prejudice against doing this, and a large part of the colored people gave themselves new names. When the teacher called the roll, I noticed that he called each pupil by two names, that is a given name and a surname. When he came to me he asked for my full name, and I told him to put me down as "Booker Washington," and that name I have borne ever since. It is not every school boy who has the privilege of choosing his own name. In introducing me to an audience in Essex Hall, London, during my visit to Europe, in the summer of 1899, Honorable Joseph H. Choate, the American Ambassador, said that I was one of the few Americans that had had the opportunity of choosing his own name, and in exercising the rare privilege I had very naturally chosen the best name there was in the list.

My step-father seemed to be over careful that I should continue my work in the salt furnace until nine o'clock each day. This practice made me late at school, and often caused me to miss my lessons. To overcome this I resorted to a practice of which I am not now very proud, and it is one of the few things I did as a child of which I am now ashamed. There was a large clock in the salt furnace that kept the time for hundreds of workmen connected with the salt furnace and coal mine. But, as I found myself continually late at school, and after missing some of my lessons, I yielded to the temptation to move forward the hands on the dial of the clock so as to give enough time to permit me to get to school in time. This went on for several days, until the manager found the time so unreliable that the clock was locked up in a case.

It was in Malden that I first found out what a Sunday school meant. I remember that I was playing marbles one Sunday morning in the road with a number of other boys, and an old colored man passed by on his way to Sunday school. He spoke a little harshly to us about playing marbles on Sunday, and asked why we did not go to Sunday school. He explained in a few broken though plain words what a Sunday school meant and what benefit we would get from it by going. His words impressed me so that I put away my marbles and followed him to Sunday school, and thereafter was in regular attendance. I remember that, some years afterwards, I became one of the teachers in this Sunday school and finally became its superintendent.

No matter how dark the days or how discouraging the circumstances, there was never a time in my youth when the firm resolution to secure an education, at any cost, did not constantly remain with me. Next came the unpleasant coal mine experience.

My step-father was not able, however, to permit me to continue in school long, even for a half day at the time. I was soon taken out of school and put to work in the coal mine. As a child I recall now the fright which, going a long distance under the mountain into a dark and damp coal mine, gave me. It seemed to me that the distance from the opening of the mine to the place where I had to work was at least a mile and a half. Although I had to leave school I did not give up my search for knowledge. I took my book into the coal mine, and during the spare minutes I tried to read by the light of the little lamp which hung on my cap. Not long after I began to work in the mines my mother hired some one to teach me at night, but often, after walking a considerable distance for a night's lesson, I found that my teacher knew but little more than I did. This, however, was not the case with Mr. William Davis, my first teacher.

After working in the coal mine for some time, my mother secured a position for me as house boy in the family of General Lewis Ruffner. I went to live with this family with a good many fears and doubts. General Ruffner's wife, Mrs. Viola Ruffner, had the reputation of being very strict and hard to please, and most of the boys who had been employed by her had remained only a short time with her. After remaining with Mrs. Ruffner a while, I grew weary of her exact manner of having things done, and, without giving her any notice, I ran away and hired myself to a steamboat captain who was plying a boat between Malden and Cincinnati. Mrs. Ruffner was a New England woman, with all the New England ideas about order, cleanliness and truth. The boat captain hired me as a waiter, but before the boat had proceeded many miles towards Cincinnati he found that I knew too little about waiting on the table to be of any service, so he discharged me before I had been on his boat for many hours.

In some way, however, I persuaded him to take me to Cincinnati and return me to Malden. As soon as I returned home, I returned to Mrs. Ruffner, acknowledged my sins, and secured my old position again. After I had lived with Mrs. Ruffner for a while she permitted me to attend school for a few hours in the afternoons during three months, on the condition that I should work faithfully during the forenoon. She paid me, or rather my step-father, six dollars per month and board for my work. When I could not get the opportunity to attend school in the afternoon I resorted to my old habit of having some one teach me at night, although I had to walk a good distance after my work was done in order to do this.

While living with Mrs. Ruffner I got some very valuable experience in another direction, that of marketing and selling vegetables. Mrs. Ruffner was very fond of raising grapes and vegetables, and, although I was quite a boy, she entrusted me with the responsibility of selling a large portion of these products. I became very fond of this work. I remember that I used to go to the houses of the miners and prevail upon them to buy these things. I think at first Mrs. Ruffner doubted whether or not I would be honest in these transactions, but as time went on and she found the cash from these sales constantly increasing, her confidence grew in me, and before I left her service she willingly trusted me with anything in her possession. I always made it a special point to return to her at the end of each campaign as a salesman every cent that I had received and to let her see how many vegetables or how much fruit was brought back unsold.

At one time I remember that, when I passed by an acquaintance of mine when I had a large basket of peaches for sale, he took the liberty of walking up to me and taking one of the ripest and most tempting peaches. Although he was a man and I was but a boy, I gave him to understand in the most forceful manner that I would not permit it. He seemed greatly surprised that I would not let him take one peach. He tried to explain to me that no one would miss it and that I would be none the worse off for his taking it. When he could not bring me to his way of thinking he tried to frighten me by force into yielding, but I had my way, and I am sure that this man respected me all the more for being honest with other people's property. I told him that if the peaches were mine I would gladly let him have one; but under no circumstances could I consent to let him take without a protest that which was entrusted to me by others. It happened very often that as I would pass through the streets with a large basket of grapes or other fruit, many of the larger boys tried by begging and then by force to dispossess me of a portion of what had been given me to sell, but I think there was no instance when I yielded. From my earliest childhood I have always had it implanted in me that it never pays to be dishonest, and that reward, at some time, in some manner, for the performance of conscientious duty, will always come, and in this I have never been disappointed.

I wish to add here that there are few instances of a member of my race betraying a specific trust. One of the best illustrations of this which I know of, is in the case of an ex-slave from Virginia, whom I met not long ago in a little town in the state of Ohio. I found that this man had made a contract with his master, two or three years previous to the Emancipation Proclamation, to the effect that the slave was to buy himself, by paying so much per year for his body; and while he was paying for himself, he was to be permitted to labor where and for whom he pleased. Finding that he could secure better wages in Ohio, he went there. When freedom came, he was still in debt to his master some three hundred dollars. Notwithstanding that the Emancipation Proclamation freed him from any obligation to his master, this black man walked the greater portion of the distance back to where his old master lived in Virginia, and placed the last dollar, with interest, in his hands. In talking to me about this, the man told me that he knew he did not have to pay the debt, but he had given his word to his master, and his word he had never broken. He felt that he could not enjoy his freedom till he had fulfilled his promise.

In all, I must have spent about four years in the employ of Mrs. Ruffner, and I here repeat what I have said more than once, that aside from the training I got at the Hampton Institute under General Armstrong, Mrs. Ruffner gave me the most valuable part of my education. Her habit of requiring everything about her to be clean, neat and orderly, gave me an education in these respects that has been most valuable to me in the work that I have since tried to accomplish. At first I thought that her idea of strict honesty and punctuality in everything meant unkindness, but I soon learned to understand her and she to understand me, and she has from the first time that I knew her until this day proven one of the best friends I ever possessed.

One day, while I was at work in the coal mine, I heard some men talking about a school in Virginia, where they said that black boys and girls were permitted to enter, and where poor students were given an opportunity of working for their board, if they had not money with which to pay for it. As soon as I heard of this institution, I made up my mind to go there. After I had lived with Mrs. Ruffner about four years I decided to go to the Hampton Institute, in Virginia, the school of which I had heard. I had no definite idea about where the Hampton Institute was, or how long the journey was. Some time before starting for Hampton, I remember, I joined the little Baptist church, in Malden, of which I am still a member.

Of my ancestry I know almost nothing. While in slave quarters, and even later, I heard whispered conversations among the colored people of the tortures which the slaves, including, no doubt, my ancestors on my mother's side, suffered in the middle passage of the slave ship while being conveyed from Africa to America. I have been unsuccessful in securing information that would throw any accurate light upon the history of my family beyond my mother. She, I remember, had a half-brother and a half-sister. In the days of slavery, not very much attention was given to family history and family records—that is, black family records. My mother, I suppose, attracted the attention of a purchaser who was afterward my owner and hers. Her addition to the slave family attracted about as much attention as the purchase of a new horse or cow. Of my father I know even less than of my mother. I only know that he was a white man, but whoever he was, I never heard of his taking the least interest in me, or providing in any way for my rearing. But I do not find especial fault with him. He was simply another unfortunate victim of the institution which the nation unhappily had engrafted upon it at that time.

THE HOUSE IN VIRGINIA WHERE BOOKER T. WASHINGTON WAS BORN. (STILL STANDING.)

BOOKER'S MOTHER PRAYING TO BE DELIVERED
FROM BONDAGE

CHAPTER III.
LIFE AT HAMPTON INSTITUTE.

After my mother and brother John had secured me a few extra garments, with what I could provide for myself, I started for Hampton about the first of October, 1872. How long I was on this journey I have at this time no very definite idea. Part of the way I went by railroad, part in a stage, and part on foot. I remember that when I got as far as Richmond, Virginia, I was completely out of money, and knew not a single person in the city. Besides, I had never been in a city before. I think it was about nine o'clock at night that I reached Richmond. I was hungry, tired and dirty, and had no where to go. I wandered about the streets until about midnight, when I felt completely exhausted.

By chance I came to a street that had a plank sidewalk, and I crept under this sidewalk and spent the night. The next morning I felt very much rested, but was still quite hungry, as it had been some time since I had a good meal. When I awoke, I noticed some ships not far from where I had spent the night. I went to one of these vessels and asked the captain to permit me to work for him, so that I could earn some money to get some food. The captain very kindly gave me work, which was that of helping to unload pig iron from the vessel. In my rather weak and hungry condition I found this hard work, but I stuck to it, and was given enough money to buy a little food. My work seemed to have pleased the master of the vessel so much that he furnished me with work for several days, but I continued to sleep under the sidewalk each night, for I was anxious to save enough money to pay my passage to Hampton.

After working on this vessel for some days, I started again for Hampton, and arrived there in a day or two, with a surplus of fifty cents in my pocket. I did not let any one know how forlorn my condition was. I feared that if I did, I would be rejected as one that was altogether too unpromising. The first person I saw after reaching the Hampton Institute was Miss Mary F. Mackie, the Lady Principal. After she had asked me many searching questions, with a good deal of doubt and hesitation in her manner, I was assigned to a room. She remarked at the same time that it would be decided later whether I could be admitted as a student. I shall not soon forget the impression that the sight of a good, clean, comfortable room and bed made upon me, for I had not slept in a bed since

I left my home in West Virginia. Within a few hours I presented myself again before Miss Mackie to hear my fate, but she still seemed to be undecided. Instead of telling me whether or not I could remain, I remember, she showed me a large recitation room and told me to sweep it. I felt at once that the sweeping of that room would decide my case. I knew I could sweep, for Mrs. Ruffner had taught me that art well. I think that I must have swept that room over as many as three times, and dusted it the same number of times. After awhile Miss Mackie came into the room and rubbed her handkerchief over the tables and benches to see if I had left any dust, but not a particle could she find. She remarked with a smile, "I guess we will try you as a student." At that moment I think I was the happiest individual that ever entered the Hampton Institute.

After I had been at the Hampton Institute a day or two I saw General Armstrong, the Principal, and he made the impression upon me of being the most perfect specimen of man, physically, mentally and spiritually, that I had ever seen; and I have never had occasion to change my first impression. In fact, as the years went by and as I came to know him better, the feeling grew. I have never seen a man in whom I had such confidence. It never occurred to me that it was possible for him to fail in anything that he undertook to accomplish. I have sometimes thought that the best part of my education at Hampton was obtained by being permitted to look upon General Armstrong day by day. He was a man who could not endure for a minute hypocrisy or want of truth in any one. This moral lesson he impressed upon every one who came in contact with him.

After I had succeeded in passing my "sweeping examination," I was assigned by Miss Mackie to the position of assistant janitor. This position, with the exception of working on the farm for awhile, I held during the time I was a student at Hampton. I took care of four or five class rooms; that is, I swept and dusted them and built the fires when needed. A great portion of the time I had to rise at four o'clock in the morning in order to do my work and find time to prepare my lessons.

Everything was very crude at Hampton when I first went there. There were about two hundred students. There was but one substantial building, together with some old government barracks. There were no table cloths on the meal tables, and that which was called tea or coffee was served to us in yellow bowls. Corn bread was our chief food. Once a week we got a taste of white bread.

While taking the regular literary and industrial courses at Hampton, next to my regular studies I was most fond of the debating societies, of which there were two or three. The first subject that I debated in public was whether or not the execution of Maj. Andre was justifiable. After I had been at Hampton a few months I helped to organize the "After Supper Club." I noticed that the students usually had about twenty minutes after tea when no special duty called them; so about twenty-five of us agreed to come together each evening and spend those twenty minutes in the discussion of some important subject. These meetings were a constant source of delight, and were most valuable in preparing us for public speaking.

While at Hampton my best friends did not know how badly off I was for clothing during a large part of the time, but I did not fret about that. I always had the feeling that if I could get knowledge in my head, the matter of clothing would take care of itself afterwards. At one time I was reduced to a single ragged pair of cheap socks. These socks I had to wash over night and put them on the next morning.

After I had remained at Hampton for two years I went back to West Virginia to spend my four months of vacation. Soon after my return to Malden my mother, who was never strong, died. I do not remember how old I was at this time, but I do remember that it was during my vacation from Hampton. I had been without work for some time, and had been off several miles looking for work. On returning home at night I was very tired, and stopped in the boiler-room of one of the engines used to pump salt water into the salt furnace near my home. I was so tired that I soon fell asleep. About two or three o'clock in the morning some one, my brother John, I think, found me and told me that our mother was dead. It has always been a source of indescribable pain to me that I was not present when she passed away, but the lessons of truth, honor and thrift which she implanted in me while she lived have remained with me, and I consider them among my most precious possessions. She seemed never to tire of planning ways for me and the other children to get an education and to make true men and women of us, although she herself was without education. This was the severest trial I had ever experienced, because she always sympathized with me deeply in every effort that I made to get on in the world. My sister Amanda was too young to know how to take care of the house, and my step-father was too poor to hire anyone. Sometimes we had food cooked for our meals and sometimes we did not. During the whole of the summer, after the death of my mother, I do not think there was a time when the whole family sat down to a meal together. By working for Mrs. Ruffner and others, and by the aid of my brother John, I obtained money enough to return to Hampton in the fall, and graduated in the regular course in the summer of 1875.

Aside from Gen. Armstrong, Gen. Marshall and Miss Mackie, the persons who made the deepest impression upon me at Hampton were Miss Nathalie Lord and Miss Elizabeth Brewer, two teachers from New England. I am especially indebted to these two for being helped in my spiritual life and led to love and understand the Bible. Largely by reason of their teaching, I find that a day rarely, if ever, passes when I am at home, that I do not read the Bible. Miss Lord was the teacher of reading, and she kindly consented to give me many extra lessons in elocution. These lessons I have since found most valuable to me.

Life at Hampton was a constant revelation to me; it was constantly taking me into a new world. The matter of having meals at regular hours, of eating on a tablecloth, using a napkin, the use of the bath-tub and of the tooth-brush, as well as the use of sheets upon the bed, were all new to me.

I sometimes feel that the most valuable lesson

I learned at the Hampton Institute was the use of the bath. I learned there for the first time some of its value, not only in keeping the body healthy, but in inspiring self-respect and promoting virtue. In all my travels in the South and elsewhere, since leaving Hampton, I have always in some way sought my daily bath. To get it sometimes when I have been the guest of my own people in a single-roomed cabin has not always been easy to do, except by slipping away to some stream in the woods. I have always tried to teach my people that some provision for bathing should be a part of every house.

After finishing the course at Hampton, I went to Saratoga Springs, in New York, and was a waiter during the summer at the United States Hotel, the same hotel at which I have several times since been a guest upon the invitation of friends.

CHAPTER IV.

HOW THE FIRST SIX YEARS AFTER GRADUATION FROM HAMPTON WERE SPENT.

In the fall of 1875 I returned to Malden and was elected as the teacher in the school at Malden, the first school that I ever attended. I taught this school for three years. The thing that I recall most pleasantly in connection with my teaching was the fact that I induced several of my pupils to go to Hampton and that most of them have become strong and useful men. One of them, Dr. Samuel E. Courtney, is now a successful physician in Boston and has been a member of the Boston Board of Education. While teaching I insisted that each pupil should come to school clean, should have his or her hands and face washed and hair combed, and should keep the buttons on his or her clothing.

I not only taught school in the day, but for a great portion of the time taught night school. In addition to this I had two Sunday schools, one at a place called Snow Hill, about two miles from Malden, in the morning, and another in Malden in the afternoon. The average attendance in my day school, was, I think, between eighty and ninety. As I had no assistant teacher it was a very difficult task to keep all the pupils interested and to see that they made progress in their studies. I had few unpleasant experiences, however, in connection with my teaching. Most of the parents, notwithstanding the fact that they and many of the children knew me as a boy, seemed to have the greatest confidence in me and respect for me, and did everything in their power to make the work pleasant and agreeable.

One thing that gave me a great deal of satisfaction and pleasure in teaching this school was the conducting of a debating society which met weekly and was largely attended both by the young and older people. It was in this debating society and the societies of a similar character at Hampton that I began to cultivate whatever talent I may have for public speaking. While in Malden, our debating society would very often arrange for debates with other similar organizations in Charleston and elsewhere.

Soon after I began teaching, I resolved to induce my brother John to attend the Hampton Institute. He had been good enough to work for the family while I was being educated, and besides had helped me in all the ways he could, by working in the coal mines while I had been away. Within a few months he started for Hampton and by his own efforts and my aid he went through the institution. After both of us had gotten through Hampton we sent our adopted brother James there, and had the satisfaction of having him educated under Gen. Armstrong.

In 1878 I went to Wayland Seminary, in Washington, and spent a year in study there. Rev. G. M. P. King, D. D., was President of Wayland Seminary while I was a student there. Notwithstanding I was there but a short time, the high Christian character of Dr. King made a lasting impression upon me. The deep religious spirit which pervaded the atmosphere at Wayland made an impression upon me which I trust will always remain.

Soon after my year at Wayland was completed, I was invited by a committee of gentlemen in Charleston, West Virginia, to stump the state of West Virginia in the interest of having the capital of the state moved from Wheeling, West Virginia, to Charleston. For some time there had been quite an agitation in the state on the question of the permanent location of the capital. A law was passed by the legislature providing that three cities might be voted for; these were, I think, Charleston, Parkersburg and Martinsburg. It was a three-cornered contest and great energy was shown by each city. After about three months of campaigning the voters declared in favor of Charleston as the permanent capital, by a large majority. I went into a large number of the counties of West Virginia and had the satisfaction of feeling that my efforts counted for something in winning success for Charleston, which is only five miles from my old home, Malden.

The speaking in connection with the removal of the capital rather fired the slumbering ambition which I had had for some time to become a lawyer, and after this campaign was over I began in earnest to study law, in fact read Blackstone and several elementary law books preparatory to the profession of the law. A good deal of my reading of the law was done under the kind direction of the Hon. Romes H. Freer, a white man who was then a prosperous lawyer in Charleston and who has since become a member of Congress. But notwithstanding my ambition to become a lawyer, I always had an unexplainable feeling that I was to do something else, and that I never would have the opportunity to practice law. As I analyze at the present time the feeling that seemed to possess me then, I was impressed with the idea that to confine myself to the practice of law would be going contrary to my teaching at Hampton, and would limit me to a much smaller sphere of usefulness than was open to me if I followed the work of educating my people after the manner in which I had been taught at Hampton. The course of events, however, very soon placed me where I found an opportunity to begin my life's work.

My work in connection with the removal of the capital had not been completed long when I received an invitation from Gen. Armstrong, much to my surprise, to return to Hampton and deliver the graduates' address at the next commencement. I chose as the subject of this address, "The Force that Wins." All who heard the address seemed pleased with what I said. After the address I was further surprised by being asked by Gen. Armstrong to return to the Hampton Institute and take a position, partly as a teacher and partly as a post-graduate student. This I gladly consented to do. Gen. Armstrong had decided to start a night class at Hampton for students who wanted to work all day and study for two hours at night. He asked me to organize and teach this class. At first there were only about a half dozen students, but the number soon grew to about thirty. The night class at Hampton has since grown to the point where it now numbers six or seven hundred. It seems to me that the teaching of this class was almost the most satisfactory work I ever did. The students who composed the class worked during the day for ten hours in the saw mill, on the farm, or in the laundry. They were a most earnest set. I soon gave them the name of the "Plucky Class." Several of the members of this "Plucky Class" now fill prominent and useful positions. While I was teaching I was given lessons in advanced subjects, among those who assisted me in that way being Dr. H. B. Frissell, who was then chaplain, but who is now the honored and successful successor of Gen. Armstrong.

About the time the night class was organized at Hampton, Indians for the first time were permitted to enter the institution. The second year that I worked at Hampton, in connection with other duties I was placed in charge of the Indian boys, who at that time numbered about seventy-five, I think. I lived in their cottage with them and looked after all their wants. I grew to like the Indians very much, and placed great faith in them. My daily experience with them convinced me that the main thing that any oppressed people needed was a chance of the right kind, and they would cease to be savages.

I have often wondered if there is a white institution in this country whose students would have welcomed the incoming of more than a hundred companions of another race in the cordial way that the black students at Hampton welcomed the red ones. How often have I wanted to say to white students that they lift themselves up in proportion as they help to lift others, and that the more unfortunate the race and the lower in the scale of civilization, the more does one raise one's self by giving the assistance.

This reminds me of a conversation which I once had with the Hon. Frederick Douglass. At one time Mr. Douglass was traveling in the state of Pennsylvania, and was forced, on account of his color, to ride in the baggage-car, in spite of the fact that he had paid the same fare as the other passengers. When some of the white passengers went to the baggage-car to console Mr. Douglass, and one of them said to him, "I am sorry, Mr. Douglass, that you have been degraded in this manner," Mr. Douglass straightened himself up on the box upon which he was sitting, and replied: "They cannot degrade Frederick Douglass. The soul that is within me no man can degrade. I am not the one that is being degraded on account of this treatment, but those who are inflicting it upon me."

My experience has been, that the time to test a true gentleman is to observe him when he is in contact with individuals of a race that is less fortunate than his own. This is illustrated in no better way than by observing the conduct of the old-school type of Southern gentleman when he is in contact with his former slaves or their descendants.

An example of what I mean is shown in a story told of George Washington, who, meeting a colored man in the road once, who politely lifted his hat, lifted his own in return. Some of his white friends who saw the incident, criticised Washington for his action. In reply to their criticism, George Washington said: "Do you suppose that I am going to permit a poor, ignorant colored man to be more polite than I am?"

At the end of my second year at Hampton as a teacher, in 1881, there came a call from the little town of Tuskegee, Alabama, to Gen. Armstrong for some one to organize and become the Principal of a Normal School, which the people wanted to start in that town. The letter to Gen. Armstrong was written on behalf of the colored people of the town of Tuskegee by Mr. Geo. W. Campbell, one of the foremost white citizens of Tuskegee. Mr. Campbell is still the president of the Board of Trustees of the Tuskegee Normal and Industrial Institute, and has from the first been one of its warmest and most steadfast friends. When Mr. Campbell wrote to Gen. Armstrong he had in mind the securing of a white man to take the principalship of the school. Gen. Armstrong replied that he knew of no suitable white man for the position, but that he could recommend a colored man. Mr. Campbell wrote in reply that a competent colored man would be

*Hon. Seth Low is President Board of Trustees.

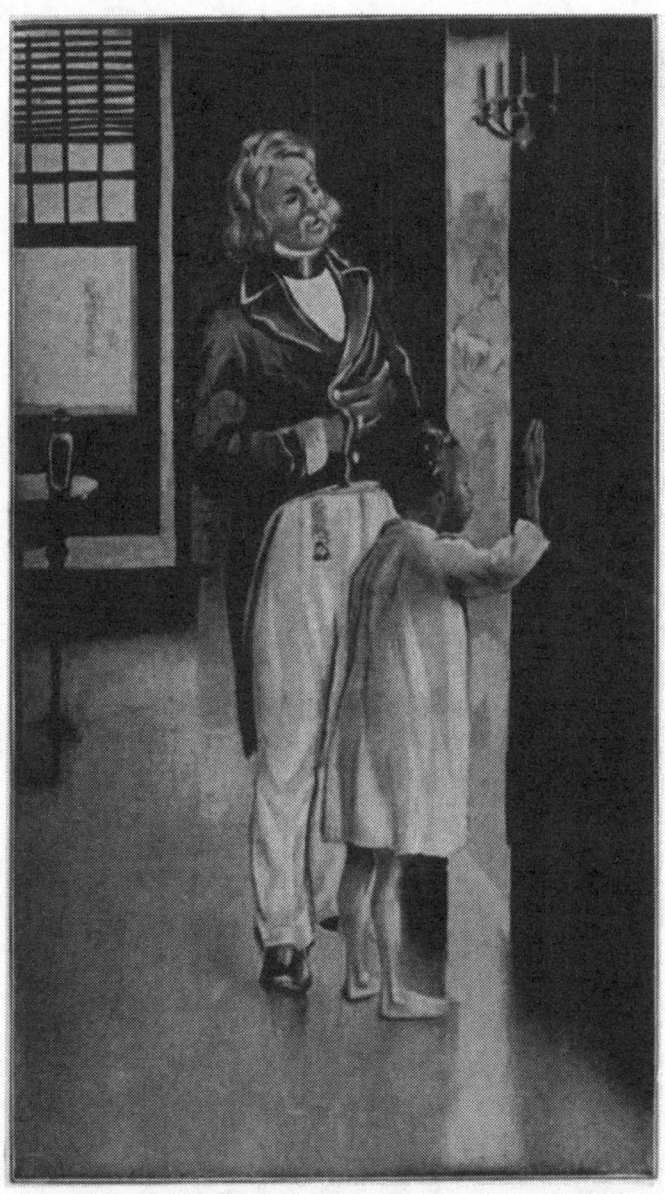

LITTLE BOOKER, A FAVORITE WITH HIS MASTER, IS ALLOWED TO PEEP INTO THE PARLOR OF THE "BIG HOUSE."

"THIS FIRED MY AMBITION TO LEARN TO READ, AS NOTHING HAD DONE BEFORE."

acceptable. Gen. Armstrong asked me to give up my work at Hampton and go to Tuskegee in answer to this call. I decided to undertake the work, and after spending a few days at my old home in Malden, West Virginia, I proceeded to the town of Tuskegee, Alabama.

I wish to add here that, in later years, I do not envy the white boy as I once did. I have learned that success is to be measured, not so much by the position that one has reached in life, as by the obstacles which he has overcome while trying to succeed. Looked at from this standpoint, I almost reach the conclusion that often the Negro boy's birth and connection with an unpopular race are an advantage, so far as real life is concerned. With few exceptions, the Negro youth must work harder and perform his tasks even better than a white youth in order to secure recognition. But out of the hard and unusual struggle through which he is compelled to pass, he gets a strength, a confidence that one misses whose pathway is comparatively smooth by reason of birth and race.

From any point of view, I had rather be what I am, a member of the Negro race, than to be able to claim membership with the most favored of any other race. I have always been made sad when I have heard members of my race claiming rights and privileges, or certain badges of distinction, on the ground simply that they were members of this or that race, regardless of their own individual worth or attainments.

CHAPTER V.

THE BEGINNING OF THE WORK AT TUSKEGEE.

Before starting for Tuskegee I found it almost impossible to find the town on any map, and had difficulty in learning its exact location. I reached Tuskegee about the middle of June, 1881. I found it to be a town of some 2,000 inhabitants, about half of whom were Negroes, and located in what is commonly called the "Black Belt," that is, the section of the South where the Negro race largely outnumbers the white population. The county in which Tuskegee is located is named Macon. Of Tuskegee and Macon County I prefer to quote the words of Maj. W. W. Screws, the editor of the "Montgomery (Alabama) Daily Advertiser," who visited Tuskegee in 1898, seventeen years after the Tuskegee Institute was founded. Maj. Screws says:

"Just at this time there is probably no place in the United States, of similar size, so well known to the people of the country, as this lovely little city. It has always possessed merits which brought it conspicuously before Alabamians, for in every locality in this and many Southern

States are noble men and women who received their educational training here.

"Thomas S. Woodward was one of the earliest white settlers in Macon County, and was one of the commissioners appointed to lay off the site for the court house. He built the first house in the new town, which they called Tuskekee, a corruption of the old Indian name, Tuskigi, which is said by Dr. Gatschet to be a contraction of Taskialgi (warriors). The old Indian town stood in the fork of the Coosa and was the home, part of the time, of the famous half-breed statesman, Alexander McGillivray. The name passed in its present form to the county seat of the new county.

"Tuskegee was settled by men who were well to do in a material point of view. They owned rich lands on the creeks and streams and in the prairie section of the county. This point is on a high, dry ridge, and from time immemorial has been noted for its healthfulness. Here came those who wished to build homes for their families, to have congenial company and to give their children educational advantages. They did not desire the projectors of the Montgomery and West Point Railroad to put the town on its route, because of the interruption it was feared would be occasioned to the schools. From the very beginning of its existence, education has been the main feature of Tuskegee, and through its schools and colleges a population gathered here which has never been excelled in point of refinement, politeness and all the gentle amenities which tend to make life comfortable.

"The town of Tuskegee was first settled about 1830. James Dent built the first house. The town was first laid out in 1833. Mr. G. W. Campbell came to the county with his father from Montgomery in 1835, and at that time perhaps 150 people were in and about what now comprises Tuskegee's territorial limits. There was no court house building, and court sessions were held in a small log house with a dirt floor. When court was not in session the building was used as a school house. The Creek Indians were in great numbers in the neighborhood, but they were friendly and peaceful, and in 1836 commenced to move to their far Western home, going overland to Montgomery, where they took steamer for New Orleans. Tuskegee is one of the model towns in the way of good order.

"Among the white settlers here are Dr. W. J. Gautier, and Messrs. G. W. Campbell, J. W. Bilbro, J. O. A. Adams and W. H. Wright. They have a perfect wealth of interesting reminiscence connected with the early days of all East Alabama. Although they have passed the three score years, they are hale, healthy men, engaged in business, and set a splendid example of energy and active life to the younger generation. The firm of Campbell & Wright has been in existence, possibly, longer than any other in Alabama.

"The Montgomery and West Point Railroad is about five miles distant from Tuskegee, the nearest station being Chehaw. From there to Tuskegee, until about twenty years ago, the usual mode of conveyance for passengers and baggage was stage coach and omnibus, while all goods were transported by wagon. It was a tiresome, troublesome and expensive method. This difficulty has been overcome through the Tuskegee Railroad which now connects the two points.

"The population of Macon County before 1860, was largely heavy landed proprietors. They suffered immensely by the results of the war from disorganized labor, and reverses stripped them of much of their property. The county is almost exclusively agricultural, and the average yield year by year, of corn, cotton, peas, potatoes and other things grown on well regulated farms, is fairly good."

When I reached Tuskegee, I found that Mr. Lewis Adams, a colored man of great intelligence and thrift, who was born a slave near Tuskegee, had first started the movement to have some kind of Normal School in Tuskegee for the education of colored youth. At the time he conceived this idea Hon. W. F. Foster and Hon. A. L. Brooks, both white Democrats, were members of the Alabama Legislature, and Mr. Adams so interested them in the movement that they promised to use their influence in the Legislature to secure an annual appropriation of $2,000 toward the expenses of a Normal School, provided one could be properly organized and started. Mr. Foster and Mr. Brooks were successful in their efforts to secure the appropriation, which was limited in its use to helping to pay teachers. A Board of three Commissioners was appointed to control the expenditure of this $2,000. When the school was first started this board consisted of Mr. Geo. W. Campbell, Mr. M. B. Swanson and Mr. Lewis Adams. After the death of Mr. Swanson, Mr. C. W. Hare was elected in his stead.

When I reached Tuskegee, the only thing that had been done toward the starting of a school was the securing of the $2,000. There was no land, building, or apparatus. I opened the school, however, on the 4th of July, 1881, in an old church and a little shanty that was almost ready to fall down from decay. On the first day there was an attendance of thirty students, mainly those who had been engaged in teaching in the public schools of that vicinity. But these little buildings, inadequate as they were, were most gladly furnished by the colored people, who from the first day that I went to Tuskegee to the present time have done everything within their power to further the interests of the school.

One curious thing that happened in connection with the students was, as additional pupils began to come in, that some of them had been attending schools taught by some of those who came to the Tuskegee school, and, in several cases, it happened that former pupils entered higher classes than their former teachers.

CHAPTER VI.

THE FIRST YEAR AT TUSKEGEE.

After the school had been in session in the old church and little shanty for several months, I began to see the necessity of having a permanent location for the institution, where we could have the students not only in their class rooms, but get hold of them in their home life, and teach them how to take care of their bodies in the matter of bathing, care of the teeth, and in general cleanliness. We also felt that we must not only teach the students how to prepare their food, but how to serve and eat it properly. So long as we had the students only a few hours in the class room during the day, we could give attention to none of these important matters, which our students had not had an opportunity of learning before leaving their homes. Few of the students who came during the first year were able to remain during the nine months' session, for lack of money, so we felt the necessity of having industries where the students could pay a part of their board in cash. It was rather noticeable that, notwithstanding the poverty of most of the students who came to us in the earlier months of the institution, most of them had the idea of getting an education in order that they might find some method of living without manual labor; that is, they had the feeling that to work with the hands was not conducive to the development of the highest type of lady or gentleman. This feeling we wanted to change as fast as possible, by teaching students the dignity, beauty and civilizing power of intelligent labor.

After a few months had passed, I wrote Gen. J. F. B. Marshall, at that time treasurer of the Hampton Institute, and put our condition before him, telling him that there was an abandoned farm about a mile from the town of Tuskegee in the market which I could secure at a very cheap price for our institution. As I had absolutely no money with which to make the first payment on the farm, I summoned the courage to ask Gen. Marshall to lend me $500 with which to make the first payment. To my surprise a letter came back in a few days enclosing a check for $500. A contract was made for the purchase of the farm, which at that time consisted of 100 acres. Subsequent purchases and gifts of adjacent lands have increased the number of acres at this place to 700, and this is the present site of the Tuskegee Institute. This has again been enlarged from time to time by purchases and gifts of land not adjacent until at present the school owns farm lands to the number of about 2,500 acres.

After the school had been in session three months, Miss Olivia A. Davidson, a graduate of the Hampton Institute and later a graduate of the Framingham, Mass., Normal School, was employed as an assistant teacher.

Miss Davidson was teaching among her people near Memphis, Tennessee, in 1879, when the yellow fever drove her away. She went to Hampton, entered the senior class and graduated the following spring. She did not go to Hampton, however, until her application to return to Memphis to help nurse the yellow fever patients had been refused by the authorities there. Through friends she was able to enter the Normal School at Framingham, Massachusetts, and graduated in the summer of 1881; and, when an assistant at Tuskegee was called for, she accepted the work. Her enthusiasm had won the admiration of her schoolmates, and from them she received much assistance for the school at Tuskegee in after years.

The success of the school, especially during the first half dozen years of its existence, was due more to Miss Davidson than any one else. During the organization of the school and in all matters of discipline she was the one to bring order out of every difficulty. When the last effort had apparently been exhausted and it seemed that things must stop, she was the one to find a way out. Not only was this true at the school, but when a campaign for money had ended unsuccessfully, she would start for the North, and money was sure to be found.

Our hardest struggle began after we had made the first payment on the farm. We not only had to secure the money within a few months with which to repay Gen. Marshall's loan, but had to get the means with which to meet future payments, and also to erect a building on the farm. Miss Davidson went among the white and colored families in Tuskegee and told them our plans and needs, and there were few of either race who did not contribute either something in cash or something that could be turned into cash at the many festivals and fairs which were held for the purpose of raising money to help the school. In many cases the white ladies in Tuskegee contributed chickens or cakes that were sold for the benefit of our new enterprise. I do not believe there was a single Negro family or scarcely an individual in Tuskegee or its vicinity that did not contribute something in money or in kind to the school. These contributions were most gladly made, and often at a great sacrifice.

Perhaps I might as well say right here that one of the principal things which made it easy to start such a school as now exists near the town of Tuskegee was the fact that Tuskegee is inhabited by some of the most cultured and liberal white people to be found in any portion of the South. I have been into a good many Southern towns, but I think I have never seen one where the general average of culture and intelligence is so high as that of the people of Tuskegee. We have in this town and the surrounding country a good example of the friendly relations that exist between the two races when both races are enlightened and educated. Not only are the white people above the average, but the same is true of the general intelligence and acquirements of the colored people.

The leading colored citizen in Tuskegee is Mr. Lewis Adams, to whom should largely be given the honor for securing the location of the Tuskegee Normal and Industrial Institute in the town. Mr. Adams is not only an intelligent and successful business man, but is one who combines with his business enterprise rare common sense and discretion. In the most trying periods of the growth of the Tuskegee Institute I have always found Mr. Adams a man on whom I could rely for the wisest advice. He enjoys the highest respect and confidence of the citizens of both races, and it is largely through his power and influence that the two races live together in harmony and peace in the town.

After we had raised all the money we could in Tuskegee for the purpose of paying for the farm and putting up the new building, Miss Davidson went to Boston, where she had many friends and acquaintances, and after some months of hard work she secured enough money to complete the payment on the farm and return Gen. Marshall's loan. In addition she secured means to complete the payment on our first building, Porter Hall. This building was named after Mr. H. A. Porter, of Brooklyn, N. Y., who was instrumental in assisting us to secure the largest gifts for its erection.

All the while the farm was being paid for we were holding school daily in the old church and shanty. The latter at least was well ventilated. There was one thickness of boards above and around us, and this was full of large cracks. Part of the windows had no sashes and were closed with rough wooden shutters that opened upward by leather hinges. Other windows had sashes, but with little glass in them. Through all these openings the hot sun or cold wind and rain came pouring in upon us. Many a time a storm would leave scarcely a dry spot in either of the two rooms into which the shanty was divided to make room for separate classes. These rooms were small, but into them large classes of thirty or forty had to be crowded for recitations. More than once, I remember, when Miss Davidson and I were hearing recitations, and the rain would begin pouring down, one of the larger pupils would very kindly cease his lessons and come and hold an umbrella over us so that we could continue our work. I also remember that at our boarding place, on several occasions when it rained while we were eating our meals, our good landlady would kindly get an umbrella and hold it over us while we were eating.

During the summer of 1882, at the end of our first year's work, I was married to Miss Fannie N. Smith, of Malden, West Virginia, and we began housekeeping in Tuskegee early in the fall. This made a home for our teachers, who had now been increased to four in number. My wife was also a graduate of the Hampton Institute. After earnest and constant work in the interest of the school, together with her housekeeping duties, she passed away in May, 1884. One child, Portia M. Washington, was born during our marriage. From the first my wife most earnestly devoted her thought and time to the work of the school, and was completely one with me in every interest and ambition. She died, however, before she had an opportunity of seeing what the school was destined to be.

The following account of her death is taken

from the Alumni Journal, published at the time at Hampton:

"The numerous friends of Mr. B. T. Washington will be pained to learn of the death of his beloved wife, Mrs. Fannie (Smith) Washington, class of '82, which occurred at Tuskegee, Alabama, Sunday, May 4th.

"Her death is indeed a serious bereavement to Mr. Washington, whose acquaintance and regard for the deceased had begun in their childhood. Their happy union had done much to lighten the arduous duties devolving upon him in the management of his school. To his friends he had several times expressed the great comfort his family life was to him.

"We know that all our readers will join us in extending to him the warmest sympathy in this sad hour.

"A bright little girl, not a year old, is left to sustain with her father a loss which she can never know."

READING OF THE EMANCIPATION PROCLAMATION. THE SMALL LAD WITH SLOUCH HAT, AND STICK IN RIGHT HAND, IS BOOKER.—Text page 13.

LITTLE, BOOKER LEAVING HOME FOR HAMPTON INSTITUTE.

CHAPTER VII.

THE STRUGGLES AND SUCCESS OF THE WORKERS AT TUSKEGEE FROM 1882 TO 1884.

Soon after securing possession of the farm we set about putting it into a condition so that a crop of some kind might be secured from it during the next year. At the close of school hours each afternoon, I would call for volunteers to take their axes and go into the woods to assist in clearing up the grounds. The students were most anxious to give their service in this way, and very soon a large acreage was put into condition for cultivation. We had no horse or mule with which to begin the cultivation of the farm. Mr. George W. Campbell, however, the president of the Board of Trustees, very kindly gave us a horse. This was the first animal that the school ever possessed. On the farm there was an old building that had formerly been used as a stable, another that had been used as a chicken coop, and still a third that had been used as a kitchen during ante-bellum days. All of these three buildings or shanties were duly repaired and made to do service as class-rooms and dormitories.

We had our first services in Porter Hall on Thanksgiving Day, 1882. Rev. R. C. Bedford, who was then pastor of the Congregational Church in Montgomery, and who has since been one of our trustees and warmest friends, preached the Thanksgiving sermon. This was the first Thanksgiving service, I think, that was ever held in the town of Tuskegee, and a joyous one it was to the people.

By the middle of the second year's work the existence of the school had begun to be advertised pretty thoroughly through the state of Alabama and even in some of the adjoining states. This brought to us an increasing number of students, and the problem as to what to do with them was becoming a serious one. We put the girls who did not live in town on the third floor of Porter Hall to sleep. The boys we scattered around in whatever places we were able to secure. In order to provide a dining room, kitchen and laundry, to be used by the boarding department, our young men volunteered to dig out the basement under Porter Hall, which was soon bricked up and made to answer its purpose very well. Old students, however, who to-day return to Tuskegee and see the large new dining room, kitchen, and laundry run by steam, are very much interested in noting the change and contrast.

Sometimes during the winter of the second year of the school, we were compelled to put large numbers of young men in shanties or huts to sleep, where there was almost no protection from rain and cold weather. Often during the very cold nights I have gone into the rooms of these students at midnight to see how they were getting along, and have found them sitting up by the fire, with blankets wrapped about them, as the only method of keeping warm. One morning, when I asked at the opening exercises how many had been frost-bitten during the cold weather, not less than ten hands went up. The teachers were not surprised at this. Still, notwithstanding these inconveniences and hardships, I think I never heard a complaint from the lips of a single student. They always seemed filled with gratitude for the opportunity to go to school under any circumstances.

Very early in the history of the school we made it a rule that no student, however well off he might be, was to be permitted to remain unless he did some work, in addition to taking studies in the academic department. At first quite a number of students and a large number of parents did not like this rule; in fact, during the first three or four years, a large proportion of the students brought either verbal or written messages from their parents that they wanted their children taught books, but did not want them taught work. Notwithstanding these protests, we still stuck to our rule. As the years went on and as the students and parents began to see and appreciate the value of our industrial teaching, these protests grew less frequent and less strong. It is a sufficient explanation to say in regard to this matter, that it has been ten years since a single objection has been raised by parents or students against anyone's taking part in our industrial work. In fact, there is a positive enthusiasm among parents and students over our industrial work, and we are compelled to refuse admission to hundreds every year who wish to prepare themselves to take up industrial pursuits. If we had the room and the means we could give industrial training to a much larger number of students than are now receiving it. The main burden of the letters which now come from parents is that each wants his daughter or son taught some industry or trade in connection with the academic branches. I also remember, during the early history of this institution, that students coming here who had to pass through the larger cities, or pass in the vicinity of other institutions, had the finger of scorn pointed at them because they were going to a school where it was understood that one had to labor. At the present time, however, this feeling is so completely changed that there is almost no portion of the South where there is any objection brought against industrial education of the Negro on the part of the colored people themselves. On the other hand, the feeling in favor of it is strong and most enthusiastic.

Almost from the first I determined to have the students do practically all the work of putting up the buildings and carrying on the various departments of the institution. Many of our best friends, however, doubted the practicability of this, but I insisted that it could be done. I held that while the students at first might make very poor bricks and do poor brick-masonry, the lesson of self-help would be more valuable to them in the long run than if they were put into a building which had been wholly the creation of the generosity of some one else. By the end of the third year the number of students had increased from 30, with which we began, to 169; most of them, however, coming from nearby counties and other sections of Alabama.

In February, 1883, the State Legislature of Alabama increased the state appropriation for the school from two to three thousand dollars annually, on recommendation of the State Superintendent of Public Instruction, Hon. H. Clay Armstrong. The Committee on Education reported the bill unanimously to the House, and the Governor recommended its passage. As some of the members were not acquainted with the character of the school, they raised objection to this increase at a time when, by defalcation of the state treasurer, reported only the day before, the state had lost a quarter of a million dollars. The Speaker of the House, Hon. W. F. Foster, a member from Tuskegee, and an ex-Confederate soldier, left the chair, and in an eloquent and effective speech in praise of the work of the school at Tuskegee, urged the passage of the bill. On conclusion of Col. Foster's speech the bill passed by a large majority vote. Col. Foster not only interested himself in the passage of the first bill which gave support from the state to this institution, but has been one of the warmest and most helpful friends from that time until the present.

In reference to the passage of the bill for an increased appropriation for the school, Rev. R. C. Bedford, at that time residing in Montgomery as pastor of the Congregational Church, wrote to Gen. Armstrong as follows:

"Gen. S. C. Armstrong, Dear Sir:—

"A short time ago I made a trip to Tuskegee, Ala., for the purpose of visiting the State Normal School for colored people located there, four of whose five teachers, together with the wife of the Principal, were once pupils of yours at Hampton Institute. I attended the session of the school for two days and was exceedingly pleased with the enthusiastic spirit of both teachers and pupils. One of the encouraging features of the school is the warm interest it has inspired in many of the leading white citizens of Tuskegee. Mr. G. W. Campbell and Mr. Wm. B. Swanson are among the oldest and most respected citizens of Macon County. They with Mr. Lewis Adams, a prominent colored man, constitute the State Board of Commissioners for the school. Col. Bowen, Mr. Varner, and Col. W. F. Foster, speaker of the present Legislature, all citizens of Tuskegee and familiar with the school, are among its warmest friends. A short time ago, in conversation with Hon. H. Clay Armstrong, our State Superintendent of Education, I learned that he was so much pleased with the work of Mr. Washington and his associates as to recommend to the Committee on Education to report a bill giving $1,000 per year additional to the school. I was present during the debate on the bill. So interested was Col. Foster in its passage that he left the speaker's chair, and upon the floor of the House, in an eloquent and effective speech, urged that it pass. He sat down, and by a vote of 59 to 18, the bill was passed; and it is now a law.

"With this example before us, we need have no fear as to what the colored people can do if, like Mr. Washington and his associates, they will take hold to win."

In April, 1883, the school enjoyed a pleasant visit from Gen. J. F. B. Marshall, the treasurer of Hampton Institute, and the one who had been generous enough to lend us $500 with which to make the first payment on the farm. Gen. Marshall's visit gave us the greatest hope and encouragement. He wrote, while at the school, to the Southern Workman, a paper published at Hampton Institute, as follows, concerning his visit:

"A few days' rest from office duties being enjoined upon me recently, I determined to pay a visit to the Tuskegee school, in which the faculty and teachers of Hampton Institute naturally feel a special interest.

"The Tuskegee farm contains 140 acres and the boys are at work clearing a field for sugar cane, which grows well here. They also raise cotton, sweet potatoes, peaches, etc. To enable them to train the students properly they must have them board at the school. A building is very much needed for the accommodation of 100 young men. Mr. Washington says that it will cost $8,000, if student labor can be made available in its construction. For this purpose he proposes to build of brick made on the farm, which has excellent clay. The young men are impatient to set to work on their building.

"Tuskegee is one of the very old towns in the state, an attractive place of about 2500 inhabitants, having several colleges and academies of high repute for the white youth of both sexes. I was glad to find a very strong temperance sentiment here. There were only two bars in town and they pay a license of about $900 a year each. No better location could have been chosen.

"The leading white citizens of the place appreciate the importance of Mr. Washington's work, and speak of him in high terms. He has evidently won the esteem and confidence of all. Mr. Foster, the present speaker of the House, in the State Legislature, lives here, and rendered valuable aid in getting the increased appropriation of the state for Mr. Washington, of whom he spoke to me in high praise.

"I am reminded by everything I see here of our own beginning and methods at Hampton. I found on my arrival at the school, which is about a mile from the village center, a handsome frame building of two stories with a mansard roof. Though not yet finished it is occupied as a school building and is very conveniently planned for the purpose, reminding me of the Academic Hall at Hampton. The primary school on the Normal School grounds bears the same relation to it as a practice school that the Butler does to the Hampton Institute. It has 250 on the roll. They are stored away in what was the stable, close as crayons in a Waltham box. Let us hope they will all make their mark.

"All six teachers of the Normal and Training Schools are colored; and to their race belongs all credit for the work accomplished here and of the judicious use of the funds which the friends of the school, through the efforts of Mr. Washington and Miss Davidson, have contributed.

"The experiment, thus far so successful, is one of deep interest to all who have the welfare of the race at heart, and should not be suffered to fail for want of means for its completion. It is vital to the success of this school that the students should all be brought under the training and supervision of the teachers by being boarded and lodged on the premises. Our experience at Hampton has shown us the necessity of this. I know of no more worthy object, or one conducive to more important results, than this school enterprise, and I trust the friends of Negro advancement and education will not suffer it to languish or be hampered for funds. They may rest assured that these may be wisely expended and most worthily bestowed.

"My three days' visit to Tuskegee was eminently satisfactory and has inspired me with new hope for the future of the race."

The next event in the history of the school was

the celebration of its second anniversary, combined with the dedication of Porter Hall, cornerstone of which had been laid the year before. The dedication address was delivered by Rev. Geo. L. Chaney, of Atlanta, now of Boston, one of the Trustees of the school; and eloquent speeches were also made by Rev. Morgan Calloway, the associate in Emory College of its president, Dr. Atticus G. Haygood, author of "Our Brother in Black." Rev. Mr. Owens, of Mobile, also made an interesting address.

During the following summer a small frame cottage with four rooms was put up to hold sixteen young men, and three board shanties near the grounds were rented, affording accommodations for about thirty-six additional students. In September a boarding department was opened for both sexes, and as many young men as could be provided for gladly availed themselves of the privilege of working out about half of their board at the school.

In 1883 Mr. Warren Logan, a graduate of the Hampton Institute, who had received special training in book-keeping under Gen. Marshall at Hampton, came to Tuskegee as a teacher. He had not been here long, however, before it was clearly seen that he could serve the school effectively in another capacity, as well as a class room teacher, and he was soon given the position of Treasurer and book-keeper, in addition to his duties as an instructor. Mr. Logan has now been connected with the school sixteen years, and has been its Treasurer during thirteen years of this time. In addition to the position of treasurer, he fills the position of Acting Principal in the absence of the Principal. All of these various and delicate, as well as responsible, duties he has performed with great ability and satisfaction.

Mr. J. H. Washington, my brother, came to the school from West Virginia in 1885 and took the position of Business Agent. He was afterwards made Superintendent of Industries and has held that position ever since. In the meantime the school has grown, and his duties as well as those of Mr. Logan, have broadened and increased in responsibility. Both he and Mr. Logan, during the absence of the Principal, are in a large measure the mainstay and dependence of the institution for counsel and wise direction.

These two men, Mr. Logan and my brother John, have been from the beginning very important forces in the school management. As Treasurer and Superintendent of Industries respectively their responsibilities are heavy, and how much credit they deserve will never be fully known till the necessity arises some day to fill their places. They, with James N. Calloway, a graduate of Fisk University, who is the manager of

Marshall Farm, Mr. G. W. Carver, Director of the Agricultural Department, and Mr. M. T. Driver, Business Agent, constitute the Finance Committee of the Institute, a sort of cabinet for the Principal.

In September, 1883, a very pleasant surprise came to the workers in the form of $1,100, secured through Rev. R. C. Bedford from the Trustees of the Slater Fund. I might add right here that the interest of the Trustees of the Slater Fund, now under the control of Dr. J. L. M. Curry, Special Agent, has continued from that time until this, so that the institution now receives $11,000 from the Slater Fund instead of $1,100 at the beginning. With this impetus, a carpenter shop was built and started, a windmill set up to pump water into the school building, a sewing machine bought for the girls' industrial room, mules and wagons for the farm, and the farm manager's salary was also paid for nine months.

All during the summer, as was true of th previous one, Miss Davidson and myself had been earnestly presenting our cause at the North with so much encouragement that the work on the new building, called Alabama Hall, was vigorously pushed during the fall and winter. In February, 1884, about three years after the school was opened, $5,000 had been secured towards the erection of Alabama Hall, which eventually cost about $10,000.

In March, 1884, Gen. Armstrong did one of those generous things which he was noted for all through his life. In fact, from the beginning of Tuskegee's life until Gen. Armstrong's death, he seemed to take as much interest in the work of Tuskegee as in the Hampton Institute, and I am glad to say the same generous spirit is constantly shown by the successor of Gen. Armstrong, Dr. Frissell. I received a letter from Gen. Armstrong stating that he had decided to hold a number of public meetings in such cities as Baltimore, Philadelphia, New York and Boston, and wished me to accompany him and speak in the interest of Tuskegee. These meetings were advertised to be in the interest of Hampton and Tuskegee jointly, but in reality they turned out to be meetings in the interest of Tuskegee, so generous was Gen. Armstrong in his words and actions at these meetings. The special object aimed at in these meetings was to secure money with which to complete Alabama Hall.

I quote from an address made at one of these meetings by myself: "Our young men have already made two kilns of bricks, and will make all required for the needed building, Alabama Hall. From the first we have carried out the plan at Tuskegee of asking help for nothing that we could do for ourselves. Nothing has been bought that the students can produce. The boys have done the painting, made the bricks, the chairs, tables and desks, have built a stable, and are now moving the carpenter shop. The girls do the entire housekeeping, including the washing, ironing and mending of the boys' clothing. Besides, they make garments to sell, and give some attention to flower gardening."

In due time, however, by hard work, the remainder of the money, $10,000 in all, necessary to complete Alabama Hall, was secured, largely in the North, although not a little was gotten from friends in and about Tuskegee, especially through the holding of festivals and other entertainments.

In April, 1884, we received a visit from the Lady Principal of the Hampton Institute, Miss Mary F. Mackie, who was the first one to receive me when I went to Hampton as a student. I will say here that, from the visit of Gen. Marshall up to the present time, we have received constant visits and encouragement from the officers and teachers of the Hampton Institute. Miss Mackie, writing to a friend at Hampton, said:

"The wish constantly on my lips or in my heart, since I reached here last evening, is that you could see this school. I am sure you would feel, as I do, that the dial of time must have turned back twelve years in its course. In many respects it is more like the Hampton I first knew than the one of today is; I was particularly struck with the plantation melodies which Mr. Washington called for at the close of the evening prayers; there is more of the real wail in their music than I ever heard elsewhere. The teachers here laugh over their exact imitation of the alma mater; even the night school feature has sprouted; to be sure it only numbers two students, but it is on the same plan as ours. Do you know that Mr. ———— has lately given them 440 acres of land, making their farm now 580 acres?"

The June number of the Southern Letter, a little paper published by the Institute, contained the following account of commencement, which took place May 29, 1884: "Many visitors were present, white and colored. The great interest was in the development of the department of industrial training, which now includes the farm, the Slater carpenter shop and blacksmith shop, the printing office, the girls' industrial room, and the brick yard, where the students were making brick for Alabama Hall. The morning exercises, were, as usual, inspection, recitations and review of the current news. The speaker of the afternoon was Prof. R. T. Greener, of Washington, who delivered a very practical and eloquent ad-

BOOKER T. WASHINGTON REHEARSING HIS GRADUATING ORATION AT HAMPTON. HIS FIRST SPEECH.

STUDENTS GATHERING SWEET POTATOES, TUSKEGEE INSTITUTE.

dress. Reporters were present from Montgomery and Tuskegee."

In the spring of 1884 I was very pleasantly surprised to receive an invitation from the President of the National Educational Association, Hon. Thos. W. Bicknall, of Boston, asking me to deliver an address before that body at its next meeting during the summer. The Association assembled at Madison, Wisconsin, and I think I am safe in saying that there were at least five thousand teachers present, representing every portion of the United States. This was the first opportunity I had had of presenting the work of the school to any large audience, especially of a national character. It was rather late in the evening before my time to speak came. Several speakers had preceded me, and one especially had proven himself to be rather tedious and tiresome by his long and rather unprepared address, but this did not discourage me. I determined to make the best address that I possibly could, although I was beset by fear and trembling. The many kind words, however, which I received after my address, assured me that in some measure my effort had not been a failure. Among other things I said:

"I repeat that any work looking toward the permanent improvement of the Negro in the South must have for one of its aims the fitting of him to live friendly and peaceably with his white neighbors, both socially and politically. In spite of all talk of exodus, the Negro's home is permanently in the South, for, coming to the bread and meat side of the question, the white man needs the Negro and the Negro needs the white man. His home being permanently in the South, it is our duty to help him prepare himself to live there, an independent, educated citizen. In order that there may be the broadest development of the colored man, and that he may have an unbounded field in which to labor, the two races South must be brought to have faith in each other. The teachings of the Negro, in various ways, for the last twenty years, have tended too much to array him against his white brother, rather than to put the races in co-operation with each other. Thus, Massachussetts, supports the Republican party because the Republican party supports Massachusetts with a protective tariff; but the Negro supports the Republican party simply because Massachusetts does. When the colored man is educated up to the point of seeing that Alabama and Massachusetts are a long way apart, that the conditions of life in them are very different, and that if free trade enables my white brother across the street to buy his plows at a cheaper rate it will enable me to do the same, he will act in a different way. More than once I have noticed that when the whites were in favor of prohibition, the blacks, led even by sober, upright ministers, voted against prohibition, simply because the whites were in favor of it, and for this reason the blacks said that they knew it was a 'democratic trick.' If the whites vote to lay a tax to build a school house, it is a signal for the blacks to oppose the measure, simply because the whites favor it. I venture the assertion that the sooner the colored man, South, learns that one political party is not composed altogether of angels and the other altogether of devils, and that all his enemies do not live in his own town or neighborhood and all his friends in some other distant section of the country, the sooner will his educational advantages be enhanced many fold. But matters are gradually changing in this respect. The black man is beginning to find out that there are those even among the Southern whites who desire his elevation. The Negro's new faith in the white man is being reciprocated in proportion as the Negro is rightly educated. The white brother is beginning to learn by degrees that all Negroes are not liars and chicken thieves.

"Now in regard to what I have said about the relations of the two races, there should be no unmanly cowering or stooping to satisfy unreasonable whims of Southern white men; but it is charity and wisdom to keep in mind the two hundred years of schooling in prejudice against the Negro which the ex-slaveholders are called on to conquer. A certain class of whites object to the general education of the colored man on the ground that when he is educated he ceases to do manual labor, and there is no avoiding the fact that much aid is withheld from Negro education in the South by the states on these grounds. Just here the great mission of industrial education, coupled with mental, comes in. It kills two birds with one stone, viz., it secures the co-operation of the whites and does the best possible thing for the black man."

Unknown to me, there were a large number of people present from Alabama, and some from my own home, Tuskegee. These white people frankly told me afterward that they went to the meeting expecting to hear the South roundly abused, but were pleasantly surprised to find that there was no word of adverse criticism in my address. On the other hand, the South was given due credit for all the good things they had done towards aiding the Negro. A white lady, who was a teacher in a college in Tuskegee, wrote back to the local paper that she was pleased, as well as surprised, to note the credit which I gave the white people of Tuskegee for their aid in getting the school started. This address at Madison, Wisconsin, was the first that I had delivered, that, in any large measure, dealt with the general problem of the races. Those who heard the address seemed to be pleased with what I said, and with the position I took.

After this address I began receiving invitations from a good many portions of the country to deliver addresses on the subject of educating the Negro. At the present time these applications have increased to such an extent, and they come in such large numbers, that if I were to try to answer even one-third of the calls that come to me from all parts of the United States, as well as other countries, to speak, I would scarcely spend a single day at Tuskegee.

CHAPTER VIII.

THE HISTORY OF TUSKEGEE FROM 1884 TO 1894.

From 1884 to 1894 comparatively little was heard of the school in the public press, yet that was a period of constant and solid growth. In 1884 the enrollment was 169. In 1894 the enrollment had increased to 712, and 54 officers and teachers were employed. Besides the growth in the number of students and instructors, there had also been quite an increase in the number of buildings, and in every way the students were made more comfortable in their surroundings. By 1893 we had upon the school grounds thirty buildings of various kinds and sizes, practically all built by the labor of the students.

Between 1884 and 1894, I think, the hardest work was done in securing money. Regularly, during this period, we were compelled, on account of lack of accommodations, to refuse many students, but very often they would come to us under such circumstances that, though lacking in accommodations, we could not have the heart to turn them away, especially after they had traveled long distances, as was true in many cases. Students seemed willing to put up with almost any kind of accommodations if they were given a chance to secure an education.

During this period either Miss Davidson or myself, or sometimes both of us, spent a great deal of time in the North getting funds with which to meet our ever increasing demands. This, of course, was the hardest and most trying part of the work. Beginning early in the morning, the day was spent in seeing individuals at their homes or in their offices; and in the evening, and sometimes during the day, too, addresses were delivered before churches, Sunday Schools, or other organizations. On many occasions I have spoken as many as five times at different churches on the same Sabbath.

The large increase in the number of students tempted us often to put up buildings for which we had no money. In the early days of the institution by far the larger proportion of the buildings were begun on faith. I remember at one time we began a building which cost in the end about $8,000, and we had only $200 in cash with which to pay for it; nevertheless the building was completed after a hard struggle and is now in constant use.

I remember at one time we were very much in need of money with which to meet pressing obligations. I borrowed $400 from a friend, with the understanding that the money must be returned within thirty days. On the morning of the day that the thirty days expired we were without the $400 with which to repay the loan, and were, of course, very much depressed in consequence. The mail, however, came in at about eleven o'clock, and brought a check from a friend for exactly $400. I could give a number of other such instances illustrating how we were relieved from embarrassing circumstances in ways that have always seemed to me to have been providential. Although the institution has had occasion many times to give promissory notes in order to meet its obligations, there has never been a single instance when any of its notes have gone to protest, and its credit and general financial standing have always been good with the commercial world. I have felt deeply obligated to the white and colored citizens of Tuskegee for their kindness in helping the school financially when it did not have money to meet its obligations. We have never applied to an individual or to either of the banks in Tuskegee for aid that we did not get it when the banks or individuals were able to aid us. The banks have been more than kind, often seemingly inconveniencing themselves in order to be of service to our institution. In the earlier days of the institution, when we had little in the way of income, on several occasions I have started to the depot, when I had to make a journey away from Tuskegee, with no money in my pocket, but felt perfectly sure of meeting a friend in the town of Tuskegee from whom I could get money, and I have never been disappointed in this respect.

In 1883 we received our first donation of $500 from the Peabody Fund, through Dr. J. L. M. Curry, the General Agent. At that time Dr. Curry formed his first acquaintance with Tuskegee; and, as I have stated elsewhere, from then until now he has been one of our warmest and most helpful friends. The amount received from the Peabody Fund has since been increased until it now amounts to twelve or fifteen hundred dollars each year.

In connection with this appropriation from the Peabody Fund it may be interesting to relate a conversation which took place between Dr. Curry and one of the State officers at Montgomery, Alabama. The State officer in question was telling Dr. Curry that there were several other schools in the state that needed help more than Tuskegee did; and that, because Tuskegee, through the efforts of its teachers, was receiving money from the North and elsewhere which other schools were not getting, he thought we were not entitled to help from the Peabody Fund. Dr. Curry promptly replied that because we were making an extra effort to get funds which other schools were not getting was the strongest reason why we should be helped; in other words, he told the officer plainly that we were trying to help ourselves, and for that reason he wanted us helped from the Peabody Fund.

Through the constant efforts of Miss Davidson and myself in the North and South, the financial report for the first two years of the school showed receipts amounting to $11,679.69. The rapid increase in the growth of the school and in the confidence with the people may be shown by the fact that, during the third year of the existence of the school, the receipts nearly doubled themselves as compared with the second year; we received the third year the sum of $10,482.78, which was nearly as much as we received during the two previous years. By far the larger proportion of this amount came in small sums; very often amounts came from individuals that were as small as fifty cents. One of the things that constantly touched and encouraged us during the early years of the school was the deep interest manifested in its success by the old and ignorant colored people in and near the town of Tuskegee. They never seemed to tire in their interest and efforts. They were constantly trying to do something to help forward the institution. Whenever they had a few chickens or eggs, for example, to spare, they would bring them in and make a present of them to the school.

The income of the institution for the fifth year amounted to $20,162.13; for the ninth year, $30,326; for the eleventh year, $61,023.28; for the fourteenth year, $79,836.50.

At the end of the third year we were able to report that the school owned property unencumbered by debt that was valued at $30,000. During the third year Alabama Hall, to which I have already referred, was completed at a cost of $10,000.

The report of the school's history for the fourth year shows that we received from all sources $11,146.07. During that year we got into a very tight place financially, and hardly knew which way to turn for relief. In the midst of our perplexity I went to Gen. Armstrong, and he very kindly loaned the school money to help it out of its embarrassment, although I afterwards learned that it was nearly all of the money that he possessed in cash.

In my fourth annual report to the Trustees I used the following words: "Greater attention has been given to the industrial department this year than ever before. Three things are accomplished by the industrial system: (1) The student is enabled to pay a part of his expenses of board, books, etc., in labor; (2) He learns how to work;

(3) He is taught the dignity of labor. In all the industrial branches the students do the actual work, under the direction of competent instructors." I have not had occasion to change in any great degree the foregoing sentences as representing the purpose for which Tuskegee stands.

During the fifth year of our work we were able also to add a saw mill, through the generosity of Gen. J. F. B. Marshall, to whom I have already referred. The addition of this saw mill enabled us to saw a large part of the lumber used by the institution.

In order to give many worthy students an opportunity to secure an education by working at some trade or industry during the day and studying at night, we opened in the fall of 1883 our our first night school. The night school was opened with one teacher and one student. From this small beginning the night school has increased, until at this writing there are four hundred and fifty students. By working in the day and going to school at night, the night students earn money with which to pay their expenses the next year in day school, and if they bring a good supply of clothing they can earn enough, together with what they earn during vacation, to keep them in school two or three years after they enter day school.

I cannot better indicate the constant growth

of the school than by giving a description of our seventh anniversary, which took place May 31, 1888. There were more than 2,000 people present, in spite of rain that came in showers. During the morning, from 9:30 to 12, the regular work of the entire school was carried on in the various departments, which were open for inspection. In addition to the regular work, products of the shops and farm were exhibited. The course of study then extended over four years, with two preparatory classes. It included the English branches for the literary part, with instruction in one or more of the following industries throughout: Blacksmithing, carpentry, brickmasonry, brick making, plastering, farming, stock, poultry and bee-raising, saw-milling, wheelwrighting, printing, mattress and cabinet making, sewing, cutting and fitting, washing and ironing, cooking, and general housekeeping. From these various departments the following articles were exhibited: At the blacksmith and wheelwright shop were seen two one-horse wagons, plow stock, small tools, express wagon body, wheelbarrow, spring wagon seat and various other articles. In the carpenter shop there were wardrobes, a center and a leaf table, wash stands, book cases, bedsteads, wash boards, picture frames, chairs, paneling, moulding, laths, etc. In the printing office there was an exhibit of the general work of the office,—such as blanks, checks, catalogues, promissory notes, diploma blanks, minutes of associations and conventions, annual reports, bill and letter heads, envelopes, circulars, handbills, invitations, business cards, certificates, etc., with samples of the two monthly papers which were then printed at the institution, the "Southern Letter" and "The Gleaner." From the farm and poultry yard, there were vegetables, hogs, cattle, chickens, turkeys, guineas, geese, a peacock, eggs, bees and honey. Mattress and chair making were features that had been added to the industries that year, and were especially satisfactory. The mattresses exhibited compared favorably with those made anywhere. In the laundry there was a tastefully arranged exhibit of laundried bedding, dresses, collars and cuffs, shirts, ladies' and gentlemen's underwear, table linen and towels. The sewing room showed samples of all kinds of ladies', gentlemen's and children's clothing, with laces, mats, tidies, etc. At the brickyard there was a kiln of 120,000 bricks ready for burning. About the saw mill there were stacks of its products. The cooking class had a tempting display of its work in cakes, jellies, bread, yeast, meats and a roast pig.

Among the first things seen by a visitor coming to the school from any direction was a large new brick building—Olivia Davidson Hall. This building was almost entirely the product of student labor, under the supervision of Mr. Brown, instructor in carpentry at that time, who also planned the building. The school then had three large and comfortable buildings. Porter Hall contained recitation rooms, offices, library and reading room, chapel and dormitories for boys, with the school laundry in the basement. Alabama Hall, with a large frame annex built that year, was used for girls' dormitories, and contained, in addition, teachers' and students' parlors and dining rooms and kitchen. Armstrong Hall contained young men's dormitories, reading and sitting rooms, bath room, printing office and two recitation rooms. In addition there were several cottages on the grounds, while a new one and a large barn, the latter to cost perhaps $2,000, were in process of erection.

In the early years of the school, the anniversary exercises were held in the school chapel, which was the small chapel in Porter Hall, but from year to year the influx of patrons and friends from far and near had so increased that the chapel would no longer hold a fifth of them. That year the audience of 2,000, including the 400 students, was assembled in a rude pavilion built of rough timber and partly covered by the wide spreading branches of some mulberry trees. Here, after partaking of a substantial dinner furnished by the school and friends, students and visitors assembled. A long procession was formed of students, teachers and graduates, which marched from Alabama Hall to the pavilion to music furnished by the school band, and there the exercises of the seventh anniversary were held.

There were ten members of the graduating class of that year, as follows: Andrew J. Wilborn, Valedictorian, Tuskegee, Ala.; Letitia B. Adams, Tuskegee, Ala.; Caroline Smith, Tuskegee, Ala.; Shadrach R. Marshall, Talbotton, Ga.; Philip P. Wright, LaFayette, Ala.; William H. Clark, Brunswick, Ga.; Eugenia Lyman, Opelika, Ala.; Sarah L. Hunt, Salutatorian, Sparta, Ga.; George W. Lovejoy, Olustee Creek, Ala.; Nicholas E. Abercrombie, Montgomery, Ala.

The total enrollment for the year was 400. The school farm then contained 540 acres of farm and timber land. The saw mill had furnished most of the lumber for the buildings and other carpenter work done that year, and for that purpose saw logs had been cut from the school land. The school property was then worth about $80,000. The income for the year had been $26,755.73. This amount about covered the expenses. Including the ten mentioned above, the school then had forty-two graduates. During the year previous all the graduates had been engaged in teaching for some part of the year. All the members of

EARNEST DAVIDSON WASHINGTON, YOUNGEST SON OF DR. WASHINGTON.

SOCIAL LIFE AT TUSKEGEE INSTITUTE. THE OFFICERS ANNUAL HOP.

that year's class were Christians. They went out as teachers of various kinds in the state of Alabama. The young women had a knowledge of washing, ironing, cooking, sewing and general housekeeping, in addition to their intellectual attainments. One of the six young men was a shoemaker, one a carpenter, one had considerable knowledge of the printer's trade and one was an excellent plasterer. The annual address at that commencement was delivered by Hon. John R. Lynch, of Mississippi, and for eloquence, practical thought and helpful information could hardly have been surpassed. There were a number of Tuskegee's best white citizens present, while the colored citizens came out *en masse* to witness the exercises that launched into life three youths from their own town. Montgomery was represented by one of her military companies, the "Capital City Guards," and 124 of her best citizens, for whose accommodation special trains were sent out.

In order to emphasize the fact that people at Tuskegee during its early history were not idle, I give the daily program which was in effect in January, 1886: 5 a. m., rising bell; 5:50 a. m., warning breakfast bell; 6 a. m., breakfast bell; 6:20 a. m., breakfast over; 6:20 to 6:50 a. m., rooms are cleaned; 6:50, work bell; 7:30, morning study hour; 8:20, morning school bell; 8:25, inspection of young men's toilet in ranks; 8:40, devotional exercises in chapel; 8:55, "5 minutes" with the daily news: 9 a. m., class work begins; 12, class work closes; 12:15 p. m., dinner; 1 p. m., work bell; 1:30 p. m., class work begins; 3:30 p. m., class work ends; 5:30 p. m., bell to "knock off" work; 6 p. m., supper; 7:10 p. m., evening prayers; 7:30 p. m., evening study hours; 8:45 p. m., evening study hour closes; 9:20 p. m., warning retiring bell; 9:30 p. m., retiring bell.

Although the period of the school's history about which I have written in this chapter was one of constant and substantial growth, it nevertheless was during this period that the school sustained a great loss, as well as I a great personal bereavement, in the death of my beloved and faithful wife, Olivia Davidson Washington. In May, 1889, after four years of married life, she succumbed to the overtaxing duties of mother and assistant principal of the school and passed away. Her remains were laid to rest amid the tears of teachers and students. "Her words of caution, advice, sympathy and encouragement were given with a judgment that rarely made an error. Her life was so full of deeds, lessons and suggestions that she will live on to bless and help the institution which she helped found as long as it is a seat of learning."

Two wide-awake boys, Baker Taliaferro and Ernest Davidson, were born to us, who were then too young to know their loss. They are now twelve and ten years of age respectively; and they, with my daughter Portia, are a source of much comfort and joy to me.

Miss Davidson came to the school almost from the very beginning, she being the next person to come after myself. I have spoken in other places of the great assistance she was in helping to build up the school in its early days. As an estimate of her worth and character, I beg to quote the words of the Rev. R. C. Bedford, a friend who knew her worth and her great help to me and to Tuskegee. Commenting upon her death Mr. Bedford said:

"Olivia Davidson was born in Virginia, June 11, 1854. When only a little child she went with her parents to Ohio, where she grew up and received the education afforded by the common schools of that state. At an early age she went to Mississippi and there spent five years as a teacher on the large plantations. In 1878 she came north to her native state, and, that she might more thoroughly fit herself for the work of a teacher, she entered the Hampton Institute, from which, in one year, she graduated with great honor. Her friend, Mrs. Hemenway, of Boston, greatly desiring that she should prose-

---
*This name was changed in later years to Booker T. Jr.

cute her studies still further, at her request, she entered the Framingham, (Mass.) Normal School, from which she graduated in two years. In August following her graduation she came to Tuskegee, Ala., to act as assistant to Prof. Washington, in the State Normal School of which he had been made principal in the July previous. From the very first it became evident that she had found her field of labor for life. Everything tended to inspire her to this end. The people were poor; they were numerous; they were anxious, and aside from an act of the Legislature establishing a school, it had, literally, to be created. The story of her success has often been told, and in this brief tribute cannot be repeated.

"August 11, 1885, Miss Davidson was married to Prof. B. T. Washington, and although she at once took upon herself the cares of a very busy home life, she still retained a most important relation to the school, which no amount of warning from her friends could persuade her to drop. Her marriage with Mr. Washington proved a most happy one, and rarely has it been the lot of two individuals to be so thoroughly united in their life work. The coming of little Baker into the home was an occasion of great rejoicing, and the birth of another son just a few months before his mother's death only served to double the joy.

"It was my privilege to meet Mrs. Washington at Tuskegee when the school had been in operation but little more than a year and, as one of the trustees of the school, I have had an intimate knowledge of her work ever since. It would require more than human pen to tell how deep was her love for the school and how thoroughly her life was consecrated to it. Every grain of sand on all those beautiful grounds and every beam and brick in the walls must have felt the inspiration of her love. No more touching story could be told than that of her earnest efforts to raise money from the people about Tuskegee and of her toilsome walks in Boston, as from house to house, and with an eloquence that was rarely refused, she sought funds to provide shelter for the hundreds of students that were flocking to the school. Her character made her especially adapted to all parts of the work in which she was engaged, and the stamp of her influence on the higher life of the school no time can ever efface. Among a people who make much show of religion, but often with too little of its spirit, hers was religion indeed, but with so little of show as sometimes to make her life a mystery to those who did not really know her. The blind and the poor, and above all the aged, can tell of her religion as they recall the happy Thanksgiving and Christmas times when they have sat at her table and her own hands have ministered to their wants, and when in sickness she has visited them and relieved their sufferings. No woman ever had a truer husband or more devoted friends; and the memory of their kindness will rest, as a precious legacy, upon the school and upon all who loved her as long as time shall last."

While speaking of the financial growth of the school, I must not neglect to indicate its growth at the same time in students. As I have stated, the school opened with one teacher and 30 students. By the end of the first year we had three teachers, including Miss Davidson, Mr. John Caldwell and myself. For the third session there were 169 students and 10 teachers. For the fifth year there were 279 students and 18 teachers. For the eighth year there were 399 students and 25 teachers. For the tenth year there were 730 students and 30 teachers. For the fourteenth year, ending in June, 1895, there were 1,013 students and 63 teachers.

In the spring of 1892, at our annual commencement, we had the pleasure and the honor of a visit from Hon. Frederick Douglass, who delivered the annual address to the graduating class of that year. This was Mr. Douglass' first visit to the far South, and there was a large crowd of people from far and near to listen to the words of that grand old man. The speech was fully up to the high standard of excellence, eloquence and wisdom for which that venerable gentleman was noted.

Mr. Douglass had the same idea concerning the importance and value of industrial education that I have tried to emphasize. He also held the same views as I do in regard to the emigration of the Negro to Africa, and was opposed to the scheme of diffusion and dissemination of the Negro throughout the North and Northwest, believing as I do, that the Southern section of the country where the Negro now resides is the best place for him. In fact, the more I have studied the life of Mr. Douglass, the more I have been surprised to find his far-reaching and generous grasp of the whole condition and needs of the Negro race. Years before Hampton or Tuskegee undertook industrial education, in reply to a request for advice by Mrs. Harriet Beecher Stowe as to how she could best use a certain sum of money which had been or was about to be placed in her hands, Mr. Douglass wrote her in part as follows:

ROCHESTER, March 8, 1853.

MY DEAR MRS. STOWE:

You kindly informed me when at your house a fortnight ago, that you designed to do something which should permanently contribute to the improvement and elevation of the free colored people in the United States. You especially expressed an interest in such of this class as had become free by their own exertions, and desired most of all to be of service to them. In what manner and by what means you can assist this class most successfully, is the subject upon which you have done me the honor to ask my opinion.

. . . I assert, then, that *poverty*, *ignorance*, and *degradation* are the combined evils; or in other words, these constitute the social disease of the free colored people in the United States.

To deliver them from this triple malady is to improve and elevate them, by which I mean simply to put them on an equal footing with their white fellow-countrymen in the sacred right to "*Life*, *Liberty* and the pursuit of happiness." I am for no fancied or artificial elevation, but only ask fair play. How shall this be obtained? I answer, first, not by establishing for our use high schools and colleges. Such institutions are, in my judgment, beyond our immediate occasions and are not adapted to our present most pressing wants. High schools and colleges are excellent institutions, and will in due season be greatly subservient to our progress; but they are the result, as well as they are the demand, of a point of progress which we as a people have not yet attained. Accustomed as we have been to the rougher and harder modes of living, and of gaining a livelihood, we cannot and we ought not to hope that in a single leap from our low condition we can reach that of *Ministers*, *Lawyers*, *Doctors*, *Editors*, *Merchants*, etc. These will doubtless be attained by us; but this will only be when we have patiently and laboriously, and I may add, successfully, mastered and passed through the intermediate gradations of agriculture and the mechanic arts. Besides, there are (and perhaps there is a better reason for my views of the case) numerous institutions of learning in this country, already thrown open to colored youth. To my thinking, there are quite as many facilities now afforded to the colored people as they can spare the time, from the sterner duties of life, to judiciously appropriate. In their present condition of poverty they cannot spare their sons and daughters two or three years at boarding-schools or colleges, to say nothing of finding the means to sustain them while at such institutions. I take it, therefore, that we are well provided for in this respect; and that it may be fairly inferred from the fact, that the facilities for our education, so far as schools and colleges in the Free States are concerned, will increase quite in proportion with our future wants. Colleges have been opened to colored youth in this country during the last dozen years. Yet few, comparatively, have acquired a classical education; and even this few have found themselves educated far above a living condition, there being no methods by which they could turn their learning to account. Several of this latter class have entered the ministry; but you need not be told that an educated people is needed to sustain an educated ministry. There must be a certain amount of cultivation among the people, to sustain such a ministry. At present we have not that cultivation amongst us; and, therefore, we value in the preacher strong lungs rather than high learning. I do not say that educated ministers are not needed amongst us, far from it. I wish there were more of them; but to increase their number is *not* the largest benefit you can bestow upon us.

We have two or three colored lawyers in this country; and I rejoice in the fact; for it affords very gratifying evidence of our progress. Yet it must be confessed that, in point of success, our lawyers are as great failures as our ministers. White people will not employ them to the obvious embarrassment of their causes; the blacks, taking their cue from the whites, have not sufficient confidence in their abilities to employ them. Hence educated colored men, among the colored people, are at a very great discount. It would seem that education and emigration go together with us, for as soon as a man rises amongst us, capable, by his genius and learning, to do us great service, just so soon he finds that he can serve himself better by going elsewhere. In proof of this, I might instance the Russwurms, the Garnets, the Wards, the Crummells, and others, all men of superior ability and attainments, and capable of removing mountains of prejudice against their race, by their simple presence in the country; but these gentlemen, finding themselves embarrassed here by the peculiar disadvantages to which I have referred, disadvantages in part growing out of their education, being repelled by ignorance on one hand, and prejudice on the other, and having no taste to continue a contest against such odds, have sought more congenial climes, where they can live more peaceable and quiet lives. I regret their election, but I cannot blame them; for with an equal amount of education and the hard lot which was theirs, I might follow their example.

There is little reason to hope that any considerable number of the free colored people will ever be induced to leave this country, even if such a thing were desirable. The black man (unlike the Indian) loves civilization. He does not make very great progress in civilization himself, but he likes to be in the midst of it, and prefers to share its most galling evils, to encountering barbarism. Then the love of country, the dread of isolation, the lack of adventurous spirit, and the thought of seeming to desert their "brethren in bonds," are a powerful check upon all schemes of colonization, which look to the removal of the colored people, without the slaves. The truth is, dear madam, we are here, and here we are likely to remain. Individuals emigrate—nations never. We have grown up with this republic, and see nothing in her character, or even in the character of the American people, as yet, which compels the belief that we must leave the United States. If, then, we are to remain here, the question for the wise and good is precisely that which you have submitted to me—namely: What can be done to improve the condition of the free people of color in the United States? The plan which I humbly submit in answer to this inquiry (and the hope that it may find favor with you, and with the many friends of humanity who honor, love and co-operate with you) is the establishment in Rochester, N. Y., or in some other part of the United States equally favorable to such an enterprise, of an INDUSTRIAL COLLEGE in which shall be taught several important branches of the mechanic arts. This college shall be open to colored youth. I shall pass over the details of such an institution as I propose. . . . Never having had a day's schooling in my life, I may not be expected to map out the details of a plan so comprehensive as that involved in the idea of a college. I repeat, then, that I leave the organization and administration of the institution to the superior wisdom of yourself and the friends who second your noble efforts. The argument in favor of an Industrial College (a college to be conducted by the best men, and the best workmen which the mechanic arts can afford; a college where colored youth can be instructed to use their hands, as well as their heads; where they can be put in possession of the means of getting a living wherever their lot in after life may be cast among civilized or uncivilized men; whether they choose to stay here, or prefer to return to the land of their fathers) is briefly this: Prejudice against the free colored people in the United States has shown itself nowhere so invincible as among mechanics. The farmer and the professional man cherish no feeling so bitter as that cherished by these. The latter would starve us out of the country entirely. At this moment I can more easily get my son into a lawyer's office to study law than I can in a blacksmith's shop to blow the bellows and to wield the sledge-hammer. Denied the means of learning useful trades, we are pressed into the narrowest limits to obtain a livelihood. In times past we have been the hewers of wood and drawers of water for American society, and we once enjoyed a monopoly in menial employments, but this is so no longer. Even these employments are rapidly passing away out of out hands. The fact is, (every day begins with the lesson, and ends with the lesson) that colored men must learn trades; must find new employments; new modes of usefulness to society, or that they must decay under the pressing wants to which their condition is rapidly bringing them.

We must become mechanics; we must build as well as live in houses; we must make as well as use furniture; we must construct bridges as well as pass over them; before we can properly live or be respected by our fellow-men. We need mechanics as well as ministers. We need workers in iron, clay, and leather. We have orators, authors, and other professional men, but these reach only a certain class, and get respect for our race in certain select circles. To live here as we ought we must fasten ourselves to our countrymen through their every-day, cardinal wants. We must not only be able to black boots, but to make them. At present we are in the Northern states, unknown as mechanics. We give no proof of genius or skill at the county, state or national fairs. We are unknown at any of the great exhibitions of the industry of our fellow citizens, and being unknown, we are unconsidered.

Wishing you, dear madam, renewed health, a pleasant passage and safe return to your native land, I am, most truly, your gratified friend,

FREDERICK DOUGLASS.

In October, 1893, I was married to Miss Margaret James Murray, a graduate of Fisk University, who came to Tuskegee in 1889 as a teacher. She has been in every way as much interested in the advancement of Tuskegee as myself, and fully bears her share of the responsibilities and labor, giving especial attention to the development of the girls and to work among the women through her mothers' meetings in various parts of Alabama and elsewhere.

CHAPTER IX.

INVITED TO DELIVER A LECTURE AT FISK UNIVERSITY.

In the spring of 1895 I was pleasantly surprised to receive an invitation from the Fisk University Lecture Bureau, in Nashville, Tennessee, to deliver a lecture before that organization. Mr. Edgar Webber was the president, and presided at the meeting when I spoke. This was among the first addresses which I had delivered in the South that was fully reported by the Southern press. A full description of the meeting was given by the Nashville Daily American and the Nashville Banner, and papers throughout many portions of the South contained editorials based upon this address. It was also my first opportunity to speak before any large number of educated and representative colored people, and I accepted the invitation very reluctantly and went to Nashville with a good deal of fear and trembling, but my effort seemed to meet with the hearty approval of the greater portion of the audience.

As the address delivered at Fisk University on this occasion constitutes in a large measure the basis for many of my other addresses and much of the work I have tried to do, I give in full what the Nashville American said:

"An intelligent and appreciative audience composed of prominent colored citizens, students and quite a large number of white people, crowded the beautiful and commodious Fisk memorial chapel last night to hear Prof. Booker T. Washington lecture on 'Industrial Education.' The lecture was the first given under the auspices of the Student's Lecture Bureau of Fisk University, and was in every way a complete success. Mr. Washington is a powerful and convincing speaker. His simplicity and utter unselfishness, both in speech and action, are impressive. He speaks to the point. He does not waste words in painting beautiful pictures, but deals mostly with plain facts. Nevertheless, he is witty and caused his audience last night to laugh and applaud repeatedly the jokes and striking points of his address.

"Booker T. Washington is doing a great work for his race and the South. He has the right views.

"Prof. Washington was introduced by Edgar Webber, President of the Lecture Bureau, and among other things he said:

'I am exceedingly anxious that every young man and woman should keep a hopeful and cheerful spirit as to the future. Despite all of our disadvantages and hardships, ever since our fore-

THE FACULTY, TUSKEGEE INSTITUTE.—125 OFFICERS AND TEACHERS.

TRUSTEES OF THE TUSKEGEE INSTITUTE.

STANDING—From left to right: Warren Logan, Treasurer; Mr. Frank Trumbull, Mr. W. M. Scott, Mr. Emmett J. Scott, Mr. Charles E. Mason and Mr. Victor H. Tulane.

SITTING—From left to right: Mr. A. J. Wilborn, Mr. William G. Willcox, Mr. Julius Rosenwald, Dr. Booker T. Washington, Hon. Seth Low, Mr. R. O. Simpson, Mr. C. W. Hare and Mr. W. W. Campbell.

Picture taken during Mid-Winter Meeting of Trustees, February, 1915.

fathers set foot upon the American soil as slaves, our pathway has been marked by progress. Think of it: We went into slavery pagans; we came out Christians. We went into slavery pieces of property; we came out American citizens. We went into slavery without a language; we came out speaking the proud Anglo-Saxon tongue. We went into slavery with slave chains clanking about our wrists; we came out with the American ballot in our hands.

"'I believe that we are to reach our highest development largely along the lines of scientific and industrial education. For the last fifty years education has tended in one direction, the cementing of mind to matter.'

"The speaker then said most people had the idea that industrial education was opposed to literary training, opposed to the highest development. He wanted to correct this error. He would choose the college graduate as the subject to receive industrial education. The more mind the subject had, the more satisfactory would be the results in industrial education. It requires as strong a mind to build a Corliss engine as it does to write a Greek grammar. Without industrial education, the speaker feared they would be in danger of getting too many 'smart men' scattered through the South. A young colored man in a certain town had been pointed out to him as being exceedingly smart, and he had heard of him as being very accomplished. Upon inquiry, however, he learned the young man applied his knowledge and training to no earthly good. 'He was just a smart man, that was all.'

"Continuing, the speaker said: 'As a race there are two things we must learn to do—one is to put brains into the common occupations of life, and the other is to dignify common labor. If we do not, we cannot hold our own as a race. Ninety per cent. of any race on the globe earns its living at the common occupations of life, and the Negro can be no exception to this rule.'

"Prof. Washington then illustrated the importance of this by citing the fact that while twenty years ago every large and paying barber shop over the country was in the hands of black men, today in all the large cities you cannot find a single large or first class barber shop operated by colored men. The black men had had a monopoly of that industry, but had gone on from day to day in the same old monotonous way without improving anything about the industry. As a result the white man has taken it up, put brains into it, watched all the fine points, improved and progressed until his shop today was not known as a barber shop, but as a tonsorial parlor, and he was no longer called a barber, but a tonsorial artist. Just so the old Negro man with his bucket

of whitewash and his long pole and brush had
given way to the white man who had applied
his knowledge of chemistry to mixing materials,
his knowledge of physics to the blending of colors,
and his knowledge of geometry to figuring and
decorating the ceiling. But the white man was
not called a whitewasher; he was called a house
decorater. He had put brains into his work, had
given dignity to it, and the old colored man with
the long pole and bucket was a thing of the past.
The old Negro woman and her wash tub were
fast being supplanted by the white man with his
steam laundry, washing over a hundred shirts an
hour. The many colored men who had formerly
earned a living by cutting the grass in the front
yards and keeping the flower beds in trim were
no competitors for the white man, who, bringing
his knowledge of surveying and terracing and
plotting land, and his knowledge of botany and
blending colors into active play, had dignified and
promoted the work. He was not called a grass
cutter or a yard cleaner, but a florist or a land-
scape gardener. The old black 'mammy' could
never again enter the sick-room, where she was
once known as a peerless nurse. She had given
place to the tidy little white woman, with
her neat white cap and apron, her knowledge
of physiology, bandaging, principles of diseases
and the administration of medicine, who had

dignified, beautified and glorified the art of nursing and had turned it into a profession. Just so, too, the black cook was going out of date under the influence of the superior knowledge and art of cookery possessed by white 'chefs,' who were educated men and commanded large salaries.

"'Now,' said the speaker, 'what are we going to do? Are we going to put brains into these common occupations? Are we going to apply the knowledge we gain at school? Are we going to keep up with the world, or are we going to let these occupations, which mean our very life blood, slip from us? Education in itself is worthless; it is only as it is used that it is of value. A man might as well fill his head with so much cheap soup as with learning, unless he is going to use his knowledge.'

"Prof. Washington said that he had been told that the young colored man is cramped, and that after he gets his education there were few chances to use it. He had little patience with such argument. The idea had been too prevalent that the educated colored man must either teach, preach, be a clerk or follow some profession. The educated colored men must, more and more, go to the farms, into the trades, start brickyards, saw-mills, factories, open coal mines; in short, apply their education to conquering the forces of nature.

"One trouble with the average Negro, said the speaker, was that he was always hungry, and it was impossible to make progress along educational, moral or religious lines while in that condition. It was a hard matter to make a Christian out of a hungry man. It had often been contended that the Negro needed no industrial education, because he already knew too well how to work. There never was a greater mistake, and the speaker compared, as an illustration, the white man with his up-to-date cultivator to the 'one gallused' Negro with his old plow, patched harness and stiff-jointed mule.

"The speaker was inclined to fear that the Negro race laid too much stress on their grievances and not enough on their opportunities. While many wrongs had been perpetrated on them in the South, still it was recognized by all intelligent colored people that the black man has far better opportunity to rise in his business in the South than in the North. While he might not be permitted to ride in the first-class car in the South, he was not allowed to help build that first-class car in the North. He could sooner conquer Southern prejudice than Northern competition. The speaker found that when it came to business, pure and simple, the black man in the South was put on the same footing with the white man, and here, said he, was the Negro's great opportunity. The black man could always find a purchaser for his wares among the whites.

"Prof. Washington concluded with an appeal to his race to use the opportunities that are right about them, and thus grow independent.

"He has made a lasting impression on the minds of all who heard him. If he continues his wonderful career he will be classed with Douglass as a benefactor to the Negro race."

The Memphis Commercial-Appeal a few days after this address was delivered contained an editorial concerning it. I quote that in full because it is among the first editorials from a Southern newspaper concerning my addresses and the work at Tuskegee, and also because it shows that the efforts put forth at Tuskegee in behalf of industrial education for the Negro have had the effect of awakening not only the Negroes, but even the Southern whites, to the necessity of more education of this kind. The editorial is as follows:

"Prof. Booker T. Washington, a short time since, delivered an address before the students of Fisk University, in which he advocated industrial education for the Negro race. The address has received considerable attention and evoked many favorable comments, and the theme is one worthy of far more consideration than it has ever received in the South. Our interest in the matter, however, does not particularly concern its application to the Negro. We are chiefly interested for the Southern whites and the South itself. The South is just about to enter an era of industrial development that will be almost without parallel. Its progress will be all the more rapid because of the long delay that has allowed other fields to be exhausted before the vast wealth of our natural resources began to be developed. The one great drawback to the development of the south has been the lack of skilled and educated labor, and in the great industrial awakening that is upon us the skill to manage and operate our mills and factories and convert our abundant crude material into finished products must come from the North, unless something is done to educate our own people in the industrial arts. The opening of the eyes of the world to the vast natural wealth of the South will then simply mean that strangers will come in and dispossess our own people of their vintage and turn to their own account the opportunities we have never learned to employ. We must awake to the fact that we are face to face with a new civilization. The old order changeth, giving place to the new. We must adjust ourselves to the changed conditions, or be left behind in the march of progress. We must catch the spirit of modern progress and achievement, or be rooted out by those that have. The great men of this generation are not statesmen, lawyers, orators or poets. The richest rewards of intellectual effort go to those who know how to bring the forces of nature to aid the processes of production; in the natural era that is now upon us this will be especially true of the South. The men who have the capacity for taking active and effective part in the development of our resources, for the management of mills and factories, for contributing skilled labor to the fashioning of crude material into finished product, these are the men who will reap the mighty harvest and the men who will possess and rule our country. The same is true of the farm as well as the factory. The crude and unskilled methods of Southern agriculture must give way to more scientific tillage. If our own farmers cannot learn the lesson they must be displaced by those that know it.

"All the Southern States are doing much in the way of educating the people; but without disparaging the value of the learning obtained in our schools, how much of it goes to prepare the young for grappling with the conditions that surround them or will help to make them masters or successful workers in the great field of modern progress? Look at the vast wealth of undeveloped resources that encompasses almost every

Southern community. Look at the fertile fields or the worn lands still in bondage to ignorant labor and an ante-bellum agricultural system. Will a knowledge of grammar or of Greek convert our coal, our iron and our timber into wealth, or make our fields bountiful with the harvest? The plain truth is that much of the learning obtained in our schools is wasted erudition. The young are not only not educated with reference to the conditions of the age, but their minds are carefully and systematically trained in other directions. They see no triumphs of intellect except in politics or the 'learned professions.' Their imaginations are inflamed by stories of how men from humble beginnings became great statesmen, great orators and great lawyers. The result is that thousands miserably fail because their little book learning has diverted them from occupations in which they might have achieved honorable success and even distinction. These men who might have become machinists become pettifogging lawyers, quack doctors or small-bore politicians. Industrial education is the great need of the South, because industrial skill and educated labor are to be the factors of its future progress, and these are to reap the richest rewards it will have to bestow. If our own children cannot be prepared to take their part in the great work, strangers will reap and enjoy the harvest."

CHAPTER X.

THE SPEECH AT THE OPENING OF THE COTTON STATES' EXPOSITION, AND INCIDENTS CONNECTED THEREWITH.

So much has been said and written concerning the address which I delivered at the opening of the Atlanta Exposition in September, 1895, that it may not be out of place for me to explain in some detail how and why I received the invitation to deliver this address.

In the spring of 1895 I received a telegram at Tuskegee from prominent citizens in Atlanta, asking me to accompany a committee composed of Atlanta people,—all white, I think, except Bishop Gaines and Bishop Grant,—to Washington to appear before the Committee on Appropriations for the purpose of inducing Congress to make an appropriation to help forward the Exposition which the citizens of Atlanta were at that time planning to hold. I accepted this invitation and went to Washington with the committee. A number of the white people in the delegation spoke, among them the Mayor and other officials of Atlanta, and then Bishop Gaines and Bishop Grant were called upon. My name was last, I think, on the list of speakers. I had never before appeared before such a committee, or made any address in the capitol of the Nation, and I had many misgivings as to what I should say and the impression I would make. While I cannot recall my speech, I remember that I tried to impress upon the Committee with all the earnestness and plainness of language that I could, that if Congress wanted to help the South do something that would rid it of the race problem and make friends between the two races it should in every way encourage the material and intellectual growth of both races, and that the Atlanta Exposition would present an opportunity for both races to show what they had done in the way of development since freedom, and would at the same time prove a great encouragement to both races to make still greater progress. I tried to emphasize the fact that political agitation alone would not save the Negro, that back of politics he must have industry, thrift, intelligence and property; that no race without these elements of strength could permanently succeed and gain the respect of its fellow citizens, and that the time had now come when Congress had an opportunity to do something for the Negro and the South that would prove of real and lasting benefit, and that I should be greatly disappointed if it did not take advantage of the opportunity. I spoke for fifteen or twenty minutes and was very much surprised at the close of my address to receive the hearty congratulations and thanks of all the members of the Atlanta delegation, as well as the members of the Committee on Appropriations. I will not prolong the story, except to add that the Committee did pass the resolution unanimously, agreeing to report a bill to Congress in the interest of the Atlanta Exposition. Our work, however, did not end with making these addresses before the Committee. We remained in Washington several days. The Atlanta committee had meetings every day and the colored members were invited to these, and were given a free opportunity to express their views. Certain members of Congress were parceled out to each member of the Atlanta committee to see, and we spent some time in convincing as many individual members of Congress as possible of the justness of Atlanta's claim. We called in a body upon Speaker Thomas B. Reed. This was the first time I had ever had the pleasure of shaking hands with this great American; since then I have come to know him well and am greatly indebted to him for many kindnesses. After we had spent some time in Washington in hard effort in the interest of the bill, it was called up in Congress and was passed with very little opposition. From the moment that the bill passed Congress the success of the Atlanta Exposition was assured.

Soon after we made this trip to Washington, the directors of the Atlanta Exposition decided that it was the proper thing to give the colored people of the country every opportunity possible to show, by a separate exhibit, to what progress they had attained since their freedom. To this end the directors decided to erect a large and commodious building to be known as the Negro Building. This building in size, architectural beauty and general finish was fully equal to the other buildings on the grounds. It was entirely constructed by colored labor and was filled with the products of Negro skill, brains, and handicraft.

After it was decided to have a separate Negro exhibit it became quite a question as to the best manner of securing a representative and large exhibit from the race. I, in connection with prominent colored citizens of Georgia, was consulted on a good many occasions by the directors of the exposition. It was finally decided to appoint a Negro commissioner to represent each Southern State, who should have charge of collecting and installing the exhibit from his state. After these state commissioners were appointed, a meeting of them was called in Atlanta for the purpose of organization and forming plans to further the Negro exhibit. At the joint meeting of these State Commissioners, it was decided that a Chief Commissioner to have the general supervision of all the exhibits should be selected. A good many people insisted that I should accept the position of Chief Commissioner. I declined to permit my name to be used for this purpose, because my duties at Tuskegee would not permit me to give the time and thought to it that the position demanded. I did, however, accept the position of Commissioner for the State of Alabama. After a good deal of discussion, Mr. I. Garland Penn, of Lynchburg, Virginia, was selected by the Commissioners, and this choice was made unanimous. The success of the Negro exhibit was in a very large measure due to the energy and fidelity of Mr. Penn. No one who voted for him, I think, ever had reason to regret doing so. Most of the states, especially the Southern States, including the District of Columbia, had very creditable exhibits—exhibits that in many cases surprised not only the Negro race but the white people as well. I think the class of people who were most surprised when they went into the Negro Building were some of the Southern white people who, while they had known the Negro as a field hand and as a servant, and had seen him on the streets, had not been in any large degree into his homes and school-houses. At this Exposition, they had, I believe, the first general opportunity to see for themselves the real progress that the Negro was making in the most vital things of life, and it was very interesting as well as satisfactory to hear their constant exclamations of surprise and gratification as they walked through the Negro Building.

The Tuskegee Normal and Industrial Institute made a special effort to prepare a large and creditable exhibit, and in this the institution was most successful. The Tuskegee exhibit consisted of all forms of agricultural products, various articles made in the shops, such as two-horse wagons, one-horse wagons, single and double carriages, harness, shoes, tinware, products from the sewing rooms, laundry, printing office, and academic work, in fact all of the twenty-six industries in operation at Tuskegee were well and creditably represented. With the exception of the exhibit from the Hampton Institute, Hampton, Va., Tuskegee had the largest exhibit in the Negro Building.

As the day for the opening of the Exposition began to draw near, the Board of Directors began to prepare their programme for the opening day. A great many suggestions were made as to the kind of exercises that should be held on that day and as to the names of the speakers to take part. As the discussion went on from day to day, Mr. I. Garland Penn was bold enough to suggest to the Commissioners that, as the Negroes were taking such a prominent part in trying to make the Exposition a success, it was due them that they should have some representation on the programme on the opening day. This suggestion by Mr. Penn was discussed for several days by the Board of Directors, none, however, seeming to have any great objection to it,—the only objection being that they feared it might bring upon the Exposition hurtful criticism. The Board, however, finally voted to ask some Negro to deliver an address at the opening of the Exposition. Several names were suggested, but in some manner, largely I think due to Mr. Penn, my name was selected by the Board, and in due time I received an official communication from the President of the Exposition inviting me to deliver this address. It was the middle of August when I received this invitation. The Exposition was to open on the 18th of September. The papers throughout the country began at once discussing the action of the Board of Directors in inviting a Negro to speak, most of the newspaper comments, however, being favorable.

The delicacy and responsibility of my position in this matter can be appreciated when it is known that this was the first time in the history of the South that a Negro had been invited to take part on a programme with white Southern people on any important and national occasion. Our race should not neglect to give due credit to the courage that these Atlanta men displayed in extending this invitation; but the directors had told the Negroes from the beginning that they would give them fullest and freest opportunity to represent themselves in a creditable manner at every stage of the progress of the Exposition, and from the first day to the last this promise was kept.

The invitation to deliver this address came at a time when I am very busy every year preparing for the opening of the new school year at Tuskegee, and this made it quite difficult for me to find time in which to concentrate my thoughts upon the proper preparation of an important address, but the great reponsibility which had been entrusted to me weighed very heavily on me from day to day. I knew that what I said would be listened to by Southern white people, by people of my own race and by Northern white people. I was determined from the first not to say anything that would give undue offense to the South and thus prevent it from thus honoring another Negro in the future. And at the same time I was equally determined to be true to the North and to the interests of my own race. As the 18th of September drew nearer the heavier my heart became and the more I felt that my address would prove a disappointment and a failure. I prepared myself, however, as best I could. After preparing the address I went through it carefully, as I usually do with important utterances, with Mrs. Washington, and she approved of what I intended to say. On the 16th of September, the day before I started for Atlanta, as several of the teachers had expressed a desire to hear my address, I consented to read it to them in a body. When I had done so and heard their criticisms I felt more encouraged, as most of them seemed to be very much pleased with it.

On the morning of September 17, 1895, together with Mrs. Washington, Portia, Baker and Davidson, my children, I started for Atlanta. On the way to the depot from the school, in passing through Tuskegee, I happened to meet a white farmer who lived some distance in the country, and he in a rather joking manner said to me, "Washington, you have spoken with success before Northern white audiences, and before Negroes in the South, but in Atlanta you will have to speak before Northern white people, Southern white people and Negroes altogether. I fear they have got you into a pretty tight place." This farmer diagnosed the situation most accurately, but his words did not add to my comfort at that time. On the way to Atlanta I was constantly surprised by having both colored and white people come to the cars, stare at me and point me out and discuss in my hearing what was to take place the next day. In Atlanta we were met by a committee of colored citizens. The first thing I heard when I stepped from the cars in Atlanta was this remark by an old colored man near by: "That's the man that's gwine to make that big speech out at the Exposition tomorrow." We were taken to our boarding place by the committee and remained there until the next morning. Atlanta was literally packed at that time with people from all parts of the country, including many military and other organizations. The afternoon papers contained in large head lines a forecast of the next day's proceedings. All of this tended to add to the burden that was pressing heavily upon me.

On the morning of the day that the Exposition opened, a committee of colored citizens called at my boarding place to escort me to the point where I was to take my place in the procession which was to march to the Exposition grounds. In this same procession was Bishop W. J. Gaines, Rev. H. H. Proctor and other prominent colored citizens of Atlanta. What also added to the interest of this procession was the appearance of several colored military organizations which marched in the same procession with the white organizations. It was very noticeable that in the arrangement of the line of march the white officers who had control of the procession seemed to go out of their way to see that all of the colored people in the procession were properly placed and properly treated. The march through the streets out to the Exposition grounds occupied two or three hours, and, as the sun was shining disagreeably hot, when I got to the Exposition I felt rather fagged out, and very much feared that my address was going to prove a complete failure.

As I now recall, the only colored persons who had seats on the platform were Mr. I. Garland Penn, the Negro Commissioner, and myself, though of course there were hundreds of colored people in the audience. When I took my place on the platform the colored portion of the audience cheered vigorously, and there were faint cheers from some of the white people. Ex-Governor Bullock, of Atlanta, presided at the opening exercises. The audience room, which was very large and well suited for public speaking, was packed with humanity from bottom to top, and thousands were on the outside who could not get in.

A white gentleman who resides in the North and is one of my best friends, happened to be in Atlanta on the day that the Exposition opened. He was so nervous about the kind of reception I would receive at the hands of the audience and the effect my speech would produce that he could not bear to go into the building, but walked around the building on the outside until the exercises were over.

Gilmore's famous band played several stirring and patriotic airs, after which Gov. Bullock arose and delivered a short opening address and then the speaking occurred in the following order:

Opening address, Hon. Chas. A. Collier, President International Cotton States Exposition Company; address on behalf of the Woman's Department, Mrs. Joseph Thompson, President; address tendering Negro exhibit, Booker T. Washington; address on behalf of the State, His Excellency, Governor Atkinson; address on behalf of the city, Hon. Porter King; oration of the day, Judge Emory Speer.

After his introduction, when I arose to speak, there was considerable cheering in the audience, especially from the section of the room occupied by my own people. The sun was shining brightly in my face and I had to move about a good deal on the platform so as to reach a position that would enable me to escape the rays of the sun. I think the thing at the present time that I am most conscious of is that I saw thousands of eyes looking intently into my face. From the moment I was introduced until the end of my address I seemed to have entirely forgotten myself. The following is the address which I delivered:

"*Mr. President and Gentlemen of the Board of Directors and Citizens:*

"One third of the population of the South is of the Negro race. No enterprise seeking the material, civil, or moral welfare of this section can disregard this element of our population and reach the highest success. I but convey to you, Mr. President and Directors, the sentiment of the masses of my race when I say that in no way have the value and manhood of the American Negro been more fittingly and generously recognized than by the managers of this magnificent Exposition at every stage of its progress. It is a recognition that will do more to cement the friendship of the two races than any occurrence since the dawn of our freedom.

"Not only this, but the opportunity here afforded will awaken among us a new era of industrial progress. Ignorant and inexperienced, it is not strange that in the first years of our new life we began at the top instead of at the bottom; that a seat in Congress or the State Legislature was more sought than real estate or industrial skill; that the political convention or stump speaking had more attractions than starting a dairy farm or truck garden.

'A ship lost at sea for many days suddenly sighted a friendly vessel. From the mast of the unfortunate vessel was seen a signal: 'Water, water; we die of thirst!' The answer from the friendly vessel at once came back: 'Cast down your bucket where you are.' A second time the signal, 'Water, water; send us water!' ran up from the distressed vessel, and was answered: 'Cast down your bucket where you are.' And a third and fourth signal for water was answered: 'Cast down your bucket where you are.' The captain of the distressed vessel, at last heeding the injunction, cast down his bucket, and it came up full of fresh, sparkling water from the mouth of the Amazon River. To those of my race who depend on bettering their condition in a foreign land, or who underestimate the importance of cultivating friendly relations with the Southern white man, who is their next door neighbor, I would say: 'Cast down your bucket where you are'—cast it down in making friends in every manly way of the people of all races by whom we are surrounded.

"Cast it down in agriculture, mechanics, in commerce, in domestic service, and in the professions. And in this connection it is well to bear in mind that whatever other sins the South may be called to bear, when it comes to business, pure and simple, it is in the South that the Negro is given a man's chance in the commercial world, and in nothing is this Exposition more eloquent than in emphasizing this chance. Our greatest danger is, that in the great leap from slavery to freedom we may overlook the fact that the masses of us are to live by the productions of our hands, and fail to keep in mind that we shall prosper in proportion as we learn to dignify and glorify common labor, and put brains and skill into the common occupations of life; shall prosper in proportion as we learn to draw the line between the superficial and the substantial, the ornamental gewgaws of life and the useful. No race can prosper till it learns that there is as much dignity in tilling a field as in writing a poem. It is at the bottom of life we must begin, and not at the top. Nor should we permit our grievances to overshadow our opportunities.

"To those of the white race who look to the incoming of those of foreign birth and strange tongue and habits for the prosperity of the South, were I permitted, I would repeat what I say to my own race, 'Cast down your bucket where you are.' Cast it down among the 8,000,000 Negroes whose habits you know, whose fidelity and love you have tested in days when to have proved treacherous meant the ruin of your firesides. Cast down your bucket among these people who have, without strikes and labor wars, tilled your fields, cleared your forests, builded your railroads and cities, and brought forth treasures from the bowels of the earth, and helped make possible this magnificent representation of the progress of the South. Casting down your bucket among my people, helping and encouraging them as you are doing on these grounds, and, with education of head, hand and heart, you will find that they will buy your surplus land, make blossom the waste places in your fields, and run your factories. While doing this, you can be sure in the future, as in the past, that you and your families will be surrounded by the most patient, faithful, law-abiding, and unresentful people that the world has seen. As we have proved our loyalty to you in the past, in nursing your children, watching by the sick bed of your mothers and fathers, and often following them with tear-dimmed eyes to their graves, so in the future, in our humble way, we shall stand by you with a devotion that no foreigner can approach, ready to lay down our lives, if need be, in defense of yours, interlacing our industrial, commercial, civil, and religious life with yours in a way that shall make the interests of both races one. In all things that are purely social we can be as separate as the fingers, yet one as the hand in all things essential to mutual progress.

"There is no defense or security for any of us

except in the highest intelligence and development of all. If anywhere there are efforts tending to curtail the fullest growth of the Negro, let these efforts be turned into stimulating, encouraging, and making him the most useful and intelligent citizen. Effort or means so invested will pay a thousand per cent interest. These efforts will be twice blessed—'blessing him that gives and him that takes.'

"There is no escape through law of man or God from the inevitable:

> 'The laws of changeless justice bind
> Oppressor with oppressed;
> And close as sin and suffering joined
> We march to fate abreast.'

"Nearly sixteen millions of hands will aid you in pulling the load upwards, or they will pull against you the load downwards. We shall constitute one-third and more of the ignorance and crime of the South, or one-third its intelligence and progress; we shall contribute one-third to the business and industrial prosperity of the South, or we shall prove a veritable body of death, stagnating, depressing, retarding every effort to advance the body politic.

"Gentlemen of the Exposition, as we present to you our humble effort at an exhibition of our progress, you must not expect overmuch. Starting thirty years ago with ownership here and there in a few quilts and pumpkins and chickens (gathered from miscellaneous sources), remember the path that has led from these to the invention and production of agricultural implements, buggies, steam engines, newspapers, books, statuary, carving, paintings, the management of drug stores and banks, has not been trodden without contact with thorns and thistles. While we take pride in what we exhibit as a result of our independent efforts, we do not for a moment forget that our part in this exhibition would fall far short of your expectations but for the constant help that has come to our educational life, not only from the Southern States, but especially from Northern philanthropists, who have made their gifts a constant stream of blessing and encouragement.

"The wisest among my race understand that the agitation of questions of social equality is the extremest folly, and that progress in the enjoyment of all the privileges that will come to us must be the result of severe and constant struggle rather than of artificial forcing. No race that has anything to contribute to the markets of the world is long in any degree ostracized. It is important and right that all privileges of the law be ours, but it is vastly more important that we be prepared for the exercise of those privileges. The opportunity to earn a dollar in a factory just now is worth infinitely more than the opportunity to spend a dollar in an opera house.

"In conclusion, may I repeat that nothing in thirty years has given us more hope and encouragement, and drawn us so near to you of the white race, as this opportunity offered by the Exposition; and here bending, as it were, over the altar that represents the results of the struggles of your race and mine, both starting practically empty-handed three decades ago, I pledge that, in your effort to work out the great and intricate problem which God has laid at the doors of the South, you shall have at all times the patient, sympathetic help of my race; only let this be constantly in mind that, while from representations in these buildings of the product of field, of forest, of mine, of factory, letters, and art, much good will come, yet far above and beyond material benefits will be that higher good, that let us pray God will come, in a blotting out of sectional differences and racial animosities and suspicions, in a determination to administer absolute justice, in a willing obedience among all classes to the mandates of law. This, coupled with our material prosperity, will bring into our beloved South a new heaven and a new earth."

Some days after my speech in Atlanta at the opening of the Exposition I received the following letter from Dr. Gilman, President of Johns Hopkins University, who was chairman of the committee of jurors in connection with the Exposition:

"Johns Hopkins University,
"Baltimore, Sept. 30, 1895.
"*President's Office.*
"Dear Mr. Washington:—

"Would it be agreeable to you to be one of the Judges of Award in the Department of Education at Atlanta? If so, I shall be glad to place your name upon the list.

Yours very truly,
D. C. Gilman.

"A line by telegraph will be welcomed."

I was more surprised to receive this invitation to act on the board of jurors than to receive the invitation to speak at the opening of the Exposition, for it became a part of my duty as one of the jurors not only to pass on the exhibits from Negro schools but those from the white schools as well, throughout the country. I accepted this position and spent a month in Atlanta in connection with my duties as one of the jurors. The board was a large one, consisting in all of sixty members, including such well known persons as Dr. D. C. Gilman, of Johns Hopkins University;

Dr. I. S. Hopkins, secretary of the jury and president of the Georgia School of Technology; General Henry Abbott, United States engineer; President C. K. Adams, president of the University of Wisconsin; President Charles W. Dabney, of the University of Tennessee; Miss Grace Dodge, of New York; Dr. Charles Mohr, an expert in forestry; Mr. Gofford Pinchot, Biltmore, N. C.; Professor Ira Remsen, editor of the American Journal of Chemistry; Professor Eugene A. Smith, state geologist of Alabama; Professor C. P. Vanderford, of the University of Tennessee, and others equally prominent.

When the section of jurors on education met for organization, Mr. Thomas Nelson Page, the Southern author, who was a member of the board, made a motion that I be made secretary of the section on education. This motion was carried without a dissenting vote. Nearly half of the board of jurors were Southern men. We were quite intimately associated together for a month, and during this time our association was most pleasant and cordial in every respect. In performing my duty in connection with the inspection of the exhibits from the various white institutions, in each instance I was treated with the greatest respect. At the close of our labors a large photograph of the group of jurors was taken. We parted from each other with the greatest regret.

In making up their awards the board of jurors awarded but three gold medals to institutions of learning. The Tuskegee school received one of the three. As I was a member of the board I insisted that Tuskegee should not be permitted to compete for a medal, but I was overruled in this, and the medal given, regardless of my protests. The exhibit which the Tuskegee Normal and Industrial Institute made, except that from the Hampton Institute, was the largest and most comprehensive in the Negro Building.

I will let the newspaper war correspondent who was at that time in Atlanta as a representative of the New York World relate the impression my speech seemed to make. He wrote the following for the World:

"Mrs. Thompson, head of the Women's Department, had scarcely taken her seat, when all eyes were turned on a tall, tawny Negro sitting in the front row on the platform. It was Prof. Booker T. Washington, president of the Tuskegee (Ala.) Normal and Industrial Institute, who must rank from this time forth as the foremost man of his race in America. Gilmore's band played the 'Star Spangled Banner,' and the audience cheered.

HUNTINGTON HALL. A GIRLS' DORMITORY, TUSKEGEE INSTITUTE.

MR. WASHINGTON MAKING A SPEECH AT THE CHICAGO PEACE JUBILEE, OCT. 16, 1898, IN THE AUDITORIUM.—See page 224.

The tune was changed to 'Dixie,' and the audience roared with shrill ki-yi's. Again the music changed to 'Yankee Doodle,' and the clamor lessened.

"All this time the eyes of thousands looked straight at the Negro orator. A strange thing was to happen. A black man was to speak for his people with none to interrupt him. As Prof. Washington strode toward the edge of the stage, the low, descending sun shot fiery rays through the window into his face. A great shout greeted him. He turned his head to avoid the blinding light, and moved about the platform for relief. Then he turned his powerful countenance to the sun, without a blink of the eyelids, and began to talk.

"There was a remarkable figure, tall, bony, straight as a Sioux chief, high forehead, straight nose, heavy jaws, and strong, determined mouth, with big white teeth, piercing eyes, and a determined manner. The sinews stood out on his bronzed neck, and his muscular right arm swung high in the air, with a lead pencil grasped in the clenched brown fist. His big feet were planted squarely, with the heels together and the toes turned out. His voice rang out clear and true, and he paused impressively as he made each point. Within ten minutes the multitude was in an uproar of enthusiasm, handkerchiefs waved, canes flourished, hats tossed in the air. The fairest women in Georgia stood up and cheered. It was as if the orator had bewitched them.

"And when he held his dusky hand high above his head, with his fingers stretched wide apart, and said to the white people of the South on behalf of his race, 'In all things that are purely social we can be as separate as the fingers; yet one as the hand in all things essential to social progress,' the great wave of sound dashed itself against the walls, and the whole audience was on its feet in a delirium of applause, and I thought at that moment of the night when Henry Grady stood among the curling wreaths of tobacco smoke in Delmonico's banquet hall and said, 'I am a Cavalier among Roundheads.'

"I have heard the great orators of many countries, but not even Gladstone himself could have pleaded a cause with more consummate power than this angular Negro standing in a nimbus of sunshine, surrounded by the men who once fought to keep his race in bondage. The roar might swell ever so high, but the expression of his face never changed.

"A ragged, ebony giant, squatted on the floor in one of the aisles, watched the orator with burning eyes and tremulous face until the supreme outburst of applause came, then the tears ran down his face. Most of the Negroes in the audience were crying, perhaps without knowing just why.

"At the close of the speech Gov. Bullock rushed across the platform and seized the orator's hand. Another shout greeted this demonstration, and for a few moments the two men stood facing each other, hand in hand."

The papers all over the United States the next day after I spoke, and for months afterwards, were filled with the most complimentary accounts of and comments upon this speech. I quote a letter written by the Hon. Clark Howell to the New York World, and an editorial from the Boston Transcript, also two articles from colored papers, as fair samples of the expressions that were made throughout the country. The letter of Mr. Howell was as follows:

ATLANTA, GA., September 19.

'To the Editor of the World:

"I do not exaggerate when I say that Prof. Booker T. Washington's address yesterday was one of the most notable speeches, both as to character and the warmth of its reception, ever delivered to a Southern audience. It was an epoch-making talk, and marks distinctly a turning point in the progress of the Negro race. Its effect in bringing about a perfect understanding between whites and blacks of the South will be immediate. The address was a revelation. It was the first time that a Negro orator had appeared on a similar occasion before a Southern audience.

"The propriety of inviting a representative of the Negro race to participate in the opening exercises was fully discussed a month ago, when the opening program was being arranged. Some opposition was manifested on account of the fear that public sentiment was not prepared for such an advanced step. The invitation, however, was extended by a vote of the Board of Directors, and the cordial greeting which the audience gave Washington's address shows that the board made no mistake. There was not a line in the address which would have been changed by the most sensitive of those who thought the invitation to be imprudent. The whole speech is a platform on which the whites and the blacks can stand with full justice to each race.

"The speech is a full vindication from the mouth of a representative Negro of the doctrine so eloquently advanced by Grady and those who have agreed with him that it is to the South that the Negro must turn for his best friend, and that his welfare is so closely identified with the progress of the white people of the South that each race is mutually dependent upon the other, and that the so-called 'race problem' must be solved in the development of the natural relations growing out of the association between the whites and blacks of the South.

"The question of social equality is eliminated as a factor in the development of the problem, and the situation is aptly expressed by Washington in the statement that 'in all things that are purely social we can be as separate as the fingers, yet one as the hand in all things essential to mutual progress.'

"The speech will do good, and the unanimous approval with which it has been received demonstrates the fact that it has already done good.

Clark Howell,
Editor of the 'Constitution.' "

The Boston Transcript's editorial was as follows:

"The speech of Mr. Washington at the Atlanta Exposition this week seems to have dwarfed all the other proceedings and the exhibition itself. The crowd that listened to it was carried away with enthusiasm, and the sensation it has caused in the press has rarely been equaled. The Southern papers themselves pronounce it epoch-making, and call it the beginning of the end of the war between the races. All this is no great surprise to those who have kept themselves informed upon the development of industrial and other education for Negroes in the Negro-populated districts of the country. Intelligent and sympathetic observers have long been aware that it was through the silent and serious and steady work of the school for the Negroes that the solution of the race problem was coming, and not through the passions of politics, stirred and kept hot by tricky professional party managers for use in presidential elections. Mr. Washington is no different from what he has been: he is saying no more than he and his backers have been saying for years. But he is a great revelation to those who have hitherto regarded the Negro question as one simply calling for slang-whanging partisan and sectional abuse instead of philosophy, patience and study."

The editor of the Texas Freeman wrote as follows:

"The address made by Booker T. Washington, Principal of the Tuskegee Normal and Industrial Institute, at the formal opening of the Cotton States and International Exposition, stamps him as a most worthy representative of a large part of the country's citizenship. Without resort to hyperbolic exaggeration, it is but simple justice to call the address great. It was great. Great, in that it exhibited the speaker's qualities of head and heart; great, that he could and did discriminatingly recognize conditions as they affected his people, and greater still in the absolute modesty, self-respect and dignity with which he presented a platform upon which Clark Howell, of the Atlanta Constitution, says, 'both races, blacks and whites, can stand with full justice to each.' No better selection, among the whole number of the race's most prominent men, could have been made than Prof. Washington."

The Richmond Planet said:

"The speech of Prof. Booker T. Washington at the opening of the Atlanta Exposition was a magnificent effort and places him in the forefront of the representatives of our race in this country. Calm, dispassionate, logical, winning, it captivated the vast assemblage who heard it and caused a re-echoing sound of approval on the part of those who caught the rounded sentences and rhetorical periods as they were flashed over the wires.

"Reserved in his manner, earnest in the delivery, realizing fully the heavy responsibility resting upon him, he performed that duty with an ease that was magnetic and grace that was divine."

As soon as I had finished my address, the first thing that I remember is that Gov. Bullock rushed across the stage and took me by the hand. Others sitting on the platform did the same thing. Following my address came a brilliant and eloquent speech from Judge Emory Speer. At the close of his address the President of the United States, Hon. Grover Cleveland, touched a button in Washington which started the machinery, and the Exposition was declared open. By the time the exercises in the Auditorium were finished it was quite late in the afternoon and, in fact, dark. A large number of people, both Northern and Southern, together with numbers of colored people, congratulated me most heartily on my address; in fact, I found it quite difficult to get out of the building or away from the Exposition grounds. As soon as possible I left the Exposition and went to my boarding place.

After the opening exercises a reception was tendered me by some of the colored citizens of Atlanta. I did not in any large measure appreciate the excitement and deep impression that my address seemed to create until the next morning about ten o'clock, when I went to the city on some errand. As soon as I entered the business portion of Atlanta I was surprised to find myself pointed out, and I was very soon surrounded by a crowd of people who were bent on shaking my hand and congratulating me; in fact, this was kept up on every street where I went, until I found it impossible to move with any degree of comfort about the streets, and so I returned to my boarding place. In a few hours I began receiving telegrams and letters from all parts of the country.

One thing I always thought was rather strange in connection with this address, and that is that no officer connected with the Exposition ever asked me what ground I was going to cover in my speech, or ever suggested that I should be careful not to say anything which would harm the relations between the races, and thus cripple the success of the Exposition. It would, of course, have been very easy for me to have uttered a single sentence which would have thrown a wet blanket over the prospects of the Exposition and especially the harmonious relations of the races.

The next morning I took the train for Tuskegee. At the depot in Atlanta and at every station between Atlanta and Tuskegee I found a crowd of people anxious to shake hands with me, and who were pointed out to me as making remarks about my address.

Some days after I returned to Tuskegee, I sent the President of the United States, Hon. Grover Cleveland, a copy of the address I delivered at Atlanta, and was very much surprised as well as gratified to receive from him a letter which I here insert:

GRAY GABLES,
BUZZARD'S BAY, Mass., Oct. 6, 1895.
BOOKER T. WASHINGTON, Esq.

MY DEAR SIR:—I thank you for sending me a copy of your address delivered at the Atlanta Exposition.

I thank you with much enthusiasm for making the address. I have read it with intense interest, and I think the Exposition would be fully justified if it did not do more than furnish the opportunity for its delivery. Your words cannot fail to delight and encourage all who wish well for your race; and if our colored fellow citizens do not from your utterances gather new hope and form new determinations to gain every valuable advantage offered them by their citizenship, it will be strange indeed. Yours very truly,

GROVER CLEVELAND.

All of it was written with his own hand. From that time until the present, Mr. Cleveland has taken the deepest interest in Tuskegee and has been among my warmest and most helpful friends.

After I returned to Tuskegee I continued to be deluged with letters of congratulation and endorsement of my position. I received all kinds of propositions from lecture bureaus, editors of magazines and papers to take the lecture platform and write articles. One lecture bureau went as far as to offer me $50,000, or $200 a night, if I would place my services at its disposition for a given period of time. To all these communications I replied that my life work was at Tuskegee, and that wherever I should speak it must be in the interest of my race and the institution at Tuskegee, and that I could not accept any engagements that would seem to place a mere commercial value on my addresses. From that time until the present I have continued to receive liberal offers from lecture bureaus for my services. Only a few weeks ago the following letter came to me, but I have continued to refuse, as I expect to do in the future, to become a professional lecturer at any price:

CENTRAL LYCEUM BUREAU,
CHICAGO, Ill., November 29, 1897.
BOOKER T. WASHINGTON, Tuskegee, Ala.

MY DEAR SIR:—"If you will give us exclusive control of your lecture business for next summer and winter, season of 1898-99, I am confident I can make you more money than you have made this season on the platform. Would you consider an offer of say ten thousand dollars and all expenses for one hundred nights. Please let me hear from you and oblige, Yours very truly,
FRED PELHAM."

Soon after receiving the letter quoted above, I

received a proposition from a lecture bureau in Boston offering me at the rate of $200 per night for my lectures for as long a time as I would give them my services at this rate, but I declined. Although I refused to become a professional lecturer for personal gain, I did not keep silent, but continued to work and speak in behalf of Tuskegee.

In the fall of 1895 I continued addressing large audiences in the states of Massachusetts, New York, Pennsylvania and in the Western states. During my trip to the West I addressed the Hamilton Club and was its guest while in the city of Chicago. The Hamilton Club is one of the largest and most influential political organizations of Republican faith in the West. While in Chicago for the purpose of addressing this club, I was invited by Dr. Harper, the president of the University of Chicago, to deliver an address before the students of the University, which I did, and was treated with great consideration and kindness by all of the officers of the University.

CHAPTER XI.
AN APPEAL FOR JUSTICE.

While the Atlanta Exposition was in progress, the State Constitutional Convention of South Carolina was in session, having been convened for the specific purpose of passing a law that would result in disfranchising the greater proportion of the Negro voters. While this Convention was in session, I addressed an open letter to Senator Benj. Tillman of South Carolina, which read as follows:

"I am no politician. I never made a political speech, and do not know as I ever shall make one, so it is not on a political subject that I address you. I was born a slave; you a free man. I am but an humble member of an unfortunate race; you are a member of the greatest legislative body on earth, and of the great intelligent Caucasian race. The difference between us is great, yet I do not believe you will scorn the appeal I make to you in behalf of the 650,000 of my race in your State, who are to-day suppliants at your feet, and whose destiny and progress for the next century you hold largely in your hands. I have been told that you are brave and generous, and one too great to harm the weak and dependent; that you represent the chivalry of the South, which has claimed no higher praise than that of being the protectors of the defenseless. I address you because I believe that you and those associated with you in convention, have been misunderstood in the following dispatch to a number of papers:

"'An appalling fact that may not be obvious at a first glance, is that the course proposed means the end of Negro education and Negro progress in South Carolina. This is openly admitted by Senator Tillman and his friends.'

"It has been said that the truest test of the civilization of a race is the desire of the race to assist the unfortunate. Judged by this standard, the Southern States as a whole have reason to feel proud of what they have done in helping in the education of the Negro.

"I cannot believe that on the eve of the twentieth century, when there is more enlightenment, more generosity, more progress, more self-sacrifice, more love for humanity than ever existed in any other stage of the world's history, when our memories are pregnant with the scenes that took place at Chattanooga and Missionary Ridge but a few days ago, where brave men who wore the blue and gray clasped forgiving hands and pledged that henceforth the interests of one should be the interests of all—while the hearts of the whole South are centered upon the great city of Atlanta, where Southern people are demonstrating to the world in a practical way that it is the policy of the South to help and not to hinder the Negro—in the midst of all these evidences of good feeling among all races and all sections of the country, I cannot believe that you and your fellow members are engaged in constructing laws that will keep 650,000 of my weak, dependent and unfortunate race in ignorance, poverty and crime.

"You, honored Senator, are a student of history. Has there ever been a race that was helped by ignorance? Has there ever been a race that was harmed by Christian intelligence? It is agreed by some that the Negro schools should be practically closed because he cannot bear his proportion of this burden of taxation. Can an ignorant man produce taxable property faster than an intelligent man? Will capital and immigration be attracted to a State where three out of four are ignorant and where poverty and crime abound?

"Within a dozen years, the white people of South Carolina have helped in the education of hundreds of colored boys and girls at Clafflin University and smaller schools. Have these educated men and women hindered the State or hurt its reputation? It warms my heart as I read the messages of the Governors of Alabama, Georgia and other Southern States, and note their broad and statesman-like appeals for the education of all the people, none being so black or miserable as not to be reached by the beneficent hand of the State.

"Honored Sir, do not misunderstand me; I am not so selfish as to make this appeal to you in the interest of my race alone, for, thank God, a white man is as near to my heart as a black man; but I appeal to you in the interest of humanity. 'Whatsoever a man soweth, that shall he also reap.' It is my belief that were it the purpose of your convention, as reported, to practically close Negro school-houses by limiting the support of these schools to the paltry tax that the Negro is able to pay out of his ignorance and poverty after but thirty years of freedom, his school-houses would not close. Let the world know it, and there would be such an inflowing of money from the pockets of the charitable from all sections of our country and other countries, as would keep the light of the school-houses burning on every hill and in every valley in South Carolina. I believe, Senator Tillman, that you are too great and magnanimous to permit this. I believe the people of South Carolina prefer to have a large part in the education of their own citizens; prefer to have them educated to feel grateful to South Carolina for the larger part of their education rather than to outside parties wholly. This question I leave with you. The black yeomanry of your State will be educated. Shall South Carolina do it, or shall it be left to others? Here in my humble home, in the heart of the South, I beg to say that I know something of the great burden the Southern people are carrying, and sympathize with them; and I feel that I know the Southern people, and am convinced that the best white people in South Carolina and the South are determined to help lift up the Negro.

"In addressing you this simple message, I am actuated by no motive save a desire that your State, in attempting to escape a burden, shall not add one that will be ten fold more grievous, and that we all shall so act in the spirit of Him who when on earth went about doing good, that we shall have in every part of our beloved South, a contented, intelligent and prosperous people."

Soon after the Exposition, in reply to a request from the editor, I addressed the following letter to the Atlanta Journal on the benefits of the Exposition:

"Without doubt the Atlanta Exposition has helped the cause of the Negro. Before the event there was much honest difference of opinion among members of the race as to the advisability of our taking any part whatever. Many of the objectors earnestly advocated by word of mouth and through the press the policy of 'hands off;' others as much opposed participation, yet kept silent, and, so far as public expression was concerned, maintained a neutral position. From the one class no help was received by those trying to collect an exhibit; from the other, direct opposition was encountered. By reason of these disadvantages, the Negro exhibit, while highly creditable under the circumstances, was not by any means what it would have been had there been unanimity of purpose and concentrated action. There is, however, little difference of opinion, either within the race or outside of it, as to the good resulting from the Negro's part in the Exposition. Many, who for various reasons did not sanction a Negro exhibit, are inclined now to favor our embracing, as they are offered, these opportunities for showing of what we are capable along the various lines of activity. Others, still holding to what they consider the logic of their position, yet concede and rejoice in the good accomplished.

"In the first instance, this Exposition has given the colored people an insight into their ability to accomplish something by united effort. There are two points to consider in this statement; that the colored people have been helped to a fuller knowledge of their capabilities, and that they have been taught a practical lesson in the value of co-operation. Neither of these points can be too much emphasized. Without self-confidence, self-respect, a certain amount of self-assurance of the proper kind, nothing can be achieved, either by an individual or by a race. We must believe in ourselves, if we would have people believe in us. If we wonder, 'Can any good thing come out of Nazareth?' what must we expect of others?

"Of but little less importance is the expressive example afforded of the power of co-operation. Mutual distrust, disinclination to unite forces, and inability to carry on concentrated action, belong to the dark days and are the badges of inferiority. We shall rise largely in proportion as we learn to join hands and to further mutual interests by joint action. The very effort to do something, to make something, in connection with the Exposition, regardless of intrinsic value of the thing produced or achieved, has been helpful and developing in its tendencies. We learn by doing and 'rise on stepping stones of our dead selves to higher things.'

"The Exposition has also given thousands of white people, North and South, opportunities to see some of the best results of the Negro's advancement. It is a fact that always has been recognized and deplored by the better element of the colored people, that most white people see and know only the worse phase of Negro character. They live side by side with the brother in black and yet have no acquaintance with him beyond the slight knowledge gained of those serving them in menial capacities. So, perhaps, the entire race is judged by a few individuals who have had little or no opportunities for advancement along any of the lines that make for a higher civilization. The homes of culture, the work of the school, the progress in the industries, in the arts, in all things that tend to prove the Negro a man among men, have been as a sealed book to the vast majority of the white people in all sections of our country, and the adverse judgments that have been formed as to the Negro's worth and ability may be attributed more to an unfortunate ignorance and blindness on the subject than to any intention or desire to be unjust. Of no class of people, probably, is this truer than of the class commonly known as the 'poor whites' of the South. It was both interesting and amusing to view their surprise as they entered the Negro building at Atlanta, and to listen to the exclamations of astonishment which escaped them as they walked around and observed the exhibits. 'What, this the work of niggers!' Race prejudice received a heavy blow at Atlanta. The white man left with increased respect for the Negro, and he will show it in his future dealings with the members of the race. The Negro in turn, appreciative of the recognition accorded him, will entertain more cordial feelings toward those showing him such consideration. The Exposition brought the Negro prominently before the country. The attention of the press was drawn to him. Leading scientists and educators sat in judgment on the products of his brain and skill, ranged side by side with those of his white competitors for honors. His position as a part of the body politic was emphasized as never before. The impression his exhibit made was not such as to render him, in the eyes of the country, less desirable as a citizen than he had seemed before. On the contrary, his capabilities in various directions have been strikingly exemplified, and it has been demonstrated that he can measure up to the full stature of a man.

"As might have been anticipated, the showing made by the school was most creditable. The friends and advancers of Negro education must have felt that their bounty has not been misplaced. Especially must the great heart of the generous North have glowed with gratification. It is an interesting fact that out of the four highest awards, that of the gold medal made to educational institutions, two went to colored schools— Hampton and Tuskegee.

"In speaking of the helpful prominence which the Exposition gave to the Negro's cause, we must not omit the influence of the Negro congresses. The very presence in Atlanta of so many well-dressed, well-behaved, intelligent men and women of African descent, speaks loudly in our behalf. Besides, many wise words were uttered in the several addresses delivered and in the discussions which followed, and in all modesty, we think that we may claim that these black men and women made less perplexing some of the perplexing questions which confront us as a nation.

"Not less important among the happy results of the exposition is that the Southern white people and the Negro have learned that they can unite successfully in business enterprises. They have been shown that because men differ on some points and are not as one in all the affairs of life, they need not stand entirely aloof from one another. They may meet upon the level ground of a common interest and work together towards the accomplishment of a mutual aim without loss of dignity or self-respect to either.

"The exposition has encouraged the Negroes to become, more than ever before, producers. They have been helped to realize, as they may not have realized before, that no kind of toil is to be despised, that in every branch of industry the highest degree of proficiency should be sought, that every product of labor is valuable in proportion as it approaches the perfect ideal which should animate the mind of every worker. Agriculture, the trades, education, the arts, have all received an impetus which will be seen in the more rapid advancement of the future. Above all, we are encouraged now by the certainty that recognition will come as it deserved. It is not too much to say that the recognition which the Negro received at Atlanta was the natural result of the development he has made during these thirty years of effort. Further opportunities will present themselves. Already other expositions are projected whose plans include a prominent part to be taken by the Negro.

" 'All things come to him who waits,' but the Negro must understand that he must work and wait; not idly rest upon his oars. We must not only be prepared to make a good showing when the opportunity comes for us to let the world see what in us lies, but each opportunity must find us better prepared. With the New South the New Negro must arise and modestly, manfully, courageously, take his place in the march of progress. The old order of things has truly passed away, and side by side, white men and black men must determine to work out their destiny to a successful issue."

During the Fall and Winter of 1895-96 I addressed several audiences in various parts of the country, notably New York, Massachusetts and Pennsylvania. At the meeting in New York, which was held in Broadway Tabernacle, Hon. Joseph H. Choate presided. I also addressed during the Winter of 1896 the Hamilton Club of Brooklyn, New York. The most important meeting which I attended, however, after the Atlanta Exposition, was a large meeting held in Carnegie Hall, New York, in the interest of the Presbyterian Mission. This meeting was held under the auspices of the Presbyterian Church. The meeting was of national importance in its character, and the entire Presbyterian Church throughout the country was interested in it. The President of the United States, Hon. Grover Cleveland, was the presiding officer. The speakers included, besides the President, Rev. T. DeWitt Talmage, D. D.; Rev. Sheldon Jackson, D. D., and myself. The hall was packed from bottom to top with the best and most influential people in New York and vicinity, and much good seems to have resulted from the meeting. The following are some of the extracts from my speech delivered on that occasion:

"My word to you to-night will be based upon an humble effort during the last fourteen years to better the condition of my people in the 'black belt' of the South.

"What are some of the conditions in the South that need your urgent help and attention?" Eighty-five per cent. of my people in the Gulf States are on the plantations in the country districts, where a large majority are still in ignorance, without habits of thrift and economy; are in debt, mortgaging their crops to secure food; paying, or attempting to pay, a rate of interest that ranges between twenty and forty per cent.; living in one-room cabins on rented land, where schools are in session in these country districts from three to four months in the year, taught in places, as a rule, that have little resemblance to school houses.

"Each colored child in these States has spent on him this year, for education, about 70 cents, while each child in Massachusetts has spent on him this year, for education, between $18 and $20.

"What state of morality or practical Christianity you may expect when as many as six, eight, and even ten, cook, eat and sleep, get sick and die in one room, I need not explain. But what is the remedy for this condition? It is not practical nor desirable that the North attempt to educate, directly, all the colored people in the South, but the North can and should help the South educate strong Christian leaders who will go among our people and show them how to lift themselves up. That is the great problem before us. Can this be done? If in the providence of God the Negro got any good out of slavery, he got the habit of work. Whether the call for labor comes from the cotton fields of Mississippi, the rice swamps of the Carolinas, or the sugar bottoms of Louisiana, the Negro answers the call. Yes, toil is the badge of all his tribe, but the trouble centers here: By reason of his ignorance and want of training he does not know how to utilize the results of his labor. My people do not need charity, neither do they ask that charity be scattered among them. Very seldom in any part of this country do you see a black hand reached out for charity; but they do ask that through Lincoln and Biddle and Scotia and Hampton and Tuskegee, you send them leaders to guide and stimulate them till they are able to walk."

I also gave it as my opinion that the American Church has never yet comprehended its duty to the millions of poor whites in the South. I said: "When you help the poor whites, you help the Negro. So long as the poor whites are ignorant, so long there will be crime against the Negro and civilization."

During the same year I delivered addresses in several Western cities, including Chicago, Minneapolis, St. Paul and Milwaukee.

Immediately after my address in Carnegie

Hall, on the evening of March 3, I took the train in order to be present at the meeting of the Negro Conference which occurred on March 5, and arrived in Tuskegee just in time to take part in the discussion of this meeting.

Soon after my address at the opening of the Atlanta Exposition there began to appear adverse criticisms in some of the colored papers regarding the position I had taken in my address. Some of these colored papers felt that I had been entirely too liberal towards the South. I gave no special attention to these criticisms, but in March, 1896, I accepted an invitation to speak before the Bethel Literary Association in Washington. This, I think, is by far the most cultured literary organization in existence among our people, and Washington city had been the center of a good part of the criticisms on my Atlanta speech, so I felt that that city would be a good place in which to make my position more clearly understood and to emphasize my views. On the evening that I spoke in Washington, the meeting was held in the Auditorium of the Metropolitan Church, and I hardly need say that the building was full to such an extent that many were unable to find seats. In my address before the Literary Association I took very much the same position I had taken in my address at Atlanta, but of course went more into

174 THE STORY OF MY LIFE AND WORK,

detail. After my speech, those who heard me seemed to be entirely satisfied with my position, and the newspapers which had been criticising me, in a large measure, ceased to do so.

CHAPTER XII.
HONORED BY HARVARD UNIVERSITY.

One of the most helpful things accomplished during the year 1896 was an exhibit of the industrial products of the Tuskegee Institute made in New York City, Boston and Philadelphia, in connection with a similar exhibit from the Hampton Institute. The Armstrong Association in New York City was instrumental in bringing about this exhibit. A large number of people who had no idea of the extent of our industrial work had an opportunity at these exhibits to see for themselves just what was being done by Hampton and Tuskegee. Our industrial exhibit included wagons, carriages and wearing apparel of all kinds, manufactured by the students. The exhibit, however, was not confined to industrial products; a thorough exhibit of academic work was also made.

Some people have an idea that because industrial education is emphasized at Tuskegee and Hampton, very little attention is given to academic training. This is an error. A close examination will prove that both at Hampton and Tuskegee the academic training is very thorough and far-reaching; in fact, if we had only called this institution "University" or "College" and had given the same course of training that we now give, we would have met with no criticism on account of not giving more academic training. We are thoroughly imbued with the idea that a little training thoroughly given goes farther than to attempt to cover a great deal of ground poorly. Education after all is only valuable in giving mental grasp and culture.

Six months before he died, and nearly a year after he had been stricken with paralysis, General Armstrong visited Tuskegee. On his arrival, which was about nine o'clock in the evening, he was given a unique reception by the students. According to a pre-arranged plan, the moment that his carriage entered the school grounds, he began passing between two lines of lighted and waving "fat pine" wood knots held by over a thousand students and teachers. The General was completely overcome with happiness. He remained a guest in my home for nearly two months, and, although almost wholly without the use of voice or limb, he spent nearly every hour in devising ways to help the South. Time and time again he said to me, during this visit, that it was not only the duty of the country to assist in elevating the Negro of the South, but the poor white man as well. I resolved anew to devote myself more earnestly to the cause which was so dear to him.

Several times I have been asked what was the most surprising incident in my life. I have no hesitation in saying that it was the following letter from Harvard University, asking me to be present at the commencement at Harvard in June, 1896, for the purpose of having an honorary degree conferred upon me.

"HARVARD UNIVERSITY.
"CAMBRIDGE, May 28, 1896.

"MY DEAR SIR: Harvard University desires to confer on you at the approaching commencement an honorary degree; but it is our custom to confer degrees only on gentlemen who are present. Our commencement occurs this year on June 24th, and your presence would be desirable from about noon till about five o'clock in the afternoon. Would it be possible for you to be in Cambridge on that day?

"Believe me, with great regard,
"Very truly yours,
"CHARLES W. ELIOT.
"PRESIDENT BOOKER T. WASHINGTON."

Up to the time of receiving this letter I had not the faintest idea that any college, much less the oldest and highest educational institution in the country, was about to or would ever confer upon me any honorary degree. It took me, of course, greatly by surprise.

Commencement day at Harvard, June 24, 1896, was a memorable one, certainly one that I shall never forget. At the appointed hour I met President Eliot and the overseers of the College at the designated place on the grounds, for the purpose of being escorted in company with others to Sanders Theatre, where the commencement exercises were to take place and the degrees to be conferred. In addition to the degree to be conferred on me, among others Major-Gen. Nelson A. Miles, the Commander of the United States Army, Dr. Bell, the inventor of the Bell telephone system, Dr. M. J. Savage of Boston, and others, were invited to be present at commencement for the purpose of receiving degrees. We were assigned places in the line of march immediately behind the President and Overseers. As soon as we were placed in the line, the Governor of Massachusetts, escorted by the Lancers, arrived, and was assigned to the head of the line of march by the side of President Eliot. In this order, accompanied by the various officers clad in caps and gowns, we marched to Sanders Theatre. After the usual commencement exercises, the time for the conferring of honorary degrees came. This at Harvard is always the most interesting and exciting feature of commencement, owing largely to the fact that no one knows until commencement day on whom honorary degrees are to be conferred, and as each name is called for an honorary degree, the expectation rises to the highest pitch, and the individuals receive cheers and applause in proportion as they are popular at the college. When it came my turn I arose, and

President Eliot conferred upon me the degree of Master of Arts, in appropriate language. The whole ceremony for the first time at Harvard was performed in English.

At the close of the commencement exercises I was invited with Gen. Miles and others receiving honorary degrees to lunch with President Eliot. After the lunch at the residence of the President we were formed into line again and were escorted under the guidance of the Marshal of the Day, who in this case happened to be Bishop Lawrence of Massachusetts, through the grounds, in which at different points we were met and cheered by the students, each individual who had received an honorary degree receiving the Harvard yell. The most interesting feature of that day was the Alumni Dinner, which occurred at the close of our march through the grounds. This dinner was served in Memorial Hall, and, I think, was attended by at least a thousand graduates of Harvard from all sections of the country, many of them eminent in affairs of state, religion and the field of letters. Among the speakers at the Alumni Dinner were Governor Roger A. Wolcott, Senator Henry Cabot Lodge, Gen. Nelson A. Miles, Dr. Savage and others. When I was called upon to speak at the Alumni Dinner I delivered the following address:

"*Mr. President and Gentlemen:*—

"It would in some measure relieve my embarrassment if I could, even in a slight degree, feel myself worthy of the great honor which you do me to-day. Why you have called me from the Black Belt of the South, from among my humble people, to share in the honors of this occasion, is not for me to explain; and yet it may not be inappropriate for me to suggest that it seems to me that one of the most vital questions that touch our American life, is how to bring the strong, wealthy and learned into helpful touch with the poorest, most ignorant and humblest, and at the same time make the one appreciate the vitalizing, strengthening influence of the other. How shall we make the mansions on yon Beacon street feel and see the need of the spirits in the lowliest cabin in Alabama cotton fields or Louisiana sugar bottoms? This problem Harvard University is solving, not by bringing itself down, but by bringing the masses up.

"If through me, an humble representative, seven millions of my people in the South might be permitted to send a message to Harvard— Harvard that offered up on death's altar young Shaw, and Russell, and Lowell, and scores of others, that we might have a free and united country—that message would be, 'Tell them that the sacrifice was not in vain. Tell them that by habits of thrift and economy, by way of the industrial school and college, we are coming. We are crawling up, working up, yea, bursting up. Often through oppression, unjust discrimination and prejudice, but through them all we are coming up, and with proper habits, intelligence and property, there is no power on earth that can permanently stay our progress.'

"If my life in the past has meant anything in the lifting up of my people and the bringing about of better relations between your race and mine, I assure you from this day it will mean doubly more. In the economy of God there is but one standard by which an individual can succeed— there is but one for a race. This country demands that every race shall measure itself by the American standard. By it a race must rise or fall, succeed or fail, and in the last analysis mere sentiment counts for little. During the next half century and more, my race must continue passing through the severe American crucible. We are to be tested in our patience, our forbearance, our perseverence, our power to endure wrong, to withstand temptations, to economize, to acquire and use skill; in our ability to compete, to succeed in commerce, to disregard the superficial for the real, the appearance for the substance, to be great and yet small, learned and yet simple, high and yet the servant of all. This, this is the passport to all that is best in the life of our republic, and the Negro must possess it, or be debarred.

"While we are thus being tested, I beg of you to remember that wherever our life touches yours, we help or hinder. Wherever your life touches ours, you make us stronger or weaker. No member of your race in any part of our country can harm the meanest member of mine without the proudest and bluest blood in Massachusetts being degraded. When Mississippi commits crime, New England commits crime, and in so much, lowers the standard of your civilization. There is no escape—man drags man down, or man lifts man up.

"In working out our destiny, while the main burden and center of activity must be with us, we shall need, in a large measure in the years that are to come as we have in the past, the help, the encouragement, the guidance that the strong can give the weak. Thus helped, we of both races in the South, soon shall throw off the shackles of racial and sectional prejudice and rise, as Harvard University has risen and as we all should rise, above the clouds of ignorance, narrowness and selfishness, into that atmosphere, that pure sunshine, where it will be our highest ambition to serve man, our brother, regardless of race or previous condition."

As this was the first time that an honorary

degree had ever been conferred upon a Negro by any university in New England, of course it occasioned a great deal of newspaper comment throughout the country. I think I shall not speak further of the occurrence, but will insert a few newspaper clippings that will tell the story perhaps better than I feel like doing it.

Mr. Thos. J. Calloway, who was present on this occasion, wrote as follows to the Colored American:

"First in the history of America, a leading American university confers an honorary degree upon a colored man. Harvard has been always to the front in ideas of liberty, freedom and equality. When other colleges of the North are accepting the Negro as a tolerance, Harvard has been awarding him honors, as in the case of Clement G. Morgan, of recent date. Her present action, therefore, in placing an honorary crown upon the worthy head of Mr. Washington is but a step further in her magnanimity in recognizing merit under whatever color of skin.

"The mere announcement of this event is a great testimony to the standing of Mr. Washington, but to any black person who, as I did, saw and heard the enthusiasm and applause with which the audience cheered the announcement by President Eliot, the degree itself was insignificant. The Boston Lancers had conducted Gov. Wolcott to Cambridge, and five hundred Harvard graduates had double filed the march to Sanders Theatre. It was a great day. Latin orations, disquisitions, dissertations and essays in English were delivered by selected graduates, clad in stately and classic cap and gown. Bishops, generals, commodores, statesmen, authors, poets, explorers, millionaires and noted men of every calling, sat as earnest listeners. President Eliot had issued five hundred diplomas by handing them to representatives of the graduates in bundles of twenty to twenty-five. Then came the awarding of honorary degrees. Thirteen were issued, Bishop Vincent and General Nelson A. Miles, commander of the United States Army, being among the recipients. When the name of Booker T. Washington was called, and he arose to acknowledge and accept, there was such an outburst of applause as greeted no other name except that of the popular soldier patriot, General Miles. The applause was not studied and stiff, sympathetic and condoling; it was enthusiasm and admiration. Every part of the audience from pit to gallery joined in, and a glow covered the cheeks of those around me, proving their sincere appreciation of the rising struggle of an ex-slave and the work he has accomplished for his race.

"But the event of the day was the Alumni Dinner, when speeches formed the most enjoyable bill of fare. Two hundred Harvard alumni and their invited guests partook of this annual dinner. Four or five speeches were made, among them one from Mr. Washington.

"At the close of the speaking, notwithstanding the fact that Senator Henry Cabot Lodge, Dr. Minot J. Savage and others had spoken, President Eliot warmly grasped Mr. Washington by the hand and told him that his was the best speech of the day."

Speaking of the conferring of the degree and the toast, the papers were unusual in favorable comment. Says the Boston Post:

"In conferring the honorary degree of Master of Arts upon the principal of Tuskegee Institute, Harvard University has honored itself as well as the object of this distinction. The work which Prof. Booker T. Washington has accomplished for education, good citizenship and popular enlightenment in his chosen field of labor in the South, entitles him to rank with our national benefactors. The university which can claim him on its list of sons, whether in regular course or *honoris causa*, may be proud.

"It has been mentioned that Mr. Washington is the first of his race to receive an honorary degree from a New England University. This, in itself, is a distinction. But the degree was not conferred because Mr. Washington is a colored man, or because he was born in slavery, but because he has shown, by his work for the elevation of the people of the Black Belt of the South, a genius and a broad humanity which count for greatness in any man, whether his skin be white or black."

The Boston Globe said: "It is Harvard which, first among New England colleges, confers an honorary degree upon a black man. No one who has followed the history of Tuskegee and its work, can fail to admire the courage, persistence and splendid common sense of Booker T. Washington. Well may Harvard honor the ex-slave, the value of whose services, alike to his race and country, only the future can estimate."

The correspondent of the New York Times wrote: "All the speeches were enthusiastically received, but the colored man carried off the oratorical honors, and the applause which broke out when he had finished, was vociferous and long continued."

In July of the same year I delivered one of the addresses before the National Christian Endeavor Convention which met in Washington. This meeting of the Christian Endeavor Society was attended by thousands of people from all sections of the country and some from foreign countries. I remember that in order to be present in time to speak at this meeting, I had to make a long and tiresome trip from Spirit Lake, Iowa, to Washington, and reached Washington rather late in the evening. In fact, when I got to the church where I was to speak, I found President F. E. Clark and the audience rather nervous about my appearance. I found it a difficult matter to get into the room, owing to the fact that every seat was taken, the aisles full and people on the outside of the church clamoring for entrance. My address was finished about 10 o'clock that evening. At 11 o'clock I took a train for Buffalo, New York, where I was to speak the next night before the National Educational Association, where 20,000 teachers were present. As I now recall the incident, I think these two meetings caused me perhaps as great mental strain and anxiety as I have ever experienced. I had to prepare special and set addresses for each meeting, and coming, as they did, so near together, any one who has had experience in public speaking can easily imagine the difficulty with which I had to contend. I will give one or two short newspaper extracts that may convey an idea of the effect of these two addresses.

The Buffalo Express gave expression in part as follows:

"It was a great close. It began with music and it ended with music. Not a false note was struck. Every tone rang true, and when the gavel rose for the final fall, the audience rose with it, and with one mighty voice sang 'America.' All credit is due to Booker T. Washington for the keying up of the spirit that dominated the vast audience. His address was magnificent. There was nothing of speculation, nothing of theory, nothing of supposition in his speech. It was a truthful, convincing statement of the condition of the Negro and the remedy for his wrongs. It teemed with humor and was arrayed in a splendid cloak of eloquence. The audience was larger than at any of the other sessions. An overflow meeting was held in Concert Hall, at which the addresses of the closing session were repeated. The overflow meeting overflowed, and over 2,000 people were turned away. A thousand lingered outside until the convention ended."

On July 12th the Buffalo Courier contained the following:

"Booker T. Washington, the foremost educator among the colored people of the world, was a very busy man from the time he arrived in the city the other night from the West, and registered at the Iroquois. He had hardly removed the stains of travel when it was time to partake of supper. Then he held a public levee in the parlors of the Iroquois until eight o'clock. During that time he was greeted by over two hundred eminent teachers and educators from all parts of the

United States. Shortly after 8 o'clock, he was driven in a carriage to Music Hall, and in one hour and a half he made two ringing addresses, to as many as 5,000 people, on Negro education. Then Mr. Washington was taken in charge by a delegation of colored citizens, headed by the Rev. Mr. Watkins, and hustled off to a small, informal reception, arranged in honor of the visitor, by the people of his race."

Both in Washington at the Christian Endeavor meeting and in Buffalo at the National Educational Association meeting I was surprised as well as gratified at the large number of Southern gentlemen and ladies belonging to the white race who pressed forward to shake my hand at the close of these addresses. I have rarely spoken anywhere in the North that a number of Southern white people did not come forward and most earnestly thank me for my position and words.

A Southern man writing to the Charleston News and Courier concerning my address at Buffalo expressed himself as follows:

"Notwithstanding the fact that the gentlemen speaking were of great ability, the audience showed signs of impatience; they wanted Mr. Washington, and no one else would do. At last he came. He is quiet looking, a little nervous but determined. His face indicates that he has above all qualities, patience and self-control. His address to the second audience was very much the same as that delivered before the first. He was a little freer; told several amusing stories, and from the start carried the crowd as no one else has done during this meeting."

It has been my privilege to be invited to address the national gathering of both the Christian Endeavor Society and the National Educational Association at almost every session that these organizations have held, and I have been very glad to accept the invitation as often as I could find time to do so.

The following September I delivered the opening address before the Brooklyn Institute of Arts and Sciences, in Brooklyn, N. Y., and in October of the same year while in Durham, N. C., for the purpose of speaking at the Agricultural and Mechanical Fair held at that place by the colored people, I was invited by the President of Trinity College, located in Durham, to deliver an address before the students of that college. This was the first time that I had ever received an invitation to address a white college in the South. I accepted the invitation and was treated with every possible courtesy both by the officers and students of the college. After my address, as I was preparing to leave the grounds in company with a number of colored friends who had been kind enough to call with me, the students assembled in the front yard and gave me their usual college yell in a hearty manner.

CHAPTER XIII.

URGED FOR A CABINET POSITION.

Soon after the election of Major McKinley to the office of President in 1896, the Washington Post, to the surprise of nearly everybody, came out with a strong editorial urging the President-Elect to give me a place in his cabinet. The name of the late Hon. B. K. Bruce was also suggested in the same connection. This editorial created quite a journalistic discussion which extended to all parts of the country. I give a few extracts from newspapers that may indicate the character of this discussion.

The Washington Post, which, I think, was the first paper to discuss the propriety of my selection as a cabinet officer, opened the discussion with the following article:

"There is one problem which Mr. McKinley, if he be a just and grateful man—as we think he is —will have to consider, and consider very seriously. We have in mind the problem of what the Republican party proposes to do by way of recognizing its obligations to the colored voter. That party has owed much to the loyal and unselfish devotion of the race in times gone by, but never so much as in the campaign which it has conducted to a triumphant conclusion. What, now, will Mr. McKinley do to testify his gratitude?

"At every stage of his personal fight Mr. McKinley has been indebted to the Negro. It was the Negro contingent at St. Louis that made his nomination certain. It was the Negro's firm stand for gold that forced the sound money issue upon the convention. It was the Negro's vote in such States as Maryland, West Virginia, Kentucky, Ohio, Delaware and Indiana that made his victory possible. We all know now that McKinley would have had next to no chance at all had not the St. Louis convention declared emphatically and unequivocally for the gold standard. As between a simple declaration for tariff revision on the one hand and for free silver coinage without tariff disturbances on the other, the great Eastern and Middle States would have had but a languid choice. It was the solid sound money front presented by the colored delegates that compelled the adoption of the gold clause in the platform, and furnished Mr. McKinley with the issue upon which he rallied to his banner the merchants, the manufacturers, and the moneyed corporations throughout the land. Mr. McKinley could not have been elected but by the course pursued by the Negroes before. during, and after the assembling of the St.

PRESIDENT ELIOT CONFERRING HONORARY DEGREE UPON MR. WASHINGTON, AT HARVARD UNIVERSITY. JUNE 24. 1896.

CAP AND GOWN. BOOKER T. WASHINGTON.

Louis convention. Now, in what fashion does he intend to recognize and reward their service?

"It seems to us that at least one cabinet position should be given to the race. Let us say the portfolio of Agriculture, for example. There are many colored men of notable attainments, of large experience in public life, and of the highest personal character, eminently qualified to discharge the duties of this office with credit to the administration and honor to themselves. We might name such men as Hon. B. K. Bruce and Prof. Booker T. Washington. Mr. Bruce has been a Senator of the United States, and it may be truly said of him that in that capacity he won the respect and esteem of all his colleagues and served his country with distinction. He also served a term as Register of the Treasury and another as Recorder of Deeds under the District government, always with notable ability. Prof. Washington is universally recognized as one of the foremost educators in the country. The institute over which he presides, at Tuskegee, Ala., has become conspicuous under his management, and is to-day ranked with the most useful and admirable of our seats of learning. The appointment of either of these gentlemen to the control of one of the executive departments would be a graceful acknowledgment of the obligations which the Republican party has incurred, and which we should think it would be anxious to discharge. We do not limit Mr. McKinley to these two. There are many other colored men abundantly fitted for a Cabinet position. It happens simply that ex-Senator Bruce and Prof. Washington occurred to us first in running over the list of eligibles.

"Returning to the abstract proposition, however, it is clear to us that Mr. McKinley owes his election, first to the fidelity and wise foresight of the colored delegates at St. Louis, and secondly to the loyal support of the colored voters in half a dozen states necessary to his election, which could not possibly have been carried for him without their aid. He is under obligations, which, as a man of feeling, he cannot well ignore and which he could most felicitously acknowledge by asking some truly representative Negro to enter his official family."

The Canton (Ohio) Repository, after discussing in a long article a number of men, white and black, suitable for cabinet material, concluded as follows:

"Another able man is Prof. Booker T. Washington, the head of the Tuskegee Normal School, of Alabama. Mr. Washington has been spoken of for Secretary of Agriculture under the new administration, and is one of the foremost leaders of the colored race in this country and a pioneer in the industrial and educational development of his people. He is one of the younger leaders of the colored people and fully understands their needs and hopes. His address at the opening of the Atlanta Exposition has been favorably commented upon by all classes of people. He is the originator of the Normal college and is doing a great work in the South."

There were other articles of similar character in other papers at the time. and still others of course that opposed vigorously the idea of placing a Negro in the Cabinet of the President of the United States.

In a speech delivered to the colored citizens of Boston, Mass., soon after this discussion began, I openly declared that under no circumstances would I accept a political appointment that would result in my turning aside from the work which I had begun at Tuskegee.

In the spring of 1897 I was invited by Dr. Francis J. Grimke, pastor of the 15th St. Presbyterian Church, Washington, D. C., to deliver an address in his church. My subject on this occasion was "The Things in Hand." It was just after President McKinley had been inaugurated as President. Washington was full of people from all over the country, and among them not a few colored people seeking office. At this meeting I urged as strongly as I could that the colored people should cease depending so much on office, and give more attention to industrial or business enterprises. This created a wide discussion among the colored people, especially among those who were in Washington seeking office. I have always held that the Negro has the same right to aspire to political or appointive offices as the white man has, but in our present condition we will be more sure of laying a foundation that will result in permanent political recognition in the future by giving attention at the present time in a very large measure to education, business and industry, than merely by seeking political office. I would have the Negro give up no right guaranteed to him by the Constitution of the United States, but I am also convinced that the way for him to secure the opportunity to exercise his rights guaranteed to him by the Constitution is to make himself the most useful and independent citizen in his community.

In certain quarters, for a number of years, a certain element of our people have opposed my plan for the elevation of the Negroes, on the ground that they have felt that I was not in favor of the Negro receiving a college education. This is an error. I do not oppose college education for our people, but I do urge that a larger percentage of our young men and women, whether educated in college or not, give the strength of their education in the direction of commercial or industrial development, just the same as the white man does. I have tried to show my approval of college education by giving as many college men as possible employment, and have on our pay roll at Tuskegee, constantly, from fifteen to twenty men and women who have been educated at the leading colleges throughout the country. The best way to approve of college education is to give those educated at college something to do. The great need for the next fifty or one hundred years among our people will be the sending out among them of men and women thoroughly equipped with academic and religious training, together with industrial or hand training, so that they can lead the masses to a betterment of their present industrial and material condition. The young white man who graduates at college, in nine cases out of ten, finds a business waiting for him that he can enter into as soon as he gets his college diploma. This business has been created by his father, grandfather or great-grandfather years before, but the black boy graduating from college finds no business waiting for him; he must start a business for himself; therefore, it is important, in our present condition, that the Negro be so educated along technical and industrial lines that he can found a business for himself. In the matter of technical or industrial education the blacks are not keeping up with the whites. Every state has technical schools for white boys and girls, and we can not expect to retain our hold on the industries of the South, unless we give special attention to preparing ourselves for doing the best work. In too many cases the Negro carpenter, the Negro blacksmith, the Negro contractor, and laundry woman are being replaced by white people who have come into the South from the North. We can only retain our hold upon the industries of the South by putting into the field men and women of the highest intelligence and skill. We must learn to do the tasks about our door in a thorough manner; to do a common thing in an uncommon manner; to be sure that nobody else can improve on our work.

CHAPTER XIV.

THE SHAW MONUMENT SPEECH, THE VISIT OF SECRETARY JAMES WILSON, AND THE LETTER TO THE LOUISIANA CONVENTION.

In the spring of 1897 I received a letter from Hon. Edward Atkinson, of Boston, inviting me to deliver an address at the dedication of the Robert Gould Shaw monument in Boston. I take it for granted that my readers already know all about the history and achievements of Robert Gould Shaw. The monument dedicated to his memory stands on the historic Boston Common, facing Beacon Street, and is said to be the most perfect piece of art of the kind in this country.

The meeting in connection with the dedicatory exercises was held in Music Hall, Boston, which was packed from bottom to top with perhaps one of the most distinguished audiences that has ever assembled in Boston. In fact, there was a large number of the old anti-slavery element present than will perhaps ever assemble again in this country. Hon. Roger Wolcott, Governor of Massachusetts, was the presiding officer. On the platform were the Mayor of Boston, the Lieutenant Governor, members of the Governor's

Council and of the city government of Boston, besides hundreds of other distinguished persons.

As to the impression made by this address I shall let an editorial which appeared in the Boston Transcript the next day, together with a few other newspaper accounts, tell the story.

I spoke as follows:—

"Mr. Chairman and fellow citizens:—

"In this presence, and on this sacred and memorable day, in the deeds and death of our hero, we recall the old, old story, ever old, yet ever new, that when it was the will of the Father to lift humanity out of wretchedness and bondage, the precious task was delegated to him who among ten thousand was altogether lovely, and was willing to make himself of no reputation that he might save and lift up others.

"If that heart could throb and those lips could speak, what would be the sentiment and words that Robert Gould Shaw would have us feel and speak at this hour? He would not have us to dwell long on the mistakes, the injustice, the criticisms of the days—

> 'Of storm and cloud, of doubt and fears,
> Across the eternal sky must lower;
> Before the glorious noon appears.'

"He would have us bind up with his own undying fame and memory and retain by the side of his monument, the name of John A.

Andrew, who, with prophetic vision and strong arm, helped to make the existence of the 54th regiment possible; and that of George L. Stearns, who, with hidden generosity and a great, sweet heart, helped to turn the darkest hour into day, and in doing so freely gave service, fortune and life itself to the cause which this day commemorates. Nor would he have us forget those brother officers, living and dead, who, by their baptism in blood and fire, in defense of Union and freedom, gave us an example of the highest and purest patriotism.

"To you who fought so valiantly in the ranks, the scarred and scattered remnant of the 54th regiment, who with empty sleeve and wanting leg, have honored this occasion with your presence, to you your commander is not dead. Though Boston erected no monument, and history recorded no story, in you and the loyal race you represent, Robert Gould Shaw would have a monument which time could not wear away.

"But an occasion like this is too great, too sacred, for mere individual eulogy. The individual is the instrument national virtue the end. That which was three hundred years being woven into the warp and woof of our democratic institutions could not be effaced by a single battle, as magnificent as was that battle; that which for three centuries had bound master and slave, yea, North and South, to a body of death, could not be blotted out by four years of war, could not be atoned for by shot and sword, nor by blood and tears.

"Not many days ago, in the heart of the South, in a large gathering of the people of my race, there were heard from many lips praises and thanksgiving to God for his goodness in setting them free from physical slavery. In the midst of that assembly a Southern white man arose, with gray hair and trembling hands, the former owner of many slaves, and from his quivering lips there came the words: "My friends, you forget in your rejoicing that in setting you free, God was also good to me and my race in setting us free." But there is a higher and deeper sense in which both races must be free than that represented by the bill of sale. The black man who cannot let love and sympathy go out to the white man is but half free. The white man who would close the shop or factory against a black man seeking an opportunity to earn an honest living is but half free. The white man who retards his own development by opposing a black man is but half free. The full measure of the fruit of Fort Wagner and all that this monument stands for will not be realized until every man covered with a black skin shall by patient and natural effort, grow to that height in industry, property, intelligence and moral responsibility, where no man in all our land will be tempted to degrade himself by withholding from his black brother any opportunity which he himself would possess.

"Until that time comes this monument will stand for effort, not victory complete. What these heroic souls of the 54th regiment began we must complete. It must be completed not in malice, nor in narrowness; not in artificial progress, nor in efforts at mere temporary political gain, nor in abuse of another section or race. Standing as I do to-day in the home of Garrison and Phillips and Sumner, my heart goes out to those who wore the gray as well as to those clothed in the blue; to those who returned defeated, to destitute homes, to face blasted hopes and a shattered political and industrial system. To them there can be no prouder reward for defeat than by a supreme effort to place the Negro on that footing where he will add material, intellectual and civil strength to every department of the State.

"This work must be completed in the public school, industrial school and college. The most of it must be completed in the effort of the Negro himself, in his effort to withstand temptation, to economize, to exercise thrift, to disregard the superficial for the real, the shadow for the substance, to be great and yet small, in his effort to be patient in the laying of a firm foundation, to grow so strong in skill and knowledge that he shall place his service in demand by reason of his intrinsic and superior worth. All this makes the key that unlocks every door of opportunity, and all others fail. In this battle of peace the rich and poor, the black and white may have a part.

"What lessons has this occasion for the future? What of hope, what of encouragement, what of caution? 'Watchman, tell us of the night; what the signs of promise are.' If through me, an humble representative, nearly ten millions of my people might be permitted to send a message to Massachusetts, to the survivors of the 54th regiment, to the committee whose untiring energy has made this memorial possible, to the family who gave their only boy that we might have life more abundantly, that message would be, 'Tell them that the sacrifice was not in vain, that up from the depth of ignorance and poverty we are coming, and if we come through oppression out of the struggle, we are gaining strength. By the way of the school, the well cultivated field, the skilled hand, the Christian home, we are coming up; that we propose to invite all who will to step up and occupy this position with us. Tell them that we are learning that standing ground for a race, as for an individual, must be laid in intelligence, industry, thrift and property, not as an end, but as a means to the highest privileges; that we are learning that neither the conqueror's bullet nor the fiat of law could make an ignorant voter an intelligent voter, could make a dependent man an independent man, could give one citizen respect for another, a bank account, nor a foot of land, nor an enlightened fireside. Tell them that as grateful as we are to artist and patriotism for placing the figures of Shaw and his comrades in physical form of beauty and magnificence, that after all, the real monument, the greater monument, is being slowly but safely builded among the lowly in the South, in the struggles and sacrifices of a race to justify all that has been done and suffered for it.'

"One of the wishes that lay nearest Colonel Shaw's heart was that his black troops might be permitted to fight by the side of the white soldiers. Have we not lived to see that wish realized, and will it not be more so in the future? Not at Wagner, not with rifle and bayonet, but on the field of peace, in the battle of industry, in the struggle for good government, in the lifting up of the lowest to the fullest opportunities. In this we shall fight by the side of the white man, North and South. And if this be true, as under God's guidance it will, that old flag, that emblem of progress and security, which brave Sergeant Carney never permitted to fall upon the ground, will still be borne aloft by Southern soldier and Northern soldier, and, in a more potent and higher sense, we shall all realize that—

> 'The slave's chain and the master's alike broken;
> The one curse of the race held both in tether;
> They are rising, all are rising—
> The black and the white together.' "

From the Boston Evening Transcript of June 1st, the following is taken:

"The core and kernel of yesterday's great noon meeting in honor of the Brotherhood of Man in Music Hall, was the superb address of the Negro President of Tuskegee. Booker T. Washington received his Harvard A. M. last June, the first of his race, said Governor Wolcott, to receive an honorary degree from the oldest university in this country, and this for the wise leadership of his people. And when Mr. Washington rose up in the flag-filled, enthusiasm-warmed, patriotic and glowing atmosphere of Music Hall, people felt keenly that here was the civic justification of the old abolition spirit of Massachusetts, in his person the proof of her ancient and indomitable faith; in his strong thought and rich oratory, the crown and glory of the old war days of suffering and strife. The scene was full of historic beauty and a deep significance. 'Cold' Boston was alive with the fire that is always hot in her heart for righteousness and truth. Rows and rows of people who are seldom seen at any public function, whole families of those who are certain to be out of town on a holiday, crowded the place to overflowing. The city was at her birthright fete in the persons of hundreds of her best citizens, men and women whose lives and names stand for the virtues that make for honorable civic pride.

"Battle music had filled the air. Ovation after ovation, applause warm and prolonged had greeted the officers and friends of Colonel Shaw, the sculptor, St. Gaudens, the memorial committee, the Governor and his staff, and the Negro soldiers of the Fifty-fourth Massachusetts as they came upon the platform or entered the hall. Chief Marshal Appleton and Mr. Chaplain Hall had performed their duties. Colonel Henry Lee, of Governor Andrew's old staff, had made the noble, simple presentation speech for the committee, paying tribute to the chairman, Mr. John M. Forbes, in whose stead he served. Governor Wolcott had made his short memorable speech, saying, 'Fort Wagner marked an epoch in the history of a race and called it into manhood.' Mayor Quincy had received the monument for the city of Boston in eloquent words. Professor James, brother of Adjutant James, who fell at Fort Wagner, wounded but not killed, had told the story of Colonel Shaw and his black regiment in gallant words. He got at the soul of the day's meaning when he said that the battle-instinct is strong enough in the race, bred in our bone and blood, but what is needed is 'that lonely kind of valor, civic courage we call it in time of peace;' which blesses a nation with a continued saying, and whose 'inner mystery' the precious virtue of civil genius is preserved in perfect good temper and in power of righteous wrath. And then after the singing of

'Mine eyes have seen the glory,
Of the coming of the Lord,'

Booker Washington arose. It was, of course, just the moment for him. The multitude, shaken out of its usual Symphony concert calm, quivered with an excitement that was not suppressed. A dozen times it had sprung to its feet to cheer and wave and hurrah, as one person. When this man of culture and voice and power, as well as dark skin, began with the bibical poetic touch in his first words, and quickly uttered the names of Andrew and of Stearns, feeling began to mount. You could see tears glisten in the eyes of the soldiers and civilians on the platform. When the orator turned to the colored soldiers on the platform, to the color bearer of Fort Wagner, who smiling bore still the flag he never lowered, even when wounded, and said: 'To you, to the scarred and scattered remnants of the Fifty-fourth, who

POULTRY RAISING, TUSKEGEE INSTITUTE.

AN AGRICULTURAL AND BEE CULTURAL EXHIBIT, TUSKEGEE INSTITUTE.

with empty sleeve and wanting leg, have honored this occasion with your presence, to you, your commander is not dead. Though Boston erected no monument, and history recorded no story, in you and the loyal race you represent, Robert Gould Shaw would have a monument which time could not wear away,' then came the climax of the emotion of the day and the hour. It was Roger Wolcott as well as the Governor of Massachusetts, the individual representative of the people's sympathy, as well as the chief magistrate, who had sprung first to his feet and cried, 'Three cheers to Booker T. Washington.'"

One incident, however, I note that the newspapers do not describe fully. Most of my readers will perhaps know that Sergeant William H. Carney, of New Bedford, Mass., was the brave colored officer who at the battle of Fort Wagner, was the color bearer and held on to the American flag. Notwithstanding the fact that a large proportion of his regiment was slain, he escaped in some miraculous manner and exclaimed, after the battle was over. "The old flag never touched the ground."

Before I made this address I had never met Sergeant Carney. Sergeant Carney, however, together with a remnant of the Fifty-fourth Massachusetts Regiment, was present on a front seat, and he held in his hand the same flag which he had held on to safely during the battle of Fort Wagner. When I turned to address the colored regiment and referred to Sergeant Carney, he rose as if by instinct with the flag in his hands. It has been my privilege to witness a good many satisfactory and rather sensational demonstrations in connection with several of my public addresses, but in dramatic effect I have never seen nor experienced anything that equaled the impression made on the audience when Sergeant Carney arose. For a good many minutes the audience seemed to entirely lose control of itself, and patriotic feeling was at a high pitch.

In November, 1897, the Tuskegee Institute received its first recognition from a member of the President's cabinet, in the way of a visit from Hon. James A. Wilson, Secretary of Agriculture. A year previous to the visit of Secretary Wilson, I began making efforts, in connection with friends of the institution, to raise money enough to erect a building to be devoted wholly to the teaching of agriculture, horticulture, dairying, fruit-gardening, market gardening, etc. About $10,000 was secured for the erection of this building. Secretary Wilson, whom I had met in the West some months before, promised me that he would try to be present at the formal opening of this building, and he kept his promise. Secretary Wilson was accompanied from Washington by

Dr. J. L. M. Curry, the agent of the John F. Slater Fund, and was met at Tuskegee by Gov. Joseph F. Johnston and a large crowd of colored and white citizens. In addition to the persons named there were present, Ex-Gov. Northern, of Georgia, and the State Superintendent of Education of Georgia, Major Glenn. The occasion was widely published throughout the country and did much to place the work of the school prominently before the people. The opening of this building marked the beginning of a new era in the history of the Tuskegee Institute, as since that time we have emphasized the teaching of agriculture to our students. During the earlier years of the school we found it difficult to get students to take much interest in our farm work. They wanted to go into the mechanical trades instead.

After the opening of this agricultural building and the securing of Mr. Geo. W. Carver, a thoroughly educated man in all matters pertaining to agriculture, the Agricultural Department has been put upon such a high plane that the students no longer look upon agriculture as a drudgery, and many of our best students are anxious to enter the Agricultural Department. We have demands from all parts of the South for men who have finished our courses in agriculture, dairying, etc., in fact, the demands are far greater than we can supply. I often wonder why it is, there being such excellent openings in these directions, that so few of our young men are willing to prepare themselves for these valuable and responsible positions.

I shall not occupy much more of the reader's time in detailing accounts of my various speech-making tours; were I to do so, a good part of this volume would be occupied in a description of them. Nearly one-half of my time is spent away from Tuskegee addressing audiences of various kinds in different parts of the country; sometimes in the South, at other times in the Middle or Eastern States, and going as far West in many cases as Denver and Omaha. There is never a day that I do not receive a number of invitations urging me to go to some section of the country to make an address. When I am away from Tuskegee the portion of the time that is not spent in making addresses in behalf of Tuskegee is spent in seeing individuals. The latter work I consider very important and far-reaching.

During the winter of 1898 a State Constitutional Convention assembled in New Orleans, La., for the purpose of passing a law which would result in disfranchising a large proportion of the Negro voters. Some of the members of the Convention were very anxious to pass a law that would result in the disfranchising of the Negro voters without disfranchising any portion of the white

voters. The passing of any such law seemed to me so manifestly unjust that I addressed an open letter to the Convention, which read as follows:
"*To the Louisiana State Constitutional Convention:*

"In addressing you this letter I know that I am running the risk of appearing to meddle with something that does not concern me. But since I know that nothing but love for our beautiful southland, which I hold as near my heart as any of you can, and a sincere love for every black man and white man within her borders, is the only thing actuating me to write, I am willing to be misjudged, if need be, if I can accomplish a little good.

"But I do not believe that you, gentlemen of the Convention, will misinterpret my motives. What I say will, I believe, be considered in the same earnest spirit in which I write.

'I am no politician; on the other hand, I have always advised my race to give attention to acquiring property, intelligence and character, as the necessary bases of good citizenship, rather than to mere political agitation. But the question upon which I write is out of the region of ordinary politics; it affects the civilization of two races, not for to-day alone, but for a very long time to come; it is up in the region of duty of man to man, of Christian to Christian.

"Since the war, no State has had such an opportunity to settle for all time the race question, so far as it concerns politics, as is now given in Louisiana. Will your Convention set an example to the world in this respect? Will Louisiana take such high and just ground in respect to the Negro that no one can doubt that the South is as good a friend to the Negro as he possesses elsewhere? In all this, gentlemen of the Convention, I am not pleading for the Negro alone, but for the morals, the higher life of the white man as well. For the more I study this question, the more I am convinced that it is not so much a question as to what the white man will do with the Negro, as to what the Negro will do with the white man's civilization.

"The Negro agrees with you that it is necessary to the salvation of the South that restriction be put upon the ballot. I know that you have two serious problems before you; ignorant and corrupt government on the one hand, and on the other a way to restrict the ballot so that control will be in the hands of the intelligent, without regard to race. With the sincerest sympathy with you in your efforts to find a way out of the difficulty, I want to suggest that no State in the South can make a law that will provide an opportunity or temptation for an ignorant white man to vote, and withhold the same opportunity from an ignorant colored man, without injuring both men. No State can make a law that can thus be executed, without dwarfing for all time the morals of the white man in the South. Any law controlling the ballot, that is not absolutely just and fair to both races, will work more permanent injury to the whites than to the blacks.

"The Negro does not object to an education or property test, but let the law be so clear that no one clothed with State authority will be tempted to perjure and degrade himself, by putting one interpretation upon it for the white man and another for the black man. Study the history of the South, and you will find that where there has been the most dishonesty in the matter of voting, there you will find to-day the lowest moral condition of both races. First, there was the temptation to act wrongly with the Negro's ballot. From this it was an easy step to dishonesty with the white man's ballot, to the carrying of concealed weapons, to the murder of a Negro, and then to the murder of a white man and then to lynching. I entreat you not to pass such a law as will prove an eternal millstone about the neck of your children.

"No man can have respect for government and officers of the law when he knows, deep down in his heart, that the exercise of the franchise is tainted with fraud.

"The road that the South has been compelled to travel during the last thirty years has been strewn with thorns and thistles. It has been as one groping through the long darkness into the light. The time is not very far distant when the world will begin to appreciate the real character of the burden that was imposed upon the South when 4,500,000 ex-slaves, ignorant and improverished, were given the franchise. No people had before been given such a problem to solve. History had blazed no path through the wilderness that could be followed. For thirty years we have wandered in the wilderness. We are beginning to get out. But there is but one road out, and all makeshifts, expedients, 'profit and loss calculations,' but lead into the swamps, quicksands, quagmires and jungles. There is a highway that will lead both races out into the pure, beautiful sunshine, where there will be nothing to hide and nothing to explain, where both races can grow strong and true and useful in every fibre of their being. I believe that your convention will find this highway; that it will enact a fundamental law which will be absolutely just and fair to white and black alike.

"I beg of you, further, that in the degree that you close the ballot box against the ignorant, you open the school house. More than one-half of the people of your State are Negroes.

No State can long prosper when a large percentage of its citizenship is in ignorance and poverty, and has no interest in government. I beg of you that you do not treat us as an alien people. We are not aliens. You know us; you know that we have cleared your forests tilled your fields, nursed your children and protected your families. There is an attachment between us that few understand. While I do not presume to advise you, yet it is in my heart to say that if your convention would do something that would prevent, for all time, strained relations between the two races, and would permanently settle the matter of political relations in one State in the South, at least, let the very best educational opportunities be provided for both races; and add to this the enactment of an election law that shall be incapable of unjust discrimination, at the same time providing that in proportion as the ignorant secure education, property and character, they will be given the right of citizenship. Any other course will take from one-half of your citizens interest in the State, and hope and ambition to become intelligent producers and tax-payers—to become useful and virtuous citizens. Any other course will tie the white citizens of Louisiana to a body of death.

"The Negroes are not unmindful of the fact that the white people of your State pay the greater portion of the school taxes, and that the poverty of the State prevents it from doing all that it desires for public education; yet, I believe you will agree with me, that ignorance is more costly to the State than education; that it will cost Louisiana more not to educate the Negroes than it will to educate them. In connection with a generous provision for public schools, I believe that nothing will so help my own people in your State as provision at some institution for the highest academic and normal training in connection with thorough training in agriculture, mechanics and domestic economy. The fact is, that 90 per cent. of our people depend upon the common occupations for their living, and outside of the cities, 85 per cent. depend upon agriculture for support. Notwithstanding this, our people have been educated since the war in everything else but the very things that most of them live by. First-class training in agriculture, horticulture, dairying, stock raising, the mechanical arts and domestic economy, will make us intelligent producers, and not only help us to contribute our proportion as taxpayers, but will result in retaining much money in the State that now goes out for that which can be produced in the State. An institution that will give this training of the hand, along with the highest mental culture, will soon convince our people that their salvation is in the ownership of property, industrial and business development, rather than mere political agitation.

"The highest test of civilization of any race is in its willingness to extend a helping hand to the less fortunate. A race, like an individual, lifts itself up by lifting others up. Surely no people ever had a greater chance to exhibit the highest Christian fortitude and magnanimity than is now presented to the people of Louisiana. It requires little wisdom or statesmanship to repress, to crush out, to retard the hopes and aspirations of a people, but the highest and most profound statesmanship is shown in guiding and stimulating a people so that every fibre in the body, mind and soul shall be made to contribute in the highest degree to the usefulness and nobility of the State. It is along this line that I pray God the thoughts and activities of your Convention be guided."

This letter was sent out through the Associated Press widely through the country. The leading papers of New Orleans as well as those in many other parts of the South indorsed my position editorially. The law that was finally passed by the Convention, while not as bad as when first presented, was not by any means the law that should have been enacted. In June of the same year I delivered the annual address before the Regents of the University of New York, at Albany.

CHAPTER XV.

CUBAN EDUCATION AND THE CHICAGO PEACE JUBILEE ADDRESS.

Immediately after the close of the Spanish-American war the Tuskegee Institute started a movement to bring a number of Cuban and Porto Rican students to Tuskegee, for the purpose of receiving training. The idea was pretty generally endorsed, and within a reasonably short time enough funds were donated by individuals throughout the country to provide for the education of ten students from Cuba and Porto Rico. These students are now at Tuskegee taking the regular courses of training and are making a creditable record. It is the plan to have them return to their island homes and give their people the benefit of their education.

Perhaps no single agency has been more potent during the last ten years in assisting the Negro to better his condition than the John F. Slater Fund, to which I have already referred. The trustees of this fund are among the most successful and generous business men in the country, and they are using the fund very largely as a means of pointing the proper direction of the education of the Negro. During 1898 the Slater Fund trustees made an appropriation which was to be used in enabling Mrs. Washington and myself to go into all of the Southern cities and deliver lectures to our people, especially in the large cities, speaking to them plainly about their present material, financial, physical, educational and moral needs, and trying to point out a way by which they could improve. We spent a portion of the summer of 1898 in going into cities in North and South Carolina. Meetings were held in Greensboro, Wilmington, Columbia and Charleston, and everywhere we spoke the houses were packed full. We spoke four or five times in Charleston, and the audience rooms were crowded at every meeting with representatives of both races. We have the satisfaction of feeling that these meetings accomplished a great deal of good, and everywhere we were overwhelmed with thanks from the people for our words. The newspapers gave us all the space we desired and not only helped through their news columns, but were generous in their editorial mention.

When the Spanish-American war closed there was great rejoicing throughout the country, and many cities vied with each other in their effort to celebrate the return of peace on a scale that would command the attention of the whole country. The city of Chicago, however, seemed to have been the most successful in these celebrations. Chicago was fortunate in securing the President of the United States, together with nearly all the members of his cabinet, and various foreign ministers and other important officials. This gave the celebration in Chicago a national importance such as attached to the celebration held by no other city.

I was asked by President William R. Harper, of the University of Chicago, chairman of the committee on invitations, to deliver one of the addresses in Chicago. I accepted the invitation and delivered, in fact, two addresses, during the Jubilee week in Chicago. The principal address which I delivered on this occasion was on Sunday evening, October 16. The meeting was held in the Chicago Auditorium, and was the largest audience that I have ever spoken to in any part of the country. Besides speaking in the main auditorium, I addressed, on the same evening, two overflow audiences held in different portions of the city. It is said there were 16,000 people in the Auditorium, and it seems to me there were at least 16,000 on the outside trying to get into the building. In fact, without the aid of a policeman, it was impossible for any one to get anywhere near the entrance. The meeting was attended by President William McKinley, the members of his cabinet, foreign ministers and a large number of army and navy officers, many of whom had distinguished themselves during the Spanish-American war. The speakers, besides myself, on Sunday evening, were Rabbi Emil G. Hirsch, Father Thomas P. Hodnett and Dr. John H. Barrows.

The speech which I delivered on Sunday evening was as follows:

"*Mr. Chairman, Ladies and Gentlemen:*

"On an important occasion in the life of the Master, when it fell to Him to pronounce judgment on two courses of action, these memorable words fell from his lips: 'And Mary hath chosen the better part.' This was the supreme test in the case of an individual. It is the highest test in the case of a race or nation. Let us apply the test to the American Negro.

"In the life of our Republic, when he has had the opportunity to choose, has it been the better or worse part? When in the childhood of this nation the Negro was asked to submit to slavery or choose death and extinction, as did the aborigines, he chose the better part, that which perpetuated the race.

"When in 1776 the Negro was asked to decide between British oppression and American independence, we find him choosing the better part, and Crispus Attucks, a Negro, was the first to shed his blood on State street, Boston, that the white American might enjoy liberty forever, though his race remained in slavery.

"When in 1814, at New Orleans, the test of patriotism came again, we find the Negro choosing the better part, and Gen. Andrew Jackson himself testifying that no heart was more loyal and no arm more strong and useful in defense of righteousness.

"When the long and memorable struggle came between union and separation, when we knew that victory on one hand meant freedom, and defeat on the other his continued enslavement, with a full knowledge of the portentous meaning of it all, when the suggestion and temptation came to burn the home and massacre wife and children during the absence of the master in battle, and thus insure his liberty, we find him choosing the better part, and for four long years protecting and supporting the helpless, defenseless ones entrusted to his care.

"When in 1863 the cause of the union seemed to quiver in the balance, and there were doubt and distrust, the Negro was asked to come to the rescue in arms, and the valor displayed at Fort Wagner and Port Hudson and Fort Pillow testifies most eloquently again that the Negro chose the better part.

"When a few months ago the safety and honor

of the republic were threatened by a foreign foe, when the wail and anguish of the oppressed from a distant isle reached his ears, we find the Negro forgetting his own wrongs, forgetting the laws and customs that discriminated against him in his own country, again choosing the better part—the part of honor and humanity. And if you would know how he deported himself in the field at Santiago, apply for an answer to Shafter and Roosevelt and Wheeler. Let them tell how the Negro faced death and laid down his life in defense of honor and humanity, and when you have gotten the full story of the heroic conduct of the Negro in the Spanish-American war—heard it from the lips of Northern soldiers, and Southern soldiers, from ex-abolitionists and ex-masters—then decide within yourselves whether a race that is thus willing to die for its country should not be given the highest opportunity to live for its country.

"In the midst of all the complaints of suffering in the camp and field, suffering from fever and hunger, where is the official or citizen that has heard a word of complaint from the lips of a black soldier? The only request that has come from the Negro soldier has been that he might be permitted to replace the white soldier when heat and malaria began to decimate the ranks of the white regiment, and to occupy at the same time the post of greatest danger.

"This country has been most fortunate in her victories. She has twice measured arms with England and has won. She has met the spirit of rebellion within her borders and was victorious. She has met the proud Spaniard, and he lays prostrate at her feet. All this is well, it is magnificent. But there remains one other victory for Americans to win—a victory as far-reaching and important as any that has occupied our army and navy. We have succeeded in every conflict, except the effort to conquer ourselves in the blotting out of racial prejudices. We can celebrate the era of peace in no more effectual way than by a firm resolve on the part of Northern men and Southern men, black men and white men, that the trenches that we together dug around Santiago shall be the eternal burial place of all that which separates us in our business and civil relations. Let us be as generous in peace as we have been brave in battle. Until we thus conquer ourselves, I make no empty statement when I say that we shall have a cancer gnawing at the heart of the republic that shall one day prove as dangerous as an attack from an army without or within.

"In this presence and on this auspicious occasion, I want to present the deep gratitude of nearly ten millions of my people to our wise, patient and brave Chief Executive for the generous manner in which my race has been recognized during this conflict—a recognition that has done more to blot out sectional and racial lines than any event since the dawn of our freedom.

"I know how vain and impotent is all abstract talk on this subject. In your efforts to 'rise on stepping stones of your dead selves,' we of the black race shall not leave you unaided. We shall make the task easier for you by acquiring property, habits of thrift, economy, intelligence and character, by each making himself of individual worth in his own community. We shall aid you in this as we did a few days ago at El Caney and Santiago, when we helped you to hasten the peace we here celebrate. You know us; you are not afraid of us. When the crucial test comes, you are not ashamed of us. We have never betrayed or deceived you. You know that as it has been, so it will be. Whether in war or in peace, whether in slavery or in freedom, we have always been loyal to the Stars and Stripes."

I shall not attempt to burden the reader with newspaper comments on this address, but shall content myself with giving a description that appeared at the time in the Chicago Times-Herald.

"Booker T. Washington's address at the

Jubilee Thanksgiving services at the Auditorium contained one of the most eloquent tributes ever paid to the loyalty and valor of the colored race, and at the same time, was one of the most powerful appeals for justice to a race which has always chosen the better part.

"The speaker, who is the recognized leader of the colored race, reviewed the history of his people from the childhood of the nation to the present day. He pictured the Negro choosing slavery rather than extinction; recalled Crispus Attucks, shedding his blood at the beginning of the American revolution that white Americans might be free, while black Americans remained in slavery; rehearsed the conduct of the Negroes with Jackson at New Orleans; drew a vivid and pathetic picture of the Southern slaves protecting and supporting the families of their masters while the latter were fighting to perpetuate black slavery; recounted the bravery of colored troops at Port Hudson and Forts Wagner and Pillow, and praised the heroism of the black regiments that stormed El Caney and Santiago to give freedom to the enslaved people of Cuba, forgetting for the time being the unjust discrimination that law and custom make against them in their own country.

"In all of these things the speaker declared that his race had chosen the better part. And then he made his eloquent appeal to the consciences of white Americans: 'When you have gotten the full story of the heroic conduct of the Negro in the Spanish-American war, heard it from the lips of Northern soldier and Southern soldier, from ex-abolitionists and ex-masters, then decide within yourselves whether a race that is thus willing to die for its country, should not be given the highest opportunity to live for its country.'

"When Americans conquer race prejudice, the speaker declared, they will have won a victory greater than can be obtained through the achievements of arms. He likened the effect of race discrimination, especially in the Southern States, to a cancer gnawing at the heart of the republic, 'as dangerous as an attack from an army within or without.'

"This is not a threat, but a warning, and one to which the white race should give heed. The only solution of the 'Negro problem' which will remove all menace to the tranquillity and interest of the country, is a universal recognition of the Negro's civil rights. When law and custom cease to degrade him and place obstacles in the way of his advancement; when we cease by unjust discrimination to fill his heart with despair and hatred, but instead, give him hope and aid in his efforts to fully emancipate himself, he will solve the problem now fraught with vexation and danger.

"The race is fortunate in having a Booker T. Washington and other comparatively great men as living evidence of what education and the development of natural faculties have accomplished for the colored man, as well as what can be accomplished in the future.

"Only through the defeat of race prejudice can the colored man hope to acquire his full proportions as a citizen. And in conquering race prejudice, the white race will achieve a greater victory than both races won in the late war. They will be choosing the better part."

The portion of the speech which seemed to raise the wildest and most sensational enthusiasm was the part where I thanked the President for his recognition of the Negro in his appointments during the Spanish-American war. The President occupied a seat in a box to the right of the platform. When I addressed the President I turned toward him, and as I closed the sentence thanking him for his generosity, the whole audience arose and cheered for some time. The cheering continued with waving of hats, hand kerchieves and canes until the President himself arose in his box and bowed to me two or three times. This kindled anew the enthusiasm and the demonstration was almost beyond description.

I shall not go into all the details relating to the attention which was shown me during this three days' visit to Chicago. I would say that from the Mayor of the city down, every official connected with the Peace Jubilee seemed to give me the greatest attention, and completely put me at my ease on every occasion. I was given a position on the President's stand during the review of the parade, and dined twice with the President's party.

My address was reported in all portions of the country through the associated press dispatches. One portion of it seemed to have been misunderstood, however, by the Southern press, and some of the Southern newspapers took exception to some things that I said and criticised me rather strongly for what seemed to them a reflection upon the South. These criticisms continued for several weeks, when I received a letter from the editor of the Age-Herald, published in Birmingham, Alabama, asking me if I would say just what I meant to say in my address. I replied in the following letter, which seemed to put an end to all criticism on the part of the Southern press, and to satisfy the South:

"*To the Editor of the 'Age-Herald:'*

"Replying to your communication of recent date regarding my Chicago speech, I would say that I have made no change whatever in my attitude towards the South or in my idea of the elevation of the colored man. I have always made it a rule to say nothing before a Northern audience that I would not say before a Southern audience. I do not think it necessary to go into any extended explanation of what my position is, for if my seventeen years of work here in the heart of the South is not a sufficient explanation, I do not see how mere words can explain. Each year more and more confirms me in the wisdom of what I have advocated and tried to do.

"In Chicago, at the Peace Jubilee, in discussing the relations of the races, I made practically the same plea that I did in Nashville this summer at the Young People's Society of Christian Endeavor, where I spoke almost wholly to a Southern white audience. In Chicago I made the same plea that I did in a portion of my address at the opening of the Atlanta Exposition, for the blotting out of race prejudice in 'commercial and civil relations.' What is termed social recognition is a question I never discuss. As I said in my Atlanta address, 'The wisest among my race understand that the agitations of questions of social equality is the extremest folly, and that progress in the enjoyment of all the privileges that will come to us must be the result of severe and constant struggle rather than of artificial forcing.'

God knows that both—we, of the black race and the white race—have enough problems pressing upon us for solution without obtruding a social question, out of which nothing but harm would come.

"In my addresses I very seldom refer to the question of prejudice, because I realize that it is something to be lived down, not talked down, but at that great meeting which marked, in a large measure, the end of all sectional feeling, I thought at an opportune time to ask for the blotting out of racial prejudice as far as possible in 'business and civil relations'.

"In a portion of my address which was not sent out by the Associated Press, I made the request that the Negro be given every opportunity in proportion as he makes himself worthy. At Chicago I did not refer wholly to the South or to the Southern white people. All who are acquainted with the subject will agree that prejudice exists in the North as well as in the South. I naturally laid emphasis upon the South, because, as we all know, owing to the large proportion of blacks to whites in the South, it is in the South mainly that the problem is to be worked out. Whenever I discuss the question of race prejudice I never do so solely in the interest of the Negro; I always take higher ground. If a black man hates a white man, it narrows and degrades his soul. If a white man hates a black man it narrows and degrades his soul.

"Both races will grow stronger in morals, and prosper in business, just in proportion as in every manly way they cultivate the confidence and friendship of each other. Outbreaks of race feelings and strained relations not only injure business, but retard the moral and religious growth of both races; and it is the duty among the intelligent of both races to cultivate patience and moderation.

"Each day convinces me that the salvation of the Negro in this country will be in his cultivation of habits of thrift, economy, honesty, the acquiring of education, Christian character, property and industrial skill."

I have always made it a rule never to say anything in an address in the North that I would not say in the South. I have no sympathy with any policy which would leave one to suppose that he can help matters in the South by merely abusing the Southern white man. What the South wants is help and not abuse. Of course, when individuals, communities or states in the South do a wrong thing, they should be criticised, but it should be done in a dignified, generous manner. Mere abuse of a man because he is white or because he is black amounts to nothing and ends in harm. I have said more than once, and I here repeat, that I can sympathize as much with a white man as with a black man; I can sympathize as much with a Southern white man as with a Northern white man. I do not propose that my nature shall be lowered by my yielding to the temptation to hate a man because he is white or because he happens to live in the South. The Negro who hates a white man is usually little and narrow. The white man who hates a Negro is usually little and narrow. Both races will grow strong, useful and generous in proportion as they learn to love each other instead of hating each other. The Negro race, of all races in the world, should be the last to cultivate the habit of hating an individual on account of his race. He will gain more by being generous than by being narrow. If I can do anything to assist a member of the white race I feel just as happy as if I had done something to assist a member of the Negro race. I think I have learned that the best way to lift one's self up is to help some one else.

While writing upon this subject, it is a pleasure for me to add that in all my contact with the white people of the South, I have never received a single personal insult. The white people in and near Tuskegee, to an especial degree, seem to count it a privilege to show me all the respect within their power, and often go out of their way to do this.

Not very long ago, I was making a journey

between Dallas, Texas, and Houston. In some way it became known in advance that I was on the train. At nearly every station at which the train stopped, numbers of white people, including in most cases the officials of the town, came aboard and introduced themselves and thanked me heartily for the work that I was trying to do for the South.

On another occasion, in Georgia, I found in a Pullman car two ladies from Boston whom I knew well. These ladies, being ignorant of the customs of the South, insisted that I take a seat with them in their section. After some hesitation I consented. One of them, without my knowledge, ordered supper to be served to the three of us. When I found that supper had been ordered, I tried to excuse myself, but the ladies insisted that I must eat with them. I finally settled back in my seat with a sigh, and said to myself: "I am in for it now, sure."

At last the meal being over, I went into the smoking-room, where most of the men by that time were. In the meantime, however, it had become known in some way throughout the car who I was. When I went into the smoking-room nearly every man came up and introduced himself to me and thanked me earnestly for the work that I was trying to do for the whole South.

CHAPTER XVI.

THE VISIT OF PRESIDENT WM. McKINLEY TO TUSKEGEE.

Soon after starting the Tuskegee Institute I earnestly desired to have the President of the United States visit it. The chance of securing such a visit seemed to be so unattainable that I dared not mention it to my nearest friend; still, I resolved that such a visit should be made. The more I thought of it, the more I became convinced that there was but one way to secure the attention and the interest of the President of the United States, and that was by making the institution so useful to the country that the attention of the President would necessarily be attracted to it. From the first day that the school was opened, I tried to impress upon teachers and students the fact that by reason of our former condition of servitude, and prejudice against our color, we must try to perform every duty entrusted to us, not only as well, but better than any one else, so as to receive proper consideration. To-day this is the spirit which pervades the entire school. We strive to have our students understand that no possible prejudice can explain away the influence of a Negro living in a nicely painted house, with well kept flower yards, gardens, farm, poultry and live stock and who is at the same time a large tax-payer in his county.

After nearly eighteen years of work and struggle, I was more than ever determined to secure a visit from the highest official of my country, not only that he and the members of his cabinet might see what ex-slaves had accomplished in the way of building an institution of learning, but also for the sake of the encouragement that such a recognition from the Nation's Chief Executive would give the whole Negro race in America.

In October, 1898, I saw it mentioned in several newspapers that President McKinley was likely to visit the Atlanta Peace Jubilee, in December. I went at once to Washington, and was not there a great while before I found my way to the White House. There was quite a crowd of people in the various reception rooms, many of whom had been waiting some time for an audience with the President. The size of the crowd somewhat discouraged me, and I concluded that my chances of seeing the President were very slim. I at once sought the Secretary to the President, Mr. J. Addison Porter, and very frankly told him my errand. Mr. Porter kindly sent my card in to the President, and in a few minutes Mr.

McKinley permitted me to see him. After a most interesting conversation regarding the condition of the colored people in the South, in which he manifested his interest in their development, the President told me that, in case he saw his way clear to go to Altanta, in December, he would try hard to go to Tuskegee, which is a hundred and forty miles beyond Atlanta. At that time he did not make his promise final, but asked me to see him later.

By the middle of the following month, the President had definitely promised to attend the Peace Jubilee at Atlanta, Ga., December 14 and 15. I went again to see the President. This time Mr. Charles W. Hare, a white citizen of Tuskegee, accompanied me, and assisted in showing the President the importance of making such a visit. While the question was being discussed with cabinet officers, one of the oldest and most influential white citizens of Atlanta, one who had been a large slave-holder and who is now an active Democrat, stepped into the room. The President asked this gentleman's opinion of the wisdom of his making this visit, and as to his going one hundred and forty miles out of the way to visit such an institution. This Atlanta citizen replied that it was the thing to do. The reply was made without hesitation. Between my two visits, that active and most constant friend of the Negro race, Dr. J. L. M. Curry, agent of the Peabody and Slater Funds, hearing of my desire to have a visit from the President, made a personal call upon Mr. McKinley without my knowledge, and urged him to make the visit. I will not prolong the story, except to add that before the day of my last visit was over, the President definently decided to spend the greater part of the day of December 16 in visiting the Tuskegee Institute. In connection with this visit I had to call upon the President three or four times at the White House, and at all times I found him kind, patient and most cordial, apparently forgetful of the differences in our history. The time of my last visit was but a few days after the election riots of that year in North and South Carolina, when the colored people throughout the country were feeling gloomy and discouraged. I observed by the tenor of the President's remarks that he felt keenly and seriously for the race. Notwithstanding a large number of people were waiting to see him, he detained me some twenty minutes, discussing the condition and needs of my race in the South. When I told him that I thought a visit from the President of the United States at that time to a Negro institution would do more than almost anything else to encourage the race and show the world in what esteem he held the race, he replied that he was determined to show

ABOVE. ONE OF THE NEW ROSENWALD SCHOOL HOUSES.
BELOW. ONE OF THE OLD NEGRO SCHOOL HOUSES.

John W. Robinson. Jas. N. Calloway.
Shepard L. Harris. Allen L. Burks.

The party that went to Africa in the employ of the German Government to teach cotton raising in the German colony of Toga.

his interest in us by acts rather than by mere words, and that if I thought his visit to Tuskegee would permanently help the race and the institution he would most gladly give up one day of his administration to visit Tuskegee.

The morning of December 16 came, and at eight o'clock the President, Mrs. McKinley, with members of his cabinet, their families, besides several distinguished generals, including General Shafter, General Joseph Wheeler, General Lawton and others, arrived on special trains from Atlanta. Invitations had been extended to Gov. Joseph F. Johnston, of Alabama, and his staff, and they were present. The Alabama Legislature also was invited, and it adjourned and came to Tuskegee in a body. In all, more than six thousand visitors came. The morning was spent in an inspection of the grounds and in witnessing a parade of all the work of the school, religious, academic and industrial, represented on floats. This over, we went to the large chapel, where the President, members of his cabinet, the Governor, and others spoke. A few extracts from the addresses of the President, Secretary of the Navy Long, and Postmaster General Smith, in commendation of Tuskegee's work, may be of interest. The President said:

"Teachers and Pupils of Tuskegee: To meet you under such pleasant auspices and to have the opportunity of a personal observation of your work is indeed most gratifying. The Tuskegee Normal and Industrial Institute is ideal in its conception, and has already a large and growing reputation in the country and is not unknown abroad. I congratulate all who are associated in this undertaking for the good work which it is doing in the education of its students to lead lives of honor and usefulness, thus exalting the race for which it was established.

"Nowhere, I think, could a more delightful location have been chosen for this unique educational experiment, which has attracted the attention and won the support even of conservative philanthropists in all sections of the country.

"To speak of Tuskegee without paying special tribute to Booker T. Washington's genius and perseverance would be impossible. The inception of this noble enterprise was his, and he deserves high credit for it. His was the enthusiasm and enterprise which made its steady progress possible and established in the institution its present high standard of accomplishment. He has won a worthy reputation as one of the great leaders of his race, widely known and much respected at home and abroad as an accomplished educator, a great orator and a true philanthropist.

"What steady and gratifying advances have been made here during the past fifteen years a personal inspection of the material equipment strikingly proves. The fundamental plan of the original undertaking has been steadily followed; but new features have been added; gaps in the course of instruction have been filled in; the patronage and resources have been largely increased until even the legislative department of the State of Alabama recognized the worth of the work and of the great opportunities here afforded. From one small frame house the institution has grown until it includes the fine group of dormitories, recitation rooms, lecture halls and work shops which have so surprised and delighted us to-day. A thousand students, I am told, are here cared for by nearly a hundred teachers, altogether forming with the preparatory department a symmetrical scholastic community which has been well called a model for the industrial colored schools of the South. Certain it is that a pupil bent on fitting himself or herself for mechanical work can have the widest choice of useful and domestic occupations.

"One thing I like about this institution is that its policy has been generous and progressive; it has not been so self-centered or interested in its own pursuits and ambitions as to ignore what is going on in the rest of the country or make it difficult for outsiders to share the local advantages. I allude especially to the spirit in which the annual conferences have been held by leading colored citizens and educators, with the intention of improving the condition of their less fortunate brothers and sisters. Here, we can see, is an immense field and one which cannot too soon or too carefully be utilized. The conferences have grown in popularity, and are well calculated not only to encourage colored men and colored women in their individual efforts, but to cultivate and promote an amicable relationship between the two races—a problem whose solution was never more needed than at the present time. Patience, moderation, self-control, knowledge, character, will surely win you victories and realize the best aspirations of your people. An evidence of the soundness of the purpose of this institution is that those in charge of its management evidently do not believe in attempting the unattainable, and their instruction in self-reliance and practical industry is most valuable.

"In the day and night schools many branches can be taught at a small expense, which will give the men and the women who have mastered them immediate employment and secure their success afterwards, provided they abide by the principles of industry, morality and religion here inculcated. In common with the Hampton Institute, in Virginia, the Tuskegee Institute has been and is to-day of inestimable value in sowing the seeds of good citizenship. Institutions of their standing and worthy patronage from a steadier and more powerful agency for the good of all concerned than any yet proposed or suggested. The practical is here associated with the academic, which encourages both learning and industry. Here you learn to master yourselves, find the best adaptation of your faculties, with advantages for advanced learning to meet the high duties of life. No country, epoch or race has a monopoly upon knowledge. Some have easier but not necessarily better opportunities for self-development. What a few can obtain free most have to pay for, perhaps by hard physical labor, mental struggle and self-denial. But in this great country all can have the opportunity for bettering themselves, provided they exercise intelligence and perseverance, and their motives and conduct are worthy. Nowhere are such facilities for universal education found as in the United States. They are accessible to every boy and girl, white and black.

"Integrity and industry are the best possessions which any man can have, and every man can have them. Nobody can give them to him or take them from him. He cannot acquire them by inheritance; he cannot buy them or beg them or borrow them. They belong to the individual and are his unquestioned property. He alone can part with them. They are a good thing to have and keep. They make happy homes; they achieve success in every walk of life; they have won the greatest triumphs for mankind. No man who has them ever gets into the police court or before the grand jury or in the workhouse or the chain gang. They give one moral and material power. They will bring you a comfortable living, make you respect yourself and command the respect of your fellows. They are indispensable to success. They are invincible. The merchant requires the clerk whom he employs to have them. The railroad corporation inquires whether the man seeking employment possesses them. Every avenue of human endeavor welcomes them. They are the only keys to open with certainty the door of opportunity to struggling manhood. Employment waits on them; capital requires them. Citizenship is not good without them. If you do not already have them, get them.

"To the pupils here assembled I extend my especial congratulations that the facilities for advancing afforded to them are so numerous and so inviting. Those who are here for the time being have the reputation of the institution in charge and should, therefore, be all the more careful to guard it worthily. Others who have gone before you have made great sacrifices to reach the present results. What you do will affect not only those who come after you here, but many men and women whom you may never meet. The results of your training and work here will eventually be felt, either directly or indirectly, in nearly every part of the country.

"Most of you are young, and youth is the time best fitted for development both of the body and mind. Whatever you do, do with all your might, with will and purpose, not of the selfish kind, but looking to benefit your race and your country. In comparing the past with the present you should be especially grateful that it has been your good fortune to come within the influences of such an institution as that of Tuskegee and that you are under the guidance of such a strong leader. I thank him most cordially for the pleasure of visiting this institution, and I bring to all here associated my good will and the best wishes of your countrymen, wishing you the realization of success in whatever undertakings that may hereafter engage you."

Secretary Long said:

"*Mr. President and Students:*

"I cannot make a speech to you to-day. My heart is too full, full of hope, admiration and pride for my countrymen of both sections and both colors. I am filled with gratitude and admiration for your work, and from this time forward, I shall have absolute confidence in your progress and in the solution of the problem in which you are engaged.

"The problem, I say, has been solved. A picture has been presented to-day which should be put upon canvas with the pictures of Washington and Lincoln, and transmitted to future time and generations; a picture which the press of the country should spread broadcast over the land, a most dramatic picture, and that picture is this: The President of the United States standing on this platform; on one side, the Governor of Alabama, on the other, completing the trinity, a representative of a race only a few years ago in bondage, the colored president of the Tuskegee Normal and Industrial Institute.

"God bless the President under whose majesty such a scene as that is presented to the American people. God bless the State of Alabama which is showing that it can deal with this problem for itself. God bless the orator, philanthropist and disciple of the Great Master,—who if he were on earth would be doing the same work,—Booker T. Washington."

Postmaster General Smith closed as follows:

"We have witnessed many spectacles within the last few days. We have seen the magnificent grandeur and the magnificent achievements of one of the great metropolitan cities of the South. We have seen heroes of the war pass by in procession.

We have seen floral parades. But I am sure my colleagues will agree with me in saying that we have witnessed no spectacle more impressive and more encouraging, more inspiring for our future than that which we have witnessed here this morning.

"I have thought as I sat here this morning of two men, two great men, two great educators. One of them was the founder and creator of the Hampton Institute, in Virginia, and the other is the real creator and founder and pre-eminent head of this great industrial institution of the South. General Armstrong did a work which cannot be measured by the breadth of his philanthropy, the greatness of his unselfishness and the extent of his power in educating a people. We have for years mourned his lamented death. His memory will be preserved among that of the great benefactors of our people and our government. In the future, though long may that time be distant so far as relates to the head of this institution, in the distant future, we shall be ready to erect in the capitol of the nation, among the heroes of our country, among those who have contributed to its upbuilding and to its salvation, we shall be ready to erect a monument to these two great philanthropists and leaders of this people, General Armstrong and Booker T. Washington."

I cannot close this chapter without adding a

reference to the great pleasure and satisfaction given by the part the white and colored citizens of the town of Tuskegee took in this recognition of the school. A few years before this I had gone to Tuskegee unknown and entirely without means, but no white people, in any part of America, could have acted more cordially and co-operated more heartily with our school than did the white people of Tuskegee upon this occasion. They organized various committees, composed of both men and women, to help us in giving the President the proper reception. The town, from one end to the other, was decorated with the National colors, to say nothing of many beautiful arches and other forms of decorations. One of the many newspaper correspondents who accompanied the President remarked to me that he had never seen in any town of the size such generous and appropriate decorations.

What the President and his party thought of this visit to the Tuskegee Normal and Industrial Institute can be best told by the following letter, received from the Secretary to the President:

"Executive Mansion,
Washington, Dec. 23, 1899.

"Dear Sir:—By this mail I take pleasure in sending you engrossed copies of the souvenir of the visit of the President to your institution.

These sheets bear the autographs of the President and the members of the Cabinet who accompanied him on the trip. Let me take this opportunity of congratulating you most heartily and sincerely upon the great success of the exercises provided for and entertainment furnished us under your auspices during our visit to Tuskegee. Every feature of the program was perfectly executed and was viewed or participated in with the heartiest satisfaction by every visitor present. The unique exhibition which you gave of your pupils engaged in their industrial vocations was not only artistic but thoroughly impressive. The tribute paid by the President and his Cabinet to your work was none too high and forms a most encouraging augury, I think, for the future prosperity of your institution. I cannot close without assuring you that the modesty shown by yourself in the exercises was most favorably commented upon by all the members of our party.

"With best wishes for the continued advance of your most useful and patriotic undertaking, kind personal regards, and the compliments of the season, believe me, always,

    Very sincerely yours,
     JOHN ADDISON PORTER,
      Secretary to the President."

"To Pres. BOOKER T. WASHINGTON,
  Tuskegee Normal and Industrial Institute,
   Tuskegee, Ala."

The impression which this visit of the President, Members of his Cabinet, and other distinguished visitors made upon the teachers and students of the Tuskegee Institute, cannot be overestimated. It inspired the teachers and students with new life and hope, not only in the work of the present, but in that of the future. It did more. It inspired the older members of the community, black and white, with new and higher purposes in the hard battle of life. It made us all feel, as we had never felt before, that we were in a higher and nobler sense citizens of the great Republic, and that the President of the United States was our President, "in soberness and truth," as much as he was of the people of larger and more pretentious communities than ours.

CHAPTER XVII.

THE TUSKEGEE NEGRO CONFERENCE.

Tuesday, February 23, 1892, was a day memorable in the lives and fortunes of the great bulk of the Negro population in the "Black Belt" of the South. This day saw the beginning of a strange and altogether new movement in which the Negro was called upon to participate.

From the time I first began working at Tuskegee, I began to study closely not only the young people, but the condition, the weak points and the strong points, of the older people. I was very often surprised to see how much common sense and wisdom these older people possessed, notwithstanding they were wholly ignorant as far as the letter of the book was concerned.

About the first of January, 1892, I sent out invitations to about seventy-five of the common, hardworking farmers, as well as to mechanics, ministers and teachers, asking them to assemble at Tuskegee on the 23d of February and spend the day in talking over their present condition, their helps and their hindrances, and to see if it were possible to suggest any means by which the rank and file of the people might be able to benefit themselves.

I quote a portion of the printed invitation which was sent out to those invited to attend the Conference:

"In the Conference, two ends will be kept in view: First, to find out the actual industrial, moral and educational condition of the masses. Second, to get as much light as possible on what is the most effective way for the young men and women whom the Tuskegee Institute and other institutions are educating, to use their education in helping the masses of the colored people to lift themselves up.

"In this connection, it may be said that, in general, a very large majority of the colored people in the Black Belt cotton district are in debt for supplies secured through the 'mortgage system,' rent the land on which they live, and dwell in one-room log cabins. The schools are in session in the country districts not often longer than three months, and are taught in most cases in churches or log cabins with almost no apparatus or school furniture.

"The poverty and ignorance of the Negro, which show themselves by his being compelled to 'mortgage his crop,' go in debt for the food and clothes on which to live from day to day, are not only a terrible drawback to the Negro himself but a severe drain on the resources of the white man. Say what we will, the fact remains, that in the presence of the poverty and ignorance of the millions of Negroes in the Black Belt, the material, moral and educational interests of both races are making but slow headway."

In answer to this invitation we were surprised to find that nearly four hundred men and women of all kinds and conditions came. In my opening address I impressed upon them the fact that we wanted to spend the first part of the day in having them state plainly and simply just what their conditions were. I told them that we wanted no exaggeration, and did not want any cut-and dried or prepared speeches, we simply wanted each person to speak in a plain, simple manner, very much as he would if he were about his own fireside, speaking to the members of his own family. I also insisted that we confine our discussion to such matters as we ourselves could remedy, rather than in spending the time in complaining or faultfinding about those things which we could not directly reach. At the first meeting of this Negro Conference we also adopted the plan of having these common people themselves speak, and refused to allow people who were far above them in education and surroundings take up the time in merely giving advice to these representatives of the masses.

Very early in the history of these Conferences I found that it meant a great deal more to the people to have one individual who had succeeded in getting out of debt, ceasing to mortgage his crop, and who had bought a home and was living well, occupy the time in telling the remainder of his fellows how he had succeeded, than in having some one who was entirely out of the atmosphere of the average farmer occupy the time in merely lecturing to them.

In the morning of the first day of the Conference we had as many representatives from various parts as we had time in which to tell of the industrial condition existing in their immediate community. We did not let them generalize or tell what they thought ought to be or was existing in somebody's else community, we held each person down to a statement of the facts regarding his own individual community. For example, we had them state what proportion of the people in their community owned land, what proportion lived in one-room cabins, how many were in debt, the number that mortgaged their crops, and what rate of interest they were paying on their indebtedness. Under this head we also discussed the number of acres of land that each individual was cultivating, and whether or not the crop was diversified or merely confined to the growing of cotton. We also got hold of facts from the representatives of these people concerning their educational progress; that is, we had them state whether or not a school-house existed, what kind of teacher

Gov. Johnston, Pres. McKinley, Principal Washington, in Reviewing Stand.

WAITING FOR THE PROCESSION TO PASS AT THE TIME OF PRESIDENT McKINLEY'S VISIT TO TUSKEGEE, DECEMBER 16, 1898.

RECEPTION GIVEN BOOKER T. WASHINGTON, AFTER HIS RETURN FROM EUROPE, BY GOVERNOR G. W. ATKINSON. AT THE EXECUTIVE MANSION CHARLESTON, WEST VIRGINIA.

they had and what proportion of the children were attending school. We did not stop with these matters; we took up the moral and religious condition of the communities; had them state to what extent, for example, people had been sent to jail from their communities; how many were habitual drinkers; what kind of minister they had; whether or not he was able to lead the people in morality as well as in spiritual affairs.

After we had got hold of facts, which enabled us to judge of the actual state of affairs existing, we spent the afternoon of the first day in hearing from the lips of these same people in what way, in their opinion, the present condition of things could be improved, and it was most interesting as well as surprising to see how clearly these people saw into their present condition, and how intelligently they discussed their weak points as well their strong points. It was generally agreed that the mortgage system, the habit of buying on credit and paying large rates of interest, was at the bottom of much of the evil existing among the people, and the fact that so large a proportion of them live on rented land also had much to do with keeping them down. The condition of the schools was discussed with equal frankness, and means were suggested for prolonging the school term and building school-houses. Almost without exception they agreed that the fact that so large a proportion of the people live in one-room cabins, where there was almost no opportunity for privacy or seperation of the sexes, was largely responsible for the bad moral condition of many communities.

When I asked how many in the audience owned their homes, only twenty-three hands went up.

Aside from the colored people who were present at the Conference who reside in the "Black Belt," there were many prominent white and colored men from various parts of the country, especially representatives of the various religious organizations engaged in educational work in the South, and officers and teachers from several of the larger institutions working in the South. There were correspondents present representing such papers as the New York Independent, Evening Post, New York Weekly Witness, New York Tribune, Christian Union, Boston Evening Transcript, Christian Register, The Congregationalist, Chicago Inter-Ocean, Chicago Advance, and many others.

At the conclusion of the first Conference the following set of declarations was adopted as showing the concensus of opinion of those composing the Conference:

"We, some of the representatives of the colored people, living in the Black Belt, the heart of the South, thinking it might prove of interest and value to our friends throughout the country, as well as beneficial to ourselves, have met together in Conference to present facts and express opinions as to our industrial, moral and educational condition, and to exchange views as to how our own efforts and the kindly helpfulness of our friends may best contribute to our elevation.

"First. Set at liberty with no inheritance but our bodies, without training in self-dependence, and thrown at once into commercial, civil and political relations with our former owners, we consider it a matter of great thankfulness that our condition is as good as it is, and that so large a degree of harmony exists between us and our white neighbors.

"Second. Industrially considered, most of our people are dependent upon agriculture. The majority of them live on rented lands, mortgage their crops for the food on which to live from year to year, and usually at the beginning of each year are more or less in debt for the supplies of the previous year.

"Third. Not only is our own material progress hindered by the mortgage system, but also that of our white friends. It is a system that tempts us to buy much that we would do without if cash was required, and it tends to lead those who advance the provisions and lend the money, to extravagant prices and ruinous rates of interest.

"Fourth. In a moral and religious sense, while

we admit there is much laxness in morals and superstition in religion, yet we feel that much progress has been made, that there is a growing public sentiment in favor of purity, and that the people are fast coming to make their religion less of superstition and emotion and more a matter of daily living.

"Fifth. As to our educational condition, it is to be noted that our country schools are in session on an average only three and a half months each year; the Gulf States are as yet unable to provide school-houses, and as a result the schools are held almost out of doors or at best in such rude quarters as the poverty of the people is able to provide; the teachers are poorly paid and often very poorly fitted for their work, as a result of which both parents and pupils take but little interest in the schools; often but few children attend, and these with great irregularity.

"Sixth. That in view of our general condition, we would suggest the following remedies: (1) That as far as possible we aim to raise at home our own meat and bread; (2) that as fast as possible we buy land, even though a very few acres at a time; (3) that a larger number of our young people be taught trades, and that they be urged to prepare themselves to enter as largely as possible all the various avocations of life; (4) that we especially try to broaden the field of labor for our women; (5) that we make every sacrifice and practice every form of economy that we may purchase land and free ourselves from our burdensome habit of living in debt; (6) that we urge our ministers and teachers to give more attention to the material condition and home life of the people; (7) that we urge that our people do not depend entirely upon the State to provide schoolhouses and lengthen the time of the schools, but that they take hold of the matter themselves where the State leaves off, and by supplementing the public funds from their own pockets and by building school-houses, bring about the desired results; (8) that we urge patrons to give earnest attention to the mental and moral fitness of those who teach their schools; (9) that we urge the doing away with all sectarian prejudice in the management of the schools.

"Seventh. As the judgment of this Conference we would further declare: That we put on record our deep sense of gratitude to the good people of all sections for their assistance, and that we are glad to recognize a growing interest on the part of the best white people of the South in the education of the Negro.

"Eighth. That we appreciate the spirit of friendliness and fairness shown us by the Southern white people in matters of business in all lines of material development.

"Ninth. That we believe our generous friends of the country can best aid in our elevation by continuing to give their help where it will result in producing strong Christian leaders who will live among the masses as object lessons, showing them how to direct their own efforts towards the general uplifting of the people.

"Tenth. That we believe we can become prosperous, intelligent and independent where we are, and discourage any efforts at wholesale emigration, recognizing that our home is to be in the South, and we urge that all strive in every way to cultivate the good feeling and friendship of those about us in all that relates to our mutual elevation."

At the present writing eight of these Conferences have been held. I shall not occupy space in describing in detail each one of these annual Conferences except to say that each Conference has grown in numbers, interest and value to the people. Very often as many as two thousand representatives assemble at these meetings, which are usually held in the latter part of February. Representatives now come from not only almost all parts of Alabama, but from practically all of the Southern States. Similar Conferences have also been organized in other states, notably Texas, South Carolina and North Carolina. Aside from these state Conferences, local Conferences which meet as a rule monthly and bring together the people in each community or county are now in existence in many parts of the South, and the people find these meetings a great means of helping themselves forward. One of our teachers at the present time gives the greater part of the year to the work of organizing and stimulating these local Conferences in various parts of the South. The people look forward eagerly each year to the assembling of the large or central Negro Conference at Tuskegee, and they are always anxious to give their reports. The spirit of hopefulness and encouragement which now characterizes these Conferences, as compared with the rather depressed and hopeless feeling existing when the first one met, is most interesting. At the sessions of the Conference held in recent years many communities have been able to report that the people are ceasing to mortgage their crops, are buying land, building houses with two or three rooms, that their school terms in many cases have been extended from three to six and eight months, and that the moral atmosphere of the community has been cleansed and improved. These Conferences have served to make the people aware of their own inherent strength; to let them feel and understand how much they can do toward improving their own condition when once they make up their minds to make the effort. The results from every point of view are most gratifying.

In order to show something of the spirit and interest that characterize these gatherings, I give verbatim extracts from a few addresses delivered at a recent Conference by some of these Black Belt Negroes. "This Conference is doing untold good," said a very intelligent farmer and preacher of about fifty years of age, who has attended all the Conferences. "Since I went back home from the first one and told the people about it, they have gone to work and bought over two thousand acres of land. Much of it has already been paid for. I thank God on my knees for these Conferences. They are giving us homes." Another man who could not come himself to a recent Conference sent a letter saying that seven of his neighbors had bought themselves homes. One woman reported that she had raised four hundred pounds of pork, and had also raised corn enough to enable her to live without mortgaging her crop. Over one hundred in all reported that they had paid for homes. Another man said, "We are not what we ought to be, we are sadly lacking, but we are one hundred per cent. better than we were twenty years ago, and we are going to be better than we are." Another remarked with a great deal of emphasis, "It makes a man more truthful when he owns land, and I know when he gives his word he cannot run away. To own property is to own character." Another farmer from Macon County said: "The nigger race ain't such a bugaboo as you think. The trouble with our people is we don't understand ourselves; we don't have self-reliance and self-government. Eight years ago I didn't have even a meat skin, now I have got eighty acres of land and five mules, all paid for. You must be a man. Say sink or swim, I'm coming on top; if you don't you won't amount to anything. Some of our race is so shiftless that if their own mother should rise from the grave after twenty years, and come into the house and say, 'Son, give me a cup of coffee, I've been walking all night,' he couldn't do it. You make a mortgage, and then you get everything you want, not everything you need. I had a start once before, and I got a couple of old horses and a buggy, and I rid around too much and I got down. Then I promised the Lord if he would forgive me and help me to start again I would do better. Now I work from Monday to Saturday. A heap of our people don't like that part of the Bible which says 'six days thou shalt work.' When a colored man dies the merchant makes more than on any other day, because you have all got to dress up, hire buggies, and ride around and go to the funeral. I don't want anybody's foot on my neck. I don't go and say, 'Mas'r Joe, please sir, I wants

portance for the Negro has been represented at one or more of these Worker's Conferences. Besides these, we often have present the secretaries of the various religious organizations doing work in the South.

The subjects discussed in these Worker's Conferences are of a wide range. At the last Conference the time was occupied in a discussion of how the various educational institutions in the South could serve to bring about more satisfactory relations between the two races in the South. The discussion was free, open and most helpful. In fact, it is well understood that in all of these gatherings at Tuskegee there is the utmost frankness and liberality allowed as to opinion and discussion. The Worker's Conferences are growing in numbers and interest, and have now become a permanent part of the educational machinery of the South.

a little flour or I wants a little coffee for my old lady,' but when I want anything I just go and get it. You must not sit down and trust God; if you do you'll starve. Get up and go to work, and trust God, and you'll get rich."

Then Father Mitchell, who is a colored minister, said: "Now, keep quiet; we's gettin' along slowly. I wish our neighborhood was like dat brother's as jest spoke. You give me a good lick for a young man, Mr. President; but, sir, if we had twenty men like you we'd get happy 'fore we enter heaven. We make a heap of corn and potatoes." "How about morals?" asked some one. "Well, now, I'll tell you about dat. I'd thank my Redeemer to send me some morals down to my neighborhood. I am putting up a big Baptist Church down on the Sam road, an' I hope I'll be able to do my people some good."

At the time of the organization of the Annual Negro Farmers' Conference, it was decided to make a special effort to secure the attendance of the representatives of the various educational, religious and philanthropic institutions in the South for the elevation of the Negro. This attempt was quite successful, so much so that in addition to the regular delegates at the Negro Conference, quite a large number of educators and others began assembling to witness the proceedings of that body. During the session of the Conference it was determined to organize what is known as the "Worker's Conference," composed of educators and other persons interested in the elevation of the Negro. It was decided to ask the members of the Worker's Conference to be present and witness the proceedings of the regular Negro Conference, in order that they might get information at first hand as to the condition and needs of the colored people. The following day the Worker's Conference was called, and based its proceedings in a large measure upon the lessons learned the previous day at the Farmers' Conference. The Worker's Conference has now been in existence many years, and is a very important and far-reaching institution; in fact, it is the only organization that brings together annually the various officers and teachers connected with the large religious and educational enterprises the South. We have had regularly present at Worker's Conference representatives from institutions as the Hampton Institute, A University, Clark University, Atlanta College, Gammon Theological Seminary, Seminary, Morris Brown College, Fisk sity, Central Tennessee College, Str versity, Talladega College, Tougaloo Lincoln University, Selma Univers others which I have not space to m I think every educational institu

CHAPTER XVIII.

A VACATION IN EUROPE.

In the spring of 1899 a rather notable meeting was held in Boston, in the afternoon, at the Hollis Street Theatre. This meeting was gotten up in the interest of the Tuskegee Institute, by friends of the institution, in Boston for the purpose of raising money for the school. It was presided over by Bishop Lawrence, Bishop of Massachusetts. I invited to speak with me at this meeting Dr. W. E. B. DuBois and Mr. Paul Laurence Dunbar. Dr. DuBois read an original story, and Mr. Dunbar recited from his own poems. The theatre was filled with representatives of the most cultured and wealthy men and women in Boston, and was said to be the most successful meeting of the kind that had been held for a good while. An admission was charged at the door, and a generous sum was raised for the school. This was the first time that Mr. Dunbar had appeared in Boston, and his readings produced a most favorable effect. The same was true of Dr. DuBois.

During this same year I received an invitation which surprised me somewhat. It was an invitation from the secretary of the Birmingham, Alabama, Lyceum, a white literary organization.

composed of the best and most cultured people in the city of Birmingham, Alabama, inviting me to address the Lyceum. I accepted this invitation to deliver an address before the organization on the 30th of March. There was some adverse criticism and some protests through the newspapers, and otherwise, on the part of a certain element of white people in Birmingham; in fact, some effort was made to prevent white ladies from attending, but I was surprised and gratified when I appeared before the audience to find the room filled with representatives of the best ladies and gentlemen of Birmingham, and I have never spoken before any organization where my words were more heartily and more kindly received than was true on this occasion. This was the first time that I had ever received an invitation to address a white literary organization in the South, although during the winter of the same year I had delivered an address before the National Farmers' Association, which met at Fort Worth, Texas.

Immediately after the public meeting held in Boston in the Hollis Street Theatre, some friends of mine in Boston noted that I seemed to be rather worn out, as a result of nearly eighteen years of continuous work, without any vacation during the entire time. Without our knowledge, they quietly started a movement to raise a certain sum of money to be used in sending Mrs. Washington and myself to Europe, where we could rest for two or three months. This plan was a very great surprise to us, and it seemed difficult for us to make up our minds to leave the school for so long a time; but these friends insisted that we owed it to the work and to ourselves to take the vacation. The result was that we sailed for Europe on the 10th of May and remained abroad until the 5th of August. We had a very pleasant and delightful trip across the ocean, and made many friends on the voyage. I was called upon to speak on the steamer going and had a large and interesting audience. After a voyage of ten days we landed at Antwerp, Belgium, and remained there a short time. We then took a trip through the country in company with some New York friends whose acquaintance we made on the voyage. In Holland we traveled on the canal boats, which gave us an opportunity of seeing the home life of the country people, and also the agricultural life of the country.

I was especially anxious to study the agricultural and dairy systems, with a view to utilizing the information in our work at Tuskegee. The thorough cultivation of the soil, for which this country is noted, made a deep impression upon me. There are few other countries, if any in the world, where the soil is so thoroughly cultivated as in Holland. The dairy interests there present an interesting and valuable field for study. While in Holland we visited The Hague, where the International Peace Congress was in session, and were shown many courtesies by the American members of the Peace Conference. After remaining for some time in Holland, we returned to Antwerp and spent some time there, and afterwards proceeded to Brussels, where we had a pleasant stay. From Brussels we went to Paris, where we remained nearly six weeks. In Paris we received much kind attention from General Horace Porter, the American Ambassador, and his wife, as well as from other American and French people. Soon after reaching Paris I received an invitation to deliver an address before the American University Club, an organization composed mainly of American college men residing in Paris. The American Ambassador, Gen. Horace Porter, presided at this meeting, and in addition to myself the speakers were Ex-president Benjamin Harrison and Archbishop Ireland. I was also invited to deliver an address the following Sunday in the American chapel, which I did. Mrs. Washington and I attended a reception given by the American Ambassador, where we met many prominent people.

I went to Europe mainly for the purpose of securing complete rest, and notwithstanding the many engagements which constantly pressed themselves upon me, I succeeded in getting a great deal of needed strength, especially was this true in Paris. From Paris we went to London, and arrived there just in the midst of the social season. We had many letters of introduction from friends in America to influential people in England, and our stay in England was occupied mainly in a continual round of social engagements.

Soon after reaching London, friends insisted that I should deliver an address to the public on the race problem in the South. The American Ambassador, Hon. Joseph H. Choate, was especially anxious that I consent to do this. A meeting was arranged to take place in Essex Hall. In connection with this meeting Rev. Brooke Herford, D. D., whom I had formerly known in Boston, gave Mrs. Washington and myself a reception. The meeting was largely attended, and Mr. Choate, the American Ambassador, presided. The substance of what Mr. Choate and myself said at this meeting was widely circulated in England, and telegraphed to the American press. This meeting was attended by such well-known people as Hon. James Bryce, who also spoke, and many high officials and members of titled families in England. After this meeting I received many invitations to speak at other gatherings, but as far as possible excused myself from doing so, in order that I might secure the rest for which I went to Europe. I did, however, consent to speak at a meeting at the Crystal Palace, which was presided over by the Duke of Westminster, said to be the richest man in the world. This meeting was also largely attended. We attended, among many other social functions, receptions given by the Duke and Duchess of Sutherland, by Mr. and Mrs. T. Fischer Unwin, Mrs. Unwin being the daughter of the late Richard Cobden. Lady Henry Somerset was very kind in her attention to us.

While in London the following editorial appeared in the Daily Chronicle:

"The presence in London of Mr. Booker T. Washington, at whose address the other evening the American Ambassador presided, calls for a generous recognition of the remarkable work being done in the United States for the Negro by this gifted member of the Negro race. What Frederick Douglass was to an older generation that Mr. Washington is to the present. At the recent visit of President McKinley to the South, Mr. Washington occupied a place of honor alongside the President, and was almost as heartily acclaimed. When one recalls the tremendous 'color' feeling in America, such a fact is exceedingly striking. The great work which Mr. Washington has done has been an educational work. Orator as he is, it is not so much his power of speech as the building up of the remarkable industrial institute at Tuskegee, in Alabama, which has given this Negro leader his deserved fame. The Civil War left the Negro legally and nominally free, and the legislation after the war was over made him legally and nominally a citizen. But we know that the Negro has been in fact in a very different position from that which he occupied on paper. He has been insulted by degrading legislation, he has been in many states virtually deprived of his vote, and in not a few cases an election dispute has afforded the dominant white man an excuse for slaughter of the blacks. The Negro has retaliated in his barbarous way. Though religious in the most emotional form, he is often non-moral, and there can be no doubt that he has committed many grave offenses against social order.

"Mr. Washington, though an enthusiastic advocate of the claims of his race, is by no means blind to the faults which render so many Negroes almost unfit for American citizenship. He saw long ago, what so many American politicians who gave the suffrage to the colored population did not see—that the most important service which could be rendered to the blacks was to make useful artisans and workmen of them. As a result of his meditation on the condition of the colored people, Mr. Washington founded the Tuskegee Institute in the Black Belt of Alabama, stumped the Union for funds, interested in his great undertaking all the best minds of the Northern States, and has had the satisfaction of seeing this institution grow to its present status of the largest and most important training centre of the black race in the world. Here, where both sexes are welcomed on terms of equality, the Negro is taken in hand, given the rudiments of education, taught a useful trade, taught also, if he proves capable, the higher branches of modern culture, subjected to high intellectual and ethical influences, and made a man of in the true sense of the word. No better work is being done in America at the present hour than in this remarkable institution in Alabama.

"That the American conscience is being roused to its duty to the Negroes is evident from the recent important conference at which two leading speakers were an ex-Governor of Georgia and a Bishop of the Episcopal Church. The horrible burnings and improvised hangings by white mobs, who took the law into their hands, have awakened the people of the North, and it is very properly asked whether those who permit such brutalities in their own borders are fit to assume control of black and yellow races in the Pacific. Ex-Governor Northen, of Georgia, took the North to task for having been more responsible for the spread of slavery than the South, and he defended, but without much success, the Southern whites against the attacks made on them. The Bishop, it is gratifying to find, took the strong ground of the Declaration of Independence, and asserted the equal right of black and white to the common rights which the law and the Constitution allow. But the important principle which emerges clearly from the long discussion that took place at this conference is that a *laissez faire* policy is impossible in the case of the Negro. You cannot 'emancipate' him alone. He must be educated, his character must be formed, he must be made a useful and self-reliant being. This is precisely what is being done at the Tuskegee Institute, and therefore, its founder is solving, as far as one man can, one of the chief American problems of the time. And what a problem! The practical humanising and elevation from barbarism of dusky millions on whose own future the future of the United States largely depends."

Perhaps the most interesting and restful part of our visit to England was the time that we spent as the guests of various English people in their country homes. In order for one to appreciate what English life really is, he should have an opportunity to get into the daily life of an English gentleman in his country residence.

We visited Bristol, where we were given a reception by the Women's Liberty Club, and also Manchester, Liverpool and Birmingham. In Birmingham we spent several days as the guests of Mr. Joseph Sturge, who kindly gave us a reception, at which we met many of the prominent citizens of Birmingham. Of course we visited a great many places of historical interest and had an opportunity of looking into the methods of education in England. We were specially interested in the work of the large polytechnic institutes and the agricultural colleges, from which we got a great deal of valuable information.

While in Europe I wrote a series of letters for the American Negro press. These letters were widely published and commented upon.

During our stay in London I took special pains to inquire into the opportunities for our people to better their condition by emigrating to Africa, and convinced myself that there was little, if any, hope of this, largely because Africa is almost completely divided up among various European nations, leaving little hope for self-government in any part of Africa, except in the small republic of Liberia, which is notably unhealthy and undesirable from almost every point of view. I found out that in many cases the Negroes are treated by Europeans in Africa almost as badly as they have ever been treated in the South. The letter which I wrote from London on this subject was very widely copied and commented upon by the American press.

While I was in Europe, cases of lynching of our people were especially frequent in the South, and in order to assist in checking this injustice perpetrated upon the race, I addressed the following letter to the Southern people, which was widely published throughout the country and seemed to do much good. It was heartily commented upon editorially in the Southern press:

"Several times, during the last few months, while our country has been shocked because of the lynching of Negro citizens, I have been asked by many to say something upon the subject through the press, and have been tempted to do so. At the time of these lynchings I kept silent, because I did not believe that the public mind was in a condition to listen to a discussion of the subject in the calm judicial manner that it would be later, when there should be no undue feeling or excitement. In the discussion of this or any other matter, little good is accomplished unless we are perfectly frank. There is no white man of the South who has more sincere love for it than I have, and nothing could tempt me to write or speak that which I did not think was for the permanent good of all the people of the South. Whenever adverse criticism is made upon the South I feel it as keenly as any member of the white race can feel it. It is, therefore, my interest in everything which pertains to the South that prompts me to write as I do now. While it is true that there are cases of lynchings and outrage in the Northern and Western States, candor compels us to admit that by far the most of the cases of lynchings take place in our Southern States, and that most of the persons lynched are Negroes.

"With all the earnestness of my heart, I want to appeal, not to the President of the United States, Mr. McKinley, not to the people of New York nor of the New England States, but to the citizens of our Southern States, to assist in creating a public sentiment such as will make human life just as safe and sacred here as it is anywhere else in the world.

"For a number of years the South has appealed to the North and to Federal authorities, through the public press, from the public platform, and most eloquently through the late Henry W. Grady, to leave the whole matter of the rights and protection of the Negro to the South, declaring that it would see to it that the Negro would be made secure in his citizenship. During the last half dozen years the whole country, from the President down, has been inclined more than ever to pursue this policy, leaving the whole matter of the destiny of the Negro to the Negro himself and to the Southern white people among whom the great bulk of the Negroes live.

"By the present policy of non-interference, on the part of the North and the Federal Government, the South is given a sacred trust. How will she execute this trust? The world is waiting and watching to see. The question must be answered largely by the protection the South gives to the life of the Negro, and the provisions that are made for the development of the Negro in the organic laws of the state. I fear that but few people in the South realize to what extent the habit of lynching, or the taking of life without due process of law, has taken hold of us, and to what extent it is hurting us, not only in the eyes of the world, but in our own moral and material growth.

"Lynching was instituted some years ago, with the idea of punishing and checking outrage upon women. Let us examine the cold facts and see where it has already led us, and where it is likely further to carry us, if we do not rid ourselves of the habit. Many good people in the South, and also out of the South, have gotten the idea that lynching is resorted to for one crime only. I have the facts from an authoriative source. During last year 127 persons were lynched in the United States. Of this number, 118 were executed in the South and 9 in the North and West. Of the total number lynched, 102 were Negroes, 23 were whites and 2, Indians Now, let everyone interested in the South, his country and the cause of humanity, note this fact—that only 24 of the entire number were charged in any way with the crime of rape; that is, 24 out of 127 cases of lynching. Sixty one of the remaining cases were for murder, 13 being for suspected murder, 6 for theft, etc. During one week last spring, when I kept a careful record, 13 Negroes were lynched in three of our Southern States, and not one was even charged with rape. All of these 13 were accused of murder or house-burning, but in none of the cases were the men allowed to go before a court, so that their innocence or guilt might be proven.

"When we get to the point where four-fifths of the people lynched in our country in one year are lynched for some crime other than rape, we can no longer plead and explain that we lynch for one crime alone.

"Let us take another year, that of 1892, for example. During this year (1892) 241 persons were lynched in the whole United States. Thirty-six of this number were lynched in Northern and Western States, and 205 in our Southern States. Of the 241 lynched in the whole country, 160 were Negroes and five of these were women. The facts show that out of the 241 lynched in the entire country in 1892, but 57 were even charged with rape, even attempted rape, leaving in that year alone, 184 persons who were lynched for other causes than that of rape.

"If it were necessary, I could produce figures for other years. Within a period of six years about 900 persons have been lynched in our Southern States. This is but a few hundred short of the total number of soldiers who lost their lives in Cuba during the Spanish-American war. If we would realize still more fully how far this unfortunate habit is leading us on, note the classes of crime, during a few months, which the local papers and Associated Press say that lynching has been inflicted for—they include 'murder,' 'rioting,' 'incendiarism,' 'robbery,' 'larceny,' 'self-defense,' 'insulting women,' 'alleged stock poisoning,' 'malpractice,' 'alleged barn-burning,' 'suspected robbery,' 'race prejudice,' 'attempted murder,' 'horse stealing,' and 'mistaken identity,' etc.

"The practice has grown until we are now at the point where not only blacks are lynched in the South, but white men as well. Not only this, but within the last six years at least a half dozen colored women have been lynched. And there are a few cases where Negroes have lynched members of their own race. What is to be the end of this? Besides this, every lynching drives hundreds of Negroes from the farming districts of the South, where their services are of great value to the country, into the already over-crowded cities.

"I know that some will argue that the crime of lynching Negroes is not confined to the South. This is true, and no one can excuse such a crime as the shooting of innocent black men in Illinois, who were guilty of no crime except that of seeking labor, but my words just now are to the South, where my home is, and a part of which I am. Let other sections act as they will; I want to see our beautiful Southland free from this terrible evil of lynching. Lynching does not stop crime. In the immediate section of the South where a colored man recently committed the most terrible crime ever charged against a member of his race, but a few weeks previous to this, five colored men had been lynched for supposed incendiarism. If lynching was a cure for crime, surely the lynching of five would have prevented another Negro from committing a most heinous crime a few weeks later.

"We might as well face the facts bravely and wisely. Since the beginning of the world crime has been committed in all civilized and uncivilized countries, and a certain amount of crime will always be committed, both in the North and in the South, but I believe that the crime of rape can be stopped. In proportion to the numbers and intelligence of the population of the South, there exists little more crime than in several other sections of the country, but because of the lynching habit we are constantly advertising ourselves to the world as a lawless people. We cannot disregard the teachings of the civilized world for eighteen hundred years, that the only way to punish crime is by law. When we leave this dictum chaos begins.

"I am not pleading for the Negro alone. Lynching injures, hardens and blunts the moral sensibilities of the young and tender manhood of the South. Never shall I forget the remark by a little nine-year-old white boy, with blue eyes and flaxen hair. The little fellow said to his mother after he had returned from a lynching: 'I have seen a man hanged; now I wish I could see one burned.' Rather than hear such a remark from one of my little boys, I would prefer seeing him laid in his grave. This is not all; every community guilty of lynching, says in so many words to the governor, to the legislature, to the sheriff, to the jury, and to the judge, I have no faith in you and no respect for you. We have no respect for the law which we helped to make.

"In the South, at the present time, there is less excuse for not permitting the law to take its course, where a Negro is to be tried, than anywhere else in the world, for almost without exception the governors, the sheriffs, the judges, the juries and the lawyers are all white men, and they can be trusted, as a rule, to do their duty; otherwise it is needless to tax the people to support these officers. If our present laws are not sufficient to properly punish crime, let the laws be changed, but that the punishment may be by lawfully constituted authority is the plea I make. The history of the world proves that where law is most strictly enforced is the least crime; where people take the administration of the law into their own hands is the most crime.

"But there is another side. The white man in the South has not only a serious duty and responsibility, but the Negro has a duty and responsibility in this matter. In speaking of my own people I want to be equally frank, but I speak with the greatest kindness. There is too much crime among us. The figures for a given period show that in the United States 30 per cent. of the crime committed is by Negroes, while we constitute only about 12 per cent. of the entire population. This proportion holds good, not only in the South, but also in the Northern States and cities.

"No race that is so largely ignorant and so lately out of slavery could, perhaps, show a better record, but we must face these plain facts. He is most kind to the Negro who tells him of his faults as well as of his virtues. A large amount of the crime among us grows out of the idleness of our young men and women. It is for this reason that I have tried to insist upon some industry being taught in connection with their course of literary training. The time has come when every parent, every teacher and minister of the gospel, should teach with unusual emphasis morality and obedience to the law. At the fireside, in the school room, in the Sunday-school, from the pulpit and the Negro press, there should be such a sentiment created regarding the committing of crime against women, that no such crime shall be charged against any member of the race. Let it be understood for all time that no one guilty of rape can find sympathy or shelter with us, and that none will be more active in bringing to justice, through the proper authorities, those guilty of crime. Let the criminal and vicious element of the race have at all times our most severe condemnation. Let a strict line be drawn between the virtuous and the criminal. I condemn with all the indignation of my soul the beast in human form guilty of assaulting a woman. Let us all be alike in this particular.

"We should not as a race become discouraged. We are making progress. No race has ever gotten upon its feet without discouragements and struggles.

"I should be a great hypocrite and a coward if I did not add that which my daily experience teaches me is true, namely, that the Negro has among many of the Southern whites as good friends as he has anywhere in the world. These friends have not forsaken us. They will not do so; neither will our friends in the North. If we make ourselves intelligent, industrious, economical and virtuous, of value to the community in which we live, we can and will work out our own salvation right here in the South. In every community, by means of organized effort, we should seek in a manly and honorable way the confidence, the co-operation, the sympathy of the best white people in the South and in our respective communities. With the best white people and the best black people standing together, in favor of law and order and justice, I believe that the safety and happiness of both races will be made secure."

In closing this chapter, I repeat what I have said on another occasion. Those who fought for the freedom of the slaves performed their duty heroically and well, but a duty still remains

ON BOAT, BATON ROUGE, LA.

Reading from left to right: Major R. R. Moton, Commandant of Cadets, Hampton Institute. Dr. M. W. Dogan, President Wiley University, Marshall, Texas. Dr. Booker T. Washington. Mr. Emmett J. Scott, Secretary of Tuskegee Institute. Dr. Robert E. Jones, Editor Southwestern Christian Advocate, New Orleans, La.

THE JOHN A. ANDREWS MEMORIAL HOSPITAL OPEN FOR THE ACCOMMODATION OF COLORED PATIENTS.

for those who are left. The mere fiat of law cannot make an ignorant voter an intelligent voter; cannot make a dependent man an independent man; cannot make one citizen respect another. These results will come to the Negro, as to all races, by beginning at the bottom and gradually working up to the highest possibilities of his nature.

In the economy of God there is but one standard by which an individual can succeed; there is but one for the race.

In working out his own destiny, while the main burden of activity must be with the Negro, he will need in the years to come the help, the encouragement, the guidance, that the strong can give to the weak.

CHAPTER XIX.

THE WEST VIRGINIA AND OTHER RECEPTIONS AFTER EUROPEAN TRIP.

Early in August we sailed for America from Southampton, and had a very pleasant voyage on the magnificent ocean steamer "St. Louis" On the voyage I was called upon to speak again to the passengers, and made many friends for our cause.

While in Europe I received the following invitation:

"CHARLESTON, W. VA., May 16, 1899.

"PROF. B. T. WASHINGTON,

"Tuskegee Institute, Tuskegee, Alabama.

"*Dear Sir:*—Many of the best citizens of West Virginia have united in liberal expressions of admiration and praise of your worth and work, and desire that on your return from Europe, you should favor them with your presence and with the inspiration of your words. We most sincerely endorse this move, and on behalf of the citizens of Charleston extend to you our most cordial invitation to have you come to us, that we may honor you who have done so much by your life and work to honor us.

"We are, very truly yours,
"The Common Council of the City of Charleston,
"By W. HERMAN SMITH, Mayor."

This invitation from the City Council of Charleston was accompanied by the following:

"PROF. B. T. WASHINGTON,

"Principal, Tuskegee Institute.

"*Dear Sir:*—We, the citizens of Charleston and West Virginia, desire to express our pride in you and the splendid career you have thus far accomplished, and ask that we be permitted to show our pride and interest in a substantial way.

"Your recent visit to your old home in our midst awoke within us the keenest regret that we were not permitted to hear you and render some substantial aid to your work, before you left for Europe.

"In view of the foregoing, we earnestly invite you to share the hospitality of our city upon your return from Europe and give us the opportunity to hear you and put ourselves in touch with your work in a way that will be most gratifying to yourself, and that we may receive the inspiration of your words and presence.

"An early reply to this invitation, with an

indication of the time you may reach our city will greatly oblige,

"Yours very respectfully,

"The Charleston Daily Gazette, The Daily Mail-Tribune, G. W. Atkinson, Governor; E. L. Boggs, Secretary to Governor; Wm. M. O. Dawson, Secretary of State; L. M. LaFollette, Auditor; J. R. Trotter, Superintendent of Schools, E. W. Wilson, ex-Governor; W. A. Mac-Corkle, ex-Governor; John Q. Dickinson, President Kanawha Valley Bank; L. Prichard, President Charleston National Bank; Geo. S. Couch, President Kanawha National Bank; Ed. Reid, Cashier Kanawha National Bank; Geo. S. Laidley, Superintendent City Schools; L. E. McWhorter, President Board of Education; Chas. K. Payne, wholesale merchant; C. C. Lewis, Jr., wholesale merchant; R. G. Hubbard, wholesale merchant; Dan. D. Brawley, City Sergeant; Grant P. Hall, Clerk of Circuit Court; O. A. Petty, Postmaster; R. Douglas Roller, Rector St. John's Episcopal Church; M. M. Williamson, Cashier Citizen's National Bank; J. N. Carnes, Assistant Cashier Citizen's National Bank; J. A. Schwabe & Co., merchants; J. A. DeGruyter, ex-Mayor; A. H. Boyd, M. D.; E. W. Staunton, Clerk Kanawha County Court; M. F. Compton, Pastor State St. M. E. Church; T. C. Johnson, Pastor Charleston Baptist Church; Coyle &

Richardson, merchants; J. H. Gaines, United States District Attorney; Sterrett Brothers, merchants; N. S. Burlew, merchant; Joel H. Ruffner, merchant; M. P. Ruffner, merchant; E. G. Pierson, senator; B. R. Winkler, member City Council; Flournoy, Price & Smith, lawyers; Abney, Barnes & Co., wholesale merchants; Sam D. Littlepage, member of City Council; D. W. Shaw, Pastor Simpson M. E. Church; J. McHenry Jones, President West Virginia Colored Institute; Jas. M. Canty, J. C. Gilmer, Byrd Prillerman, S. W. Starks, J. M. Hazelwood, Phil. Waters, C. W. Hall, Judge Criminal Court; C. W. Boyd, Principal Garnet School; B. S. Morgan, member of City Council."

This invitation to accept a reception from the citizens of Charleston, W. Va., where I had spent my boyhood days, was a very satisfactory surprise. When I left Charleston, and when I left Malden, which is very near Charleston, I was quite a boy, and I had not been able to spend any great length of time there since I had first left to enter the Hampton Institute.

I accepted the invitation for the Charleston reception, and when I reached Charleston was met by a committee of citizens headed by ex-Gov. W. A. MacCorkle. The meeting in connection with this reception was held in the opera house, and was presided over by Gov. George W.

Atkinson. It was very largely attended by white and colored citizens from that vicinity, a large number of whom had known me in my boyhood days. I must refrain from giving any detailed account of all the kind and complimentary things they were kind enough to say about me at this meeting. I spent several days in Charleston, visiting the scenes of my early boyhood, and my sister in Malden, and many of the older citizens who remembered me.

After this reception in Charleston I was invited to go to Atlanta, Ga., by the white and colored citizens, to be given a reception there. The meeting in Atlanta was presided over by the Governor of the State, and was largely attended.

Receptions by the citizens of Montgomery and New Orleans soon followed. Invitations to attend receptions in other states came to me, but I was not able to accept them all.

In the fall of 1899 a meeting was held at Huntsville, Ala., the spirit of which has since been taken up by other Southern cities, which promises to prove of lasting benefit in settling the race problem in the South. In October a meeting was called at Huntsville, which had for its object the discussion of all matters relating to the upbuilding of the South. It was well attended by representatives from nearly every Southern State, and was a strong body of men. Among the other subjects discussed was the Negro problem in its relation to the industrial progress of the South.

In connection with others, I was invited to deliver an address. The audience was composed mainly of Southern white men, but in it was a large number of Southern white women, together with quite an attendance of colored men and women. The address which I delivered on that occasion attracted a great deal of attention throughout the country, and for that reason I have taken the liberty of giving it in full:

"In all discussion and legislation bearing upon the presence of the Negro in America, it should be borne in mind that we are dealing with a people who were forced to come here without their consent and in the face of a most earnest protest. This gives the Negro a claim upon your sympathy and generosity that no other race can possess. Besides, though forced from his native land into residence in a country that was not of his choosing, he has earned his right to the title of American citizen by obedience to the law, by patriotism and fidelity, and by the millions which his brawny arms and willing hands have added to the wealth of this country.

"In saying what I have to-day, although a Negro and an ex-slave myself, there is no white man whose heart is more wrapped up in every interest of the South and who loves it more dearly than is true of myself. She can have no sorrow that I do not share; she can have no prosperity that I do not rejoice in. She can commit no error that I do not deplore. She can take no step forward that I do not approve.

"Different in race, in color, in history, we can teach the world that, although thus differing, it is possible for us to dwell side by side in love, in peace, and in material prosperity. We can be one, as I believe we will be in a larger degree in the future, in sympathy, purpose, forbearance and mutual helpfulness. Let him who would embitter, who would bring strife between your race and mine, be accursed in his basket and in his store, accursed in the fruit of his body and the fruit of his land. No man can plan the degradation of another race without being himself degraded. The highest test of the civilization of any race is its willingness to extend a helping hand to the less fortunate.

"The South extends a protecting arm and a welcome voice to the foreigner, of all nationalities, languages and conditions, but in this I pray that you will not forget the black man at your door, whose habits you know, whose fidelity you have tested. You may make of others larger gatherers of wealth, but you cannot make of them more law-abiding, useful and God-fearing people than the Negro who has been by your side for three centuries, and whose toil in forest, field and mine has helped to make the South the land of promise and glorious possibility.

"Before we can make much progress we must decide whether or not the Negro is to be a permanent part of the South. With the light that is before us, I have no hesitation in declaring that the great bulk of the Negro population will reside among you. Any hesitation or doubting as to the permanent residence of the race will work infinite harm to the industrial and economic interests of both races. Here, in His wisdom, Providence has placed the Negro. Here he will remain. Here he came without a language; here he found the Anglo-Saxon tongue. Here he came in paganism; here he found the religion of Christ. Here he came in barbarism; here he found civilization. Here he came with untrained hands; here he found industry. If these centuries of contact with the American has done this, can you not trust to the wise Creator, aided by the efforts of the Negro himself, and your guidance, to do the remainder? At this point, are you willing to cease your efforts and turn the work over to others for completion? Your duty to the Negro will not be fulfilled until you have made of him the highest type of American citizen, in intelligence, usefulness and morality.

"The South has within itself the forces that are to solve this tremendous problem. You have the climate, the soil and the material wealth. You have the labor to be performed that will occupy many times our present Negro population. While the calls come daily from South Africa, from the Hawaiian Islands, from the North and the West for the strong and willing arm of the Negro in the field of industry, you, at your very door, have that which others are energetically seeking. Not only are you in possession of that which others are seeking, but more important than all, custom and contact have so knit the two races together that the black man finds in these Southern States an open sesame in labor, industry and business that is not surpassed anywhere. It is here alone, by reason of the presence of the Negro, that capital is free from tyranny and despotism that prevents you from employing whom you please and for that wage that is mutually agreeable and profitable. It is here that that form of slavery which prevents a man from selling his labor to whom he pleases on account of his color is almost unknown. We have had slavery, now dead, that forced an individual to labor without a recompense, but none that compelled a man to remain in idleness while his family starved.

"The Negro in all parts of the country is beginning to appreciate the advantage which the South affords for earning a living, for commercial development, and in proportion as this is true, it will constitute the basis for the settlement of other difficulties. The colored man is beginning to learn that the bed rock upon which every individual rests his chances for success in life is securing in every manly way—never at the sacrifice of principle—the friendship, the confidence, the respect of his next-door neighbor in the little community in which he lives. Almost the whole problem of the Negro in the South rests itself upon the question as to whether he makes himself of such indispensable service to his neighbor, to the community, that no one can fill his place better in the body politic. There is no other safe course for the Negro to pursue. If the black man in the South has a friend in his white neighbor, and a still larger number of friends in his own community, he has a protection and a guarantee of his rights that will be more potent and more lasting than any Federal Congress or any outside power can confer. While the Negro is grateful for the opportunities which he enjoys in the business of the South, you should remember that you are in debt to the black man for furnishing you with labor that is almost a stranger to strikes, lock-outs and labor wars; labor that is law-abiding, peaceful, teachable; labor that is one with you in language, sympathy, religion and patriotism; labor that has never been tempted to follow the red flag of anarchy, but always the safe flag of his country and the spotless banner of the cross.

"But if the South is to go forward and not stand still, if she is to reach the highest reward from her wonderful resources and keep abreast of the progress of the world, she must reach that point, without needless delay, where she will not be continually advertising to the world that she has a race question to settle. We must reach that point where, at every election, from the choice of a magistrate to that of a governor, the decision will not hinge upon a discussion or a revival of the race question. We must arrive at that period where the great fundamental question of good roads, education of farmers, agricultural and mineral development, manufacturing and industrial and public school education will be, in a large degree, the absorbing topics in our political campaign. But that we may get this question from among us, the white man has a duty to perform, the black man has a duty. No question is ever permanently settled until it is settled in the principles of the highest justice. Capital and lawlessness will not dwell together. The white man who learns to disregard law when a Negro is concerned will soon disregard it when a white man is concerned.

"In the evolution of the South it seems to me that we have reached that period where private philanthropy and the Christian church of the white South should, in a large degree, share directly in the elevation of the Negro. In saying this I am not unmindful of or ungrateful for what has already been done by individuals and through public schools. When we consider the past, the wonder is that so much has been done by our brothers in white. All great reforms and improvements rest, in a large measure, upon the church for success. You acknowledge that Christianity and education make a man more valuable as a citizen, make him more industrious, make him earn more, make him more upright. In this respect let me see how the three largest white denominations in the South regard the Negro.

"To elevate the ignorant and degraded in Africa, China, Japan, India, these three denominations in the South give annually about $544,000, but to elevate the ignorant, the degraded at your doors, to protect your families, to lessen your taxes, to increase their earning power; in a word, to Christianize and elevate the people at your very side, upon whom, in a large measure, your safety and property depend, these same denominations give $21,000—$21,000 for the benighted at your doors, $544,000 for the benighted abroad. That thirty-five years after slavery and a fratricidal war the master should give even $21,000 through the medium of the church for the elevation of his former slave means much. Nor would I have one dollar less go to the foreign fields, but I would plead with all the earnestness of my soul that the Christian South give increased attention to the 8,000,000 of Negroes by whom it is surrounded. All this has a most vital and direct relation to the work of this Industrial convention. Every dollar that goes into the education of the Negro is an interest-bearing dollar.

"For years all acknowlege that the South has suffered from the low price of cotton because of over-production. The economic history of the world teaches that an ignorant farming class means a single crop, and that a single crop means, too often, low prices from over-production or famine from under-production. The Negro constitutes the principal farming class of the South. So long as the Negro is ignorant in head, unskilled in hand, unacquainted with labor-saving machinery, so long will he confine himself to a single crop, and over-production of cotton will result. So long as this is true, you will be bound in economic fetters; you will be hugging the bear, while crying for some one to help you let go. Every man, black and white, in the South, with his crop mortgaged, in debt at the end of the year, buying his meat from Iowa, his corn from Illinois, his shoes from New York, his clothing from Pennsylvania, his wagon from Indiana, his plow from Massachusetts, his mule from Missouri, and his coffin from Ohio, every-one who is thus situated, is a citizen who is not producing the highest results for his state. It is argued that the South is too poor to educate such an individual so as to make him an intelligent producer. I reply that the South is too poor not to educate such an individual.

"Ignorance is many fold more costly to taxpayers than intelligence. Every black youth that is given this training of hand and strength of mind, so that he is able to grasp the full meaning and responsibility of life, so that he can go into some forest and turn the raw material into wagons and buggies, becomes a citizen who is able to add to the wealth of the state and to bear his share of the expenses of educational government. Do you suggest that this cannot be done? I answer that it is being done every day at Tuskegee, and should be duplicated in a hundred places in every Southern state. This I take to be the white man's burden just now—no, no, not his burden, but his privilege, his opportunity, to give the black man sight, to give him strength, skill of hand, light of mind and honesty of heart. Do this, my white friends, and I will paint you a picture that shall represent the future, partly as the outcome of this Industrial Convention, and will represent the land where your race and mine dwell:

"Fourteen slaves brought into the South a few centuries ago, in ignorance, superstition and weakness, are now a free people, multiplied into 8,000,000. They are surrounded, protected, encouraged, educated in hand, heart and head, given the full protection of the law, the highest justice meted out to them through courts and legislative enactment, they are stimulated and not oppressed, made citizens, and not aliens, made to understand by word and act that in proportion as they show themselves worthy to bear responsibilities, the greater opportunities will be given them. I see them loving you, trusting you, adding to the wealth, the intelligence, the renown of each Southern commonwealth. In turn, I see you confiding in them, ennobling them, beckoning them on to the highest success, and we have all been made to appreciate in full that,

'The slave's chain and the master's alike are broken,
   The one curse of the race held both in tether;
They are rising, all are rising,
   The black and white together.'"

The most encouraging thing that happened in connection with this convention was an address delivered by ex-Governor MacCorkle, of West Virginia, in which he took the position that the time had come when the Southern States must face

ADMIRAL EVANS PRESENTING BOOKER T. WASHINGTON TO PRINCE HENRY AT THE WALDORF-ASTORIA.

THOMPKIN'S DINING HALL. ERECTED AT A COST OF $160,000. COMPLETED IN 1910.

the race problem bravely and honestly; that the South could not any longer afford to get rid of the Negro's ballot by questionable methods, and that the Southern States ought to pass a law which would require an educational or property test, or both, for voting, and that this law ought to be made to apply alike to both races honestly and fairly, and that there should be no evasion permitted or attempted.

Governor MacCorkle is a Southern man, a democrat. The words which he spoke on this occasion received the most hearty cheering, and the convention on the next day passed a resolution without a dissenting vote recommending Governor MacCorkle's suggestion in the settlement of the franchise question in the Southern States. The influence of this convention was most beneficial on the minds of the Southern white people, and gave encouragement to the Negro and to his friends throughout the country.

As I write this chapter a conference is being arranged for by the leading white citizens of Montgomery, Ala., which it is intended shall be there during May of each year. The object of this conference is to afford an opportunity for free and generous discussion of the race problem from every point of view. This movement, organized as it has been at the seat of the Confederate government, is most remarkable. It seems fitting that Montgomery should be the place where from year to year the best thought of the nation can assemble and assist in working out our national problem.

In closing this chapter I simply wish to add that I see no reason why the race should not feel encouraged. Every individual or race that has succeeded has done so only by paying the price which success demands. We cannot expect to get something for nothing. We shall continue to prosper in proportion as each individual proves his usefulness in the community, as each individual makes himself such a pillar in property and character that his community will feel that he cannot be spared.

CHAPTER XX.

NATIONAL NEGRO BUSINESS LEAGUE ORIGIN AND WORK.

After advising carefully with some of the most successful colored men throughout the country, it was deemed by us that there ought to be in the United States some organization that would bring together annually the most substantial and successful colored men and women who are engaged in business and industrial enterprises, for the purpose of consultation and receiving inspiration and encouragement from each other, as well as for the purpose of arranging for the organization of local business leagues that would co-operate with the national organization. Accordingly, the first meeting was called to meet in Boston, in August, 1900. The meeting was in session three days. The following is a copy of the call sent out for the meeting:

"After careful consideration and consultation with prominent colored people throughout the country, it has been decided to organize what will be known as the National Negro Business League.

"The need of an organization that will bring the colored people who are engaged in business together for consultation, and to secure information and inspiration from each other, has long been felt. Out of this national organization it is expected will grow local business leagues that will tend to improve the Negro as a business factor.

"Boston has been selected as the place of meeting, because of its historic importance, its cool summer climate and general favorable condition. It is felt that the rest, recreation and new ideas which business men and women will secure from a trip to Boston will more than repay them for the time and money spent.

"The date of the meeting will be Thursday and Friday, August 23rd and 24th, because it is felt that this is the season when business can be left with least loss. Then, too, nearly all the steamship lines and railroads have reduced their rates to Boston to one fare for the round trip for the entire summer.

"Every individual engaged in business will be entitled to membership, but as far as possible the colored people in all the cities and towns of the country should take steps at once to organize local business leagues, where no such organizations already exist, and should see that these organizations send one or more delegates to represent them.

"It is very important that every line of business that any Negro man or woman is engaged in be represented. This meeting will present a great opportunity for us to show the world what progress we have made in business lines since our freedom.

"This organization is not in opposition to any other now in existence, but is expected to do a distinct work that no other organization now in existence can do as well.

"Another circular, giving further information as to programme and other details of the meeting, will be issued in a few weeks. All persons, whether men or women, interested in the movement, are invited to correspond with

"Yours very truly,
"BOOKER T. WASHINGTON,
"Tuskegee, Alabama, June 15, 1900."

The number and character of the men and women who responded to this call was a surprise and a source of gratification to everyone. Representatives came from two-thirds of the States in the Union, the greater proportion coming from the South. Many of them had been in slavery during a large portion of their lives and had started in a most humble way, and in most cases in poverty, and had struggled up through the greatest disadvantages to the point where they could be classed in the world of commerce. They represented many of the commercial enterprises in which white men are engaged. There were among them bankers, real estate dealers, grocers, dry goods merchants, caterers, manufacturers, contractors, druggists, undertakers, bakers, restaurant keepers, barbers, printers, plumbers, milliners, dressmakers, jewelers, publishers and farmers.

Perhaps the most gratifying feature in connection with the first session of the League was the entire absence of anything even bordering on bickering, greed for office, and "point of order." In fact, during the whole meeting, there was not a single point of order raised. The men and women composing the organization came together with an earnest purpose—that of doing something—something that would permanently benefit themselves and the race; and they would not permit anything to turn them aside from this purpose. While the League did not by any means underestimate the outrages inflicted upon the race, it was firmly of our opinion that one way to eventually end these outrages, would be to help make the Negro such a potent factor in the commercial and industrial enterprises of the community in which he lives that he would demand respect and confidence by reason of his usefulness.

It is not the object of the League to, in any way, place mere national success above the high religious character and thorough mental culture, but to make commercial success a means to the promotion of these ends.

The choice of officers for the League resulted in the following being elected:

Booker T. Washington, President, Tuskegee, Ala.; Giles B. Jackson, Vice President, Richmond, Va.; Mrs. Albreta Moore Smith, Vice President, Chicago, Ill.; Gilbert C. Harris, Treasurer, Boston, Mass.; Edward E. Cooper, Secretary, Washington, D. C.; E. A. Johnson, Compiler, Raleigh, N. C.

EXECUTIVE COMMITTEE.

T. Thomas Fortune, New York, Chairman; T. W. Jones, Chicago, Ill.; Isaiah T. Montgomery, Mound Bayou, Miss.; Booker T. Washington, Tuskegee, Ala.; E. E. Cooper, Washington, D. C.; George E. Jones, Little Rock, Ark.; W. R. Pettiford, Birmingham, Ala.; Gilbert C. Harris, Boston, Mass; Louis F. Baldwin, Boston, Mass.

Another very encouraging phase of the Boston meeting was the surprising number of highly successful men and women who appeared from different parts of the country, and who before had not been heard from. Many expressed the idea that the Business League had been long wanted and had in its power to do a work which no other organization could perform. The following editorials from various influential newspapers will give some of the value that was placed upon the Business League meeting:

From The Outlook, New York City: "The

Convention of the National Negro Business League, held in Boston last week, brought together upwards of a hundred delegates, representing over twenty different states. The members of the convention made an excellent impression upon the representatives of the Boston press, both by their appearance and the intellectual quality of their speeches. The League was organized upon the initiative of Booker T. Washington, and his common-sense philosophy permeated most of the addresses. Had these been made at a gathering of white leaders, they might justly be condemned as materialistic. Indeed, one of them, glorifying the 'almighty dollar' as the 'new king that has been born,' should be so condemned. But in the main the emphasis put upon the acquiring of property sprang from the desire to lift up the manhood of the Negro race; for there is a moral difference between the advocacy of money-getting to secure independence and advocacy of money-getting to secure power. Economic independence is to-day as much needed for the further advancement of the Negro race as was emancipation from slavery for the advance which the present generation has witnessed. Even so uncompromising an opponent of materialism as Mr. William Lloyd Garrison, Jr., recognized this and emphasized it in his address to the convention: 'The particular word I wish to leave with you,' he said, 'is this: Aim to be your own employers as speedily as possible. If you are farmers, do not rest until you control the land from which you gain your living. If you are mechanics, or traders, seek first to gain a home without a mortgage, foregoing many desirable things until you are free from debt. Independence and debt cannot long keep company. But, in the South, as in the North, possession of honestly earned property will surely bring respect and increase personal security.' Among the Negro speakers were several men who have been remarkably successful; among others, a slave of Jefferson Davis who is now mayor of his little town in Mississippi. The speeches of some of these men telling of early struggles were full of encouragement to Negroes everywhere. The fact that some Negroes have succeeded in business, as well as the fact that some have succeeded in literature and art, forces all men to distinguish between Negroes and Negroes, and opens the door of opportunity to all Negroes who aspire."

From Buffalo Express: "The recent meeting of the National Negro Business League in Boston brought to public notice a new line of endeavor advocated by the leading Negroes of the country for the betterment of their race's commercial and social position. The call for the formation of the League was issued by President

Booker T. Washington of the Tuskegee Institute, and that it was heartily responded to by Negro business men in all parts of the country, was shown by the assembling of delegates from no less than twenty-five states. The key to the discussion during this interesting conference is to be found in the address of Prof. Booker T. Washington, who said in part: 'I have faith in the timeliness of this organization. As I have noted the conditions of our people in nearly every part of our country, I have always been encouraged by the fact that almost without exception, whether in the North or South, wherever I have seen a black man who was succeeding in business, who was a tax-payer, and who possessed intelligence and high character, that individual was treated with highest respect by the members of the white race. In proportion as we can multiply those examples North and South will our problem be solved. Let every man strive to become the most useful and indispensable man in his community. A useless, idle class is a menace and a danger. We must not in any part of our country, become discouraged, notwithstanding the way often seems dark and desolate. We must maintain faith in ourselves and in our country.'

"This opens the line of work, the possibilities of which are most promising. The development of industrial life among the Negroes in the South by schools is essential to the growth of one element and is remedying the evil of idleness. The new plan goes farther and aids in developing the business instincts of the race, establishing Negroes in mercantile pursuits and in other ways making them important factors in the commercial circles of the country. Already there are many examples of the progress of the Negro in this direction. In Chicago is a large co-operative store, where groceries and meats are sold, while Philadelphia and Richmond each have a large department store conducted by Negroes. Nearly two hundred Negroes in Chicago alone are engaged in various lines of business. Still another example is found in the corporation of New Jersey of an investment and supply company in which the corporators are Negroes. This company is authorized to furnish supplies to families, establish stores, deal in real estate without limit and engage generally in commercial pursuits. It is stated in the papers that the company will carry on a portion of its business in the cities of New York, Philadelphia, Baltimore, Washington, Chicago, Cincinnati, St. Louis, Wilmington, Del., and Richmond and Norfolk, Va., as well as in other places. The capitalization of this company is $75,000."

From Springfield Republican: "The organization of the National Negro Business League by the great convention at Boston, last week, was one of the most important steps yet taken in the lifting of the Negro race to that equality proclaimed implicitly by the Declaration of Independence and explicitly by the constitutional amendments which followed the war. Between one and two hundred delegates were present; the South that made the civil war for Negro slavery was well represented; New England, New York, Pennsylvania, were now the ruling factors in this congress of men opening a new stage in the progress of the race. They came as Americans,—and who has a better right than the Negro to that title? A few days ago a Southern white said that the Negroes had no country, no birthright—not reflecting that he has been given a country by arbitrament of war, and that his birthright, in a majority of cases, was quite as clearly traceable to white ancestry as his traducer's own. But the Negro race has been compelled to a solidarity which is rare in mixed races; the man or woman so white that no one could guess from his hair or complexion the stain of black blood, perforce casts in his lot with the blackest 'Afro-American'—and be it acknowledged that he does it proudly, for the warmest advocates of the Negro race feeling are these very persons; they rightly feel that the African descent is the more honorable.

"The convention was one of such dignity and

such seriousness, such clear-headed consideration of the situation—views being taken in broader horizons than those of the 'nigger' haters,—as to win respect on all sides. And it will not be strange, indeed, it is to be expected, that the effect all over the country will be of the most valuable sort. It is scarcely possible to underrate or condemn a class of people who have so evinced their equality in what the white man especially prides himself on,—the faculty of concentrated effort, the power of organization. This has been attained by the Negro under the most adverse conditions, as we know; even when he has been most favored he has been scantily helped; he has helped himself; and his small advantages he has made the most of, proving that he has the self-same spirit and purpose that has made America, and is just as much an American and as entitled to the blessings and honors of life, as a descendant of the English Puritan or the French Huguenots, the Hollanders, the Irish, the Scandinavian and the German. And when we reflect upon the motley crowds from southern Europe that have entered our country of late years, the comparison becomes absurd.

"The most interesting address was that of A. I. Hillyer, a graduate of the University of Minnesota, a prominent citizen of the National capital, who has compiled and published three editions of a directory of the 'colored business men and women of Washington,' and founded, and was first president of the 'Union League' so described. Mr. Hillyer was appointed by the United States Commission to make up the figures of the Negro exhibit at the Paris exposition, and thus he spoke with knowledge. By the census of 1890 it appears that, twenty-five years after Emancipation, the race had a representative in every business listed in the census schedules. The numbers engaged and the capital invested in many branches were not imposing, but the beginning had been made. That census showed 20,020 persons of Negro descent in business. There were agents and collectors, auctioneers, bankers and brokers (114), druggists, dairymen, dry-goods dealers, grocers, hotel-keepers, liquor dealers, undertakers, officials of banks and insurance companies, journalists and publishers, builders and contractors, photographers, market-men, printers, blacksmiths, watch and clock-makers and of course, barbers. Outside of the business list over 20,000 are to be numbered: Over 1,700 barbers; next to these in numbers caterers, hotel and restaurant men. Mr. Hillyer noted a stove foundry in Tennessee, a cotton mill in North Carolina, a carriage factory in Ohio, and several brick-making plants with large capital. He mentioned four banks, one in Birmingham, Ala., one in Washington, D. C., and one in Richmond, Va. Nor is it true that the business patronage of these and other institutions is confined to the Negro. Giles B. Jackson of Richmond, who spoke concerning the Negroes as real estate owners in that region, said that when the city of Richmond was unable, because of its poverty, to keep its white schools open, it applied to all of the white banks for money in vain. Then an appeal was made to the colored bank. 'How much do you want?' was asked. The reply was, 'Fifty thousand dollars.' 'You can have a hundred thousand,' said the cashier, and this was the sum loaned. Mr. Jackson also said that one-twentieth of the real estate in Virginia is owned by the colored people. The doings of the convention have been fair, measured by the dispatches we have published. They show an undaunted spirit in the face of all discouragements and a ready hopefulness in their achievements. It was a great project to form this League, and its principal pusher, if not its originator, was Mr. Washington of Tuskegee, the great statesman of the Negro race, and not the less great because he is working without the help of the state, and directly for his people. Not, however, solely for them; for Mr. Washington knows, as all thoughtful men ought to see, that the white races are on their trial in this matter. They have to determine whether barbarism or civilization shall rule. Much for the future of the United States depends upon the wise counsel of Booker T. Washington, who is elevating his race, and also elevating the human family itself. He is fitly chosen the first President of the National Negro Business League."

One of the most interesting articles about the first session of the League was contributed by Mr. Henry J. Barrymore, to the Boston Transcript. It seems quite fairly the conclusion reached by most persons who attended the session of the League:

"New Orleans, New York and Akron on the one hand; the Negro business convention on the other! It is a round-about logic—but nevertheless a good one—that answers race antipathy with commercial success. Mr. J. H. Lewis got close to the root of things when he told that convention that the Negro problem was at bottom a mercantile problem; that the business world knows nothing of color, that human selfishness, the desire of every man to get money, would eventually banish prejudice. The almighty dollar is thoroughly color-blind. Money commands respect. Rare is the merchant or manufacturer who will refuse to shake hands with a hundred thousand dollars.

"'But what hope has the Negro to succeed in business?' said Mr. Lewis. 'If you can make a better article than anybody else, and sell it cheaper than anybody else, you can command the markets of the world. Produce something that somebody else wants, whether it be a shoestring or a savings bank, and the purchaser or patron will not trouble himself to ask who the seller is. This same great economic law runs through every line of industry, whether it be farming, manufacturing, mercantile or professional pursuits. Recognize this fundamental law of trade; add to it tact, good manners, a resolute will, a tireless capacity for work, and you will succeed in business. I have found in my own experience of thirty years in business, that success and its conditions lie all around us, regardless of race or color. I believe that it is possible for any man with the proper stuff in him to make a success in business wherever he may be. The best and only capital necessary to begin with is simply honesty, industry and common sense.' This is good reasoning.

"It is also both practical and practicable. Results prove it. Mr. Booker T. Washington, in his travels through widely separated regions of the United States, found so many Negroes engaged in profitable commercial pursuits that he thought the time had come to put the Negro business men on terms of mutual acquaintanceship and mutual helpfulness. Then, with that rare insight which characterizes the man's really indisputable genius, he conceived a big convention, where the Negro business world should take to itself a voice that must at once impress the white man and encourage the black man. The plan worked as per specification. Newspapers saw space in it—space, and timeliness and vital human interest, with here and there a touch of the sensational. The business Negro is, therefore, getting the public notice he so genuinely deserves. It will do us all good.

"For one, it did me good. I confess I went to the Parker Memorial with ill-stifled chuckles of expectant amusement. My chuckles ceased as I entered, for there was something impressive in the splendid show of bunting, something impressive, too, in the gravity of the colored audience, and something wonderfully earnest about the big banner at the back of the stage. That banner made plain, blunt use of the word Negro. So did the speakers. Racial pride is beginning to assert itself. These men have little to say of the 'colored' people or of the 'Afro-American.' They are outgrowing all that sort of affectation. They do, however, insist that the word Negro shall be written with a capital N. And why should they not? We capitalize the Indian, the Chinaman, the Filipino; shame to withhold so small an honor from the Negro!

"Another confession. I looked for the tall silk hat and the flashy suit of clothes. They were there, but not among the delegates. The silly, uneducated, shiftless Negro puts his pay on his back; the business Negro puts his pay in the bank. Here were men who had penetrated the real secret of success, men who understood that the only sure basis of progress is economic, men who would sacrifice to-day's indulgence for to-morrow's independence, men who cared so much for social and educational advancement that they had come to despise the puerile strut and brag of the Negro dandy.

"Their faces surprised me as much as their clothes. There is a certain contemptible type of Caucasian who affects an equally contemptible inability to tell one Negro from another. At the Negro convention he would have had no excuse for such downright stupidity. No white audience ever showed a more interesting variety of feature and countenance, and yet, for all that, I thought I could class those men by types—the cake-walk Negro, the old-Confederate-Colonel Negro, and the well-to-do-merchant Negro. The cake-walk Negro—round-faced, shavey-headed, black as a coal scuttle, clad in rainbow-tinted cheap finery—came from Pleasant street. No seat on the platform for him! The old-Confederate-Colonel Negro — gray moustache and imperial, gold-bowed spectacles and somber dress—this was the man from the South. The well-to-do merchant Negro hailed from nowhere in particular, and, save for his color, was in no striking respect very different from white men of a similar rank in the world of trade. Sometimes the color was puzzling. A gentleman from Dixie was as white as I am. A handsome fellow he was, with a firm, stocky figure and beautifully chiseled features. Readers of Mr. Charles W. Chesnutt's current series in the Transcript would view that colored Southerner with a keen ethnological interest. Which reminds me: A year or so ago I took lunch in Cleveland with Mr. Chesnutt himself. That was before his books had called world-wide attention to his color. I had read his stories in the Atlantic and said: 'Tell me, Mr. Chesnutt, how did you ever come to know the Northern darkey so well?' Mr. Chesnutt replied that he had had rather unusual opportunities for observing the Northern darkey at close range. Six months later I learned I had had the pleasure of lunching with a cultured 'Negro,' and that Mr. Chesnutt had been bubbling with merriment ever since. I did not suspect it at the time. The business convention abounded with just such unrecognizable Negroes. Under the yellow glare of the evening lights it was difficult, in many cases, to tell who was white and who was 'col-he cannot run away. To own property is to own character." Another farmer from Macon County said: "The nigger race ain't such a bugaboo as you think. The trouble with our people is we don't understand ourselves; we don't have self-reliance and self-government. Eight years ago I didn't have even a meat skin, now I have got eighty acres of land and five mules, all paid for. You must be a man. Say sink or swim, I'm coming on top; if you don't you won't amount to anything. Some of our race is so shiftless that if their own mother should rise from the grave after twenty years, and come into the house and say, 'Son, give me a cup of coffee, I've been walking all night,' he couldn't do it. You make a mortgage, and then you get everything you want, not everything you need. I had a start once before, and I got a couple of old horses and a buggy, and I rid around too much and I got down. Then I promised the Lord if he would forgive me and help me to start again I would do better. Now I work from Monday to Saturday. A heap of our people don't like that part of the Bible which says 'six days thou shalt work.' When a colored man dies the merchant makes more than on any other day, because you have all got to dress up, hire buggies, and ride around and go to the funeral. I don't want anybody's foot on my neck. I don't go and say, 'Mas'r Joe, please sir, I wants a little flour or I wants a little coffee for my old lady,' but when I want anything I just go and get it. You must not sit down and trust God; if you do you'll starve. Get up and go to work, and trust God, and you'll get rich."

Then Father Mitchell, who is a colored minister, said: "Now, keep quiet; we's gettin' along slowly. I wish our neighborhood was like dat brother's as jest spoke. You give me a good lick for a young man, Mr. President; but, sir, if we had twenty men like you we'd get happy 'fore we enter heaven. We make a heap of corn and potatoes." "How about morals?" asked some one. "Well, now, I'll tell you about dat. I'd thank my Redeemer to send me some morals down to my neighborhood. I am putting up a big Baptist Church down on the Sam road, an' I hope I'll be able to do my people some good."

At the time of the organization of the Annual Negro Farmers' Conference, it was decided to make a special effort to secure the attendance of the representatives of the various educational, religious and philanthropic institutions in the South for the elevation of the Negro. This attempt was quite successful, so much so that in addition to the regular delegates at the Negro Conference, quite a large number of educators and others began assembling to witness the proceedings of that body. During the session of the Conference it was determined to organize what is known as the "Worker's Conference," composed of educators and other persons interested in the elevation of the Negro. It was decided to ask the members of the Worker's Conference to be present and witness the proceedings of the regular Negro Conference, in order that they might get information at first hand as to the condition and needs of the colored people. The following day the Worker's Conference was called, and based its proceedings in a large measure upon the lessons learned the previous day at the Farmers' Conference. The Worker's Conference has now been in existence many years, and is a very important and far-reaching institution; in fact, it is the only organization that brings together annually the various officers and teachers connected with the large religious and educational enterprises in the South. We have had regularly present at the Worker's Conference representatives from such institutions as the Hampton Institute, Atlanta University, Clark University, Atlanta Baptist College, Gammon Theological Seminary, Spelman Seminary, Morris Brown College, Fisk University, Central Tennessee College, Straight University, Talladega College, Tougaloo University, Lincoln University, Selma University, and many others which I have not space to mention; in fact, I think every educational institution of any importance for the Negro has been represented at one or more of these Worker's Conferences. Besides these, we often have present the secretaries of the various religious organizations doing work in the South.

The subjects discussed in these Worker's Conferences are of a wide range. At the last Conference the time was occupied in a discussion of how the various educational institutions in the South could serve to bring about more satisfactory relations between the two races in the South. The discussion was free, open and most helpful. In fact, it is well understood that in all of these gatherings at Tuskegee there is the utmost frankness and liberality allowed as to opinion and discussion. The Worker's Conferences are growing in numbers and interest, and have now become a permanent part of the educational machinery of the South.

CHAPTER XVIII.

A VACATION IN EUROPE.

In the spring of 1899 a rather notable meeting was held in Boston, in the afternoon, at the Hollis Street Theatre. This meeting was gotten up in the interest of the Tuskegee Institute, by friends of the institution, in Boston for the purpose of raising money for the school. It was presided over by Bishop Lawrence, Bishop of Massachusetts. I invited to speak with me at this meeting Dr. W. E. B. DuBois and Mr. Paul Laurence Dunbar. Dr. DuBois read an original story, and Mr. Dunbar recited from his own poems. The theatre was filled with representatives of the most cultured and wealthy men and women in Boston, and was said to be the most successful meeting of the kind that had been held for a good while. An admission was charged at the door, and a generous sum was raised for the school. This was the first time that Mr. Dunbar had appeared in Boston, and his readings produced a most favorable effect. The same was true of Dr. DuBois.

During this same year I received an invitation which surprised me somewhat. It was an invitation from the secretary of the Birmingham, Alabama, Lyceum, a white literary organization.

composed of the best and most cultured people in the city of Birmingham, Alabama, inviting me to address the Lyceum. I accepted this invitation to deliver an address before the organization on the 30th of March. There was some adverse criticism and some protests through the newspapers, and otherwise, on the part of a certain element of white people in Birmingham; in fact, some effort was made to prevent white ladies from attending, but I was surprised and gratified when I appeared before the audience to find the room filled with representatives of the best ladies and gentlemen of Birmingham, and I have never spoken before any organization where my words were more heartily and more kindly received than was true on this occasion. This was the first time that I had ever received an invitation to address a white literary organization in the South, although during the winter of the same year I had delivered an address before the National Farmers' Association, which met at Fort Worth, Texas.

Immediately after the public meeting held in Boston in the Hollis Street Theatre, some friends of mine in Boston noted that I seemed to be rather worn out, as a result of nearly eighteen years of continuous work, without any vacation during the entire time. Without our knowledge, they quietly started a movement to raise a certain sum of money to be used in sending Mrs. Washington and myself to Europe, where we could rest for two or three months. This plan was a very great surprise to us, and it seemed difficult for us to make up our minds to leave the school for so long a time; but these friends insisted that we owed it to the work and to ourselves to take the vacation. The result was that we sailed for Europe on the 10th of May and remained abroad until the 5th of August. We had a very pleasant and delightful trip across the ocean, and made many friends on the voyage. I was called upon to speak on the steamer going and had a large and interesting audience. After a voyage of ten days we landed at Antwerp, Belgium, and remained there a short time. We then took a trip through the country in company with some New York friends whose acquaintance we made on the voyage. In Holland we traveled on the canal boats, which gave us an opportunity of seeing the home life of the country people, and also the agricultural life of the country.

I was especially anxious to study the agricultural and dairy systems, with a view to utilizing the information in our work at Tuskegee. The thorough cultivation of the soil, for which this country is noted, made a deep impression upon me. There are few other countries, if any in the world, where the soil is so thoroughly cultivated as in Holland. The dairy interests there present an interesting and valuable field for study. While in Holland we visited The Hague, where the International Peace Congress was in session, and were shown many courtesies by the American members of the Peace Conference. After remaining for some time in Holland, we returned to Antwerp and spent some time there, and afterwards proceeded to Brussels, where we had a pleasant stay. From Brussels we went to Paris, where we remained nearly six weeks. In Paris we received much kind attention from General Horace Porter, the American Ambassador, and his wife, as well as from other American and French people. Soon after reaching Paris I received an invitation to deliver an address before the American University Club, an organization composed mainly of American college men residing in Paris. The American Ambassador, Gen. Horace Porter, presided at this meeting, and in addition to myself the speakers were Ex-president Benjamin Harrison and Archbishop Ireland. I was also invited to deliver an address the following Sunday in the American chapel, which I did. Mrs. Washington and I attended a reception given by the American Ambassador, where we met many prominent people.

I went to Europe mainly for the purpose of securing complete rest, and notwithstanding the many engagements which constantly pressed themselves upon me, I succeeded in getting a great deal of needed strength, especially was this true in Paris. From Paris we went to London, and arrived there just in the midst of the social season. We had many letters of introduction from friends in America to influential people in England, and our stay in England was occupied mainly in a continual round of social engagements.

Soon after reaching London, friends insisted that I should deliver an address to the public on the race problem in the South. The American Ambassador, Hon. Joseph H. Choate, was especially anxious that I consent to do this. A meeting was arranged to take place in Essex Hall. In connection with this meeting Rev. Brooke Herford, D. D., whom I had formerly known in Boston, gave Mrs. Washington and myself a reception. The meeting was largely attended, and Mr. Choate, the American Ambassador, presided. The substance of what Mr. Choate and myself said at this meeting was widely circulated in England, and telegraphed to the American press. This meeting was attended by such well-known people as Hon. James Bryce, who also spoke, and many high officials and members of titled families in England. After this meeting I received many invitations to speak at other gatherings, but as far as possible excused myself from doing so, in order that I might secure the rest for which I went to Europe. I did, however, consent to speak at a meeting at the Crystal Palace, which was presided over by the Duke of Westminster, said to be the richest man in the world. This meeting was also largely attended. We attended, among many other social functions, receptions given by the Duke and Duchess of Sutherland, by Mr. and Mrs. T. Fischer Unwin, Mrs. Unwin being the daughter of the late Richard Cobden. Lady Henry Somerset was very kind in her attention to us.

While in London the following editorial appeared in the Daily Chronicle:

"The presence in London of Mr. Booker T. Washington, at whose address the other evening the American Ambassador presided, calls for a generous recognition of the remarkable work being done in the United States for the Negro by this gifted member of the Negro race. What Frederick Douglass was to an older generation that Mr. Washington is to the present. At the recent visit of President McKinley to the South, Mr. Washington occupied a place of honor alongside the President, and was almost as heartily acclaimed. When one recalls the tremendous 'color' feeling in America, such a fact is exceedingly striking. The great work which Mr. Washington has done has been an educational work. Orator as he is, it is not so much his power of speech as the building up of the remarkable industrial institute at Tuskegee, in Alabama, which has given this Negro leader his deserved fame. The Civil War left the Negro legally and nominally free, and the legislation after the war was over made him legally and nominally a citizen. But we know that the Negro has been in fact in a very different position from that which he occupied on paper. He has been insulted by degrading legislation, he has been in many states virtually deprived of his vote, and in not a few cases an election dispute has afforded the dominant white man an excuse for slaughter of the blacks. The Negro has retaliated in his barbarous way. Though religious in the most emotional form, he is often non-moral, and there can be no doubt that he has committed many grave offenses against social order.

"Mr. Washington, though an enthusiastic advocate of the claims of his race, is by no means blind to the faults which render so many Negroes almost unfit for American citizenship. He saw long ago, what so many American politicians who gave the suffrage to the colored population did not see—that the most important service which could be rendered to the blacks was to make useful artisans and workmen of them. As a result of his meditation on the condition of the colored people, Mr. Washington founded the Tuskegee Institute in the Black Belt of Alabama, stumped the Union for funds, interested in his great undertaking all the best minds of the Northern States, and has had the satisfaction of seeing this institution grow to its present status of the largest and most important training centre of the black race in the world. Here, where both sexes are welcomed on terms of equality, the Negro is taken in hand, given the rudiments of education, taught a useful trade, taught also, if he proves capable, the higher branches of modern culture, subjected to high intellectual and ethical influences, and made a man of in the true sense of the word. No better work is being done in America at the present hour than in this remarkable institution in Alabama.

"That the American conscience is being roused to its duty to the Negroes is evident from the recent important conference at which two leading speakers were an ex-Governor of Georgia and a Bishop of the Episcopal Church. The horrible burnings and improvised hangings by white mobs, who took the law into their hands, have awakened the people of the North, and it is very properly asked whether those who permit such brutalities in their own borders are fit to assume control of black and yellow races in the Pacific. Ex-Governor Northen, of Georgia, took the North to task for having been more responsible for the spread of slavery than the South, and he defended, but without much success, the Southern whites against the attacks made on them. The Bishop, it is gratifying to find, took the strong ground of the Declaration of Independence, and asserted the equal right of black and white to the common rights which the law and the Constitution allow. But the important principle which emerges clearly from the long discussion that took place at this conference is that a *laissez faire* policy is impossible in the case of the Negro. You cannot 'emancipate' him alone. He must be educated, his character must be formed, he must be made a useful and self-reliant being. This is precisely what is being done at the Tuskegee Institute, and therefore, its founder is solving, as far as one man can, one of the chief American problems of the time. And what a problem! The practical humanising and elevation from barbarism of dusky millions on whose own future the future of the United States largely depends."

Perhaps the most interesting and restful part of our visit to England was the time that we spent as the guests of various English people in their country homes. In order for one to appreciate what English life really is, he should have an opportunity to get into the daily life of an English gentleman in his country residence.

We visited Bristol, where we were given a reception by the Women's Liberty Club, and also Manchester, Liverpool and Birmingham. In Birmingham we spent several days as the guests of Mr. Joseph Sturge, who kindly gave us a reception, at which we met many of the prominent citizens of Birmingham. Of course we visited a great many places of historical interest and had an opportunity of looking into the methods of education in England. We were specially interested in the work of the large polytechnic institutes and the agricultural colleges, from which we got a great deal of valuable information.

While in Europe I wrote a series of letters for the American Negro press. These letters were widely published and commented upon.

During our stay in London I took special pains to inquire into the opportunities for our people to better their condition by emigrating to Africa, and convinced myself that there was little, if any, hope of this, largely because Africa is almost completely divided up among various European nations, leaving little hope for self-government in any part of Africa, except in the small republic of Liberia, which is notably unhealthy and undesirable from almost every point of view. I found out that in many cases the Negroes are treated by Europeans in Africa almost as badly as they have ever been treated in the South. The letter which I wrote from London on this subject was very widely copied and commented upon by the American press.

While I was in Europe, cases of lynching of our people were especially frequent in the South, and in order to assist in checking this injustice perpetrated upon the race, I addressed the following letter to the Southern people, which was widely published throughout the country and seemed to do much good. It was heartily commented upon editorially in the Southern press:

"Several times, during the last few months, while our country has been shocked because of the lynching of Negro citizens, I have been asked by many to say something upon the subject through the press, and have been tempted to do so. At the time of these lynchings I kept silent, because I did not believe that the public mind was in a condition to listen to a discussion of the subject in the calm judicial manner that it would be later, when there should be no undue feeling or excitement. In the discussion of this or any other matter, little good is accomplished unless we are perfectly frank. There is no white man of the South who has more sincere love for it than I have, and nothing could tempt me to write or speak that which I did not think was for the permanent good of all the people of the South. Whenever adverse criticism is made upon the South I feel it as keenly as any member of the white race can feel it. It is, therefore, my interest in everything which pertains to the South that prompts me to write as I do now. While it is true that there are cases of lynchings and outrage in the Northern and Western States, candor compels us to admit that by far the most of the cases of lynchings take place in our Southern States, and that most of the persons lynched are Negroes.

"With all the earnestness of my heart, I want to appeal, not to the President of the United States, Mr. McKinley, not to the people of New York nor of the New England States, but to the citizens of our Southern States, to assist in creating a public sentiment such as will make human life just as safe and sacred here as it is anywhere else in the world.

"For a number of years the South has appealed to the North and to Federal authorities, through the public press, from the public platform, and most eloquently through the late Henry W. Grady, to leave the whole matter of the rights and protection of the Negro to the South, declaring that it would see to it that the Negro would be made secure in his citizenship. During the last half dozen years the whole country, from the President down, has been inclined more than ever to pursue this policy, leaving the whole matter of the destiny of the Negro to the Negro himself and to the Southern white people among whom the great bulk of the Negroes live.

"By the present policy of non-interference, on the part of the North and the Federal Government, the South is given a sacred trust. How will she execute this trust? The world is waiting and watching to see. The question must be answered largely by the protection the South gives to the life of the Negro, and the provisions that are made for the development of the Negro in the organic laws of the state. I fear that but few people in the South realize to what extent the habit of lynching, or the taking of life without due process of law, has taken hold of us, and to what extent it is hurting us, not only in the eyes of the world, but in our own moral and material growth.

"Lynching was instituted some years ago, with the idea of punishing and checking outrage upon women. Let us examine the cold facts and see where it has already led us, and where it is likely further to carry us, if we do not rid ourselves of the habit. Many good people in the South, and also out of the South, have gotten the idea that lynching is resorted to for one crime only. I have the facts from an authoriative source. During last year 127 persons were lynched in the United States. Of this number, 118 were executed in the South and 9 in the North and West. Of the total number lynched, 102 were Negroes, 23 were whites and 2, Indians Now, let everyone interested in the South, his country and the cause of humanity, note this fact—that only 24 of the entire number were charged in any way with the crime of rape; that is, 24 out of 127 cases of lynching. Sixty one of the remaining cases were for murder, 13 being for suspected murder, 6 for theft, etc. During one week last spring, when I kept a careful record, 13 Negroes were lynched in three of our Southern States, and not one was even charged with rape. All of these 13 were accused of murder or house-burning, but in none of the cases were the men allowed to go before a court, so that their innocence or guilt might be proven.

"When we get to the point where four-fifths of the people lynched in our country in one year are lynched for some crime other than rape, we can no longer plead and explain that we lynch for one crime alone.

"Let us take another year, that of 1892, for example. During this year (1892) 241 persons were lynched in the whole United States. Thirty-six of this number were lynched in Northern and Western States, and 205 in our Southern States. Of the 241 lynched in the whole country, 160 were Negroes and five of these were women. The facts show that out of the 241 lynched in the entire country in 1892, but 57 were even charged with rape, even attempted rape, leaving in that year alone, 184 persons who were lynched for other causes than that of rape.

"If it were necessary, I could produce figures for other years. Within a period of six years about 900 persons have been lynched in our Southern States. This is but a few hundred short of the total number of soldiers who lost their lives in Cuba during the Spanish-American war. If we would realize still more fully how far this unfortunate habit is leading us on, note the classes of crime, during a few months, which the local papers and Associated Press say that lynching has been inflicted for—they include 'murder,' 'rioting,' 'incendiarism,' 'robbery,' 'larceny,' 'self-defense,' 'insulting women,' 'alleged stock poisoning,' 'malpractice,' 'alleged barn-burning,' 'suspected robbery,' 'race prejudice,' 'attempted murder,' 'horse stealing,' and 'mistaken identity,' etc.

"The practice has grown until we are now at the point where not only blacks are lynched in the South, but white men as well. Not only this, but within the last six years at least a half dozen colored women have been lynched. And there are a few cases where Negroes have lynched members of their own race. What is to be the end of this? Besides this, every lynching drives hundreds of Negroes from the farming districts of the South, where their services are of great value to the country, into the already over-crowded cities.

"I know that some will argue that the crime of lynching Negroes is not confined to the South. This is true, and no one can excuse such a crime as the shooting of innocent black men in Illinois, who were guilty of no crime except that of seeking labor, but my words just now are to the South, where my home is, and a part of which I am. Let other sections act as they will; I want to see our beautiful Southland free from this terrible evil of lynching. Lynching does not stop crime. In the immediate section of the South where a colored man recently committed the most terrible crime ever charged against a member of his race, but a few weeks previous to this, five colored men had been lynched for supposed incendiarism. If lynching was a cure for crime, surely the lynching of five would have prevented another Negro from committing a most heinous crime a few weeks later.

"We might as well face the facts bravely and wisely. Since the beginning of the world crime has been committed in all civilized and uncivilized countries, and a certain amount of crime will always be committed, both in the North and in the South, but I believe that the crime of rape can be stopped. In proportion to the numbers and intelligence of the population of the South, there exists little more crime than in several other sections of the country, but because of the lynching habit we are constantly advertising ourselves to the world as a lawless people. We cannot disregard the teachings of the civilized world for eighteen hundred years, that the only way to punish crime is by law. When we leave this dictum chaos begins.

"I am not pleading for the Negro alone. Lynching injures, hardens and blunts the moral sensibilities of the young and tender manhood of the South. Never shall I forget the remark by a little nine-year-old white boy, with blue eyes and flaxen hair. The little fellow said to his mother after he had returned from a lynching: 'I have seen a man hanged; now I wish I could see one burned.' Rather than hear such a remark from one of my little boys, I would prefer seeing him laid in his grave. This is not all; every community guilty of lynching, says in so many words to the governor, to the legislature, to the sheriff, to the jury, and to the judge, I have no faith in you and no respect for you. We have no respect for the law which we helped to make.

"In the South, at the present time, there is less excuse for not permitting the law to take its course, where a Negro is to be tried, than anywhere else in the world, for almost without exception the governors, the sheriffs, the judges, the juries and the lawyers are all white men, and they can be trusted, as a rule, to do their duty; otherwise it is needless to tax the people to support these officers. If our present laws are not sufficient to properly punish crime, let the laws be changed, but that the punishment may be by lawfully constituted authority is the plea I make. The history of the world proves that where law is most strictly enforced is the least crime; where people take the administration of the law into their own hands is the most crime.

"But there is another side. The white man in the South has not only a serious duty and responsibility, but the Negro has a duty and responsibility in this matter. In speaking of my own people I want to be equally frank, but I speak with the greatest kindness. There is too much crime among us. The figures for a given period show that in the United States 30 per cent. of the crime committed is by Negroes, while we constitute only about 12 per cent. of the entire population. This proportion holds good, not only in the South, but also in the Northern States and cities.

"No race that is so largely ignorant and so lately out of slavery could, perhaps, show a better record, but we must face these plain facts. He is most kind to the Negro who tells him of his faults as well as of his virtues. A large amount of the crime among us grows out of the idleness of our young men and women. It is for this reason that I have tried to insist upon some industry being taught in connection with their course of literary training. The time has come when every parent, every teacher and minister of the gospel, should teach with unusual emphasis morality and obedience to the law. At the fireside, in the school room, in the Sunday-school, from the pulpit and the Negro press, there should be such a sentiment created regarding the committing of crime against women, that no such crime shall be charged against any member of the race. Let it be understood for all time that no one guilty of rape can find sympathy or shelter with us, and that none will be more active in bringing to justice, through the proper authorities, those guilty of crime. Let the criminal and vicious element of the race have at all times our most severe condemnation. Let a strict line be drawn between the virtuous and the criminal. I condemn with all the indignation of my soul the beast in human form guilty of assaulting a woman. Let us all be alike in this particular.

"We should not as a race become discouraged. We are making progress. No race has ever gotten upon its feet without discouragements and struggles.

"I should be a great hypocrite and a coward if I did not add that which my daily experience teaches me is true, namely, that the Negro has among many of the Southern whites as good friends as he has anywhere in the world. These friends have not forsaken us. They will not do so; neither will our friends in the North. If we make ourselves intelligent, industrious, economical and virtuous, of value to the community in which we live, we can and will work out our own salvation right here in the South. In every community, by means of organized effort, we should seek in a manly and honorable way the confidence, the co-operation, the sympathy of the best white people in the South and in our respective communities. With the best white people and the best black people standing together, in favor of law and order and justice, I believe that the safety and happiness of both races will be made secure."

In closing this chapter, I repeat what I have said on another occasion. Those who fought for the freedom of the slaves performed their duty heroically and well, but a duty still remains

ON BOAT, BATON ROUGE, LA.

Reading from left to right: Major R. R. Moton, Commandant of Cadets, Hampton Institute. Dr. M. W. Dogan, President Wiley University, Marshall, Texas. Dr. Booker T. Washington. Mr. Emmett J. Scott, Secretary of Tuskegee Institute. Dr. Robert E. Jones, Editor Southwestern Christian Advocate, New Orleans, La.

THE JOHN A. ANDREWS MEMORIAL HOSPITAL OPEN FOR THE ACCOMMODATION OF COLORED PATIENTS.

for those who are left. The mere fiat of law cannot make an ignorant voter an intelligent voter; cannot make a dependent man an independent man; cannot make one citizen respect another. These results will come to the Negro, as to all races, by beginning at the bottom and gradually working up to the highest possibilities of his nature.

In the economy of God there is but one standard by which an individual can succeed; there is but one for the race.

In working out his own destiny, while the main burden of activity must be with the Negro, he will need in the years to come the help, the encouragement, the guidance, that the strong can give to the weak.

CHAPTER XIX.

THE WEST VIRGINIA AND OTHER RECEPTIONS AFTER EUROPEAN TRIP.

Early in August we sailed for America from Southampton, and had a very pleasant voyage on the magnificent ocean steamer "St. Louis" On the voyage I was called upon to speak again to the passengers, and made many friends for our cause.

While in Europe I received the following invitation:

"CHARLESTON, W. VA., May 16, 1899.

"PROF. B. T. WASHINGTON,

"Tuskegee Institute, Tuskegee, Alabama.

"*Dear Sir:*—Many of the best citizens of West Virginia have united in liberal expressions of admiration and praise of your worth and work, and desire that on your return from Europe, you should favor them with your presence and with the inspiration of your words. We most sincerely endorse this move, and on behalf of the citizens of Charleston extend to you our most cordial invitation to have you come to us, that we may honor you who have done so much by your life and work to honor us.

"We are, very truly yours,
"The Common Council of the City of Charleston,
"By W. HERMAN SMITH, Mayor."

This invitation from the City Council of Charleston was accompanied by the following:

"PROF. B. T. WASHINGTON,
"Principal, Tuskegee Institute.

"*Dear Sir:*—We, the citizens of Charleston and West Virginia, desire to express our pride in you and the splendid career you have thus far accomplished, and ask that we be permitted to show our pride and interest in a substantial way.

"Your recent visit to your old home in our midst awoke within us the keenest regret that we were not permitted to hear you and render some substantial aid to your work, before you left for Europe.

"In view of the foregoing, we earnestly invite you to share the hospitality of our city upon your return from Europe and give us the opportunity to hear you and put ourselves in touch with your work in a way that will be most gratifying to yourself, and that we may receive the inspiration of your words and presence.

"An early reply to this invitation, with an

indication of the time you may reach our city will greatly oblige,

"Yours very respectfully,

"The Charleston Daily Gazette, The Daily Mail-Tribune, G. W. Atkinson, Governor; E. L. Boggs, Secretary to Governor; Wm. M. O. Dawson, Secretary of State; L. M. LaFollette, Auditor; J. R. Trotter, Superintendent of Schools, E. W. Wilson, ex-Governor; W. A. MacCorkle, ex-Governor; John Q. Dickinson, President Kanawha Valley Bank; L. Prichard, President Charleston National Bank; Geo. S. Couch, President Kanawha National Bank; Ed. Reid, Cashier Kanawha National Bank; Geo. S. Laidley, Superintendent City Schools; L. E. McWhorter, President Board of Education; Chas. K. Payne, wholesale merchant; C. C. Lewis, Jr., wholesale merchant; R. G. Hubbard, wholesale merchant; Dan. D. Brawley, City Sergeant; Grant P. Hall, Clerk of Circuit Court; O. A. Petty, Postmaster; R. Douglas Roller, Rector St. John's Episcopal Church; M. M. Williamson, Cashier Citizen's National Bank; J. N. Carnes, Assistant Cashier Citizen's National Bank; J. A. Schwabe & Co., merchants; J. A. DeGruyter, ex-Mayor; A. H. Boyd, M. D.; E. W. Staunton, Clerk Kanawha County Court; M. F. Compton, Pastor State St. M. E. Church; T. C. Johnson, Pastor Charleston Baptist Church; Coyle &

Richardson, merchants; J. H. Gaines, United States District Attorney; Sterrett Brothers, merchants; N. S. Burlew, merchant; Joel H. Ruffner, merchant; M. P. Ruffner, merchant; E. G. Pierson, senator; B. R. Winkler, member City Council; Flournoy, Price & Smith, lawyers; Abney, Barnes & Co., wholesale merchants; Sam D. Littlepage, member of City Council; D. W. Shaw, Pastor Simpson M. E. Church; J. McHenry Jones, President West Virginia Colored Institute; Jas. M. Canty, J. C. Gilmer, Byrd Prillerman, S. W. Starks, J. M. Hazelwood, Phil. Waters, C. W. Hall, Judge Criminal Court; C. W. Boyd, Principal Garnet School; B. S. Morgan, member of City Council."

This invitation to accept a reception from the citizens of Charleston, W. Va., where I had spent my boyhood days, was a very satisfactory surprise. When I left Charleston, and when I left Malden, which is very near Charleston, I was quite a boy, and I had not been able to spend any great length of time there since I had first left to enter the Hampton Institute.

I accepted the invitation for the Charleston reception, and when I reached Charleston was met by a committee of citizens headed by ex-Gov. W. A. MacCorkle. The meeting in connection with this reception was held in the opera house, and was presided over by Gov. George W.

Atkinson. It was very largely attended by white and colored citizens from that vicinity, a large number of whom had known me in my boyhood days. I must refrain from giving any detailed account of all the kind and complimentary things they were kind enough to say about me at this meeting. I spent several days in Charleston, visiting the scenes of my early boyhood, and my sister in Malden, and many of the older citizens who remembered me.

After this reception in Charleston I was invited to go to Atlanta, Ga., by the white and colored citizens, to be given a reception there. The meeting in Atlanta was presided over by the Governor of the State, and was largely attended.

Receptions by the citizens of Montgomery and New Orleans soon followed. Invitations to attend receptions in other states came to me, but I was not able to accept them all.

In the fall of 1899 a meeting was held at Huntsville, Ala., the spirit of which has since been taken up by other Southern cities, which promises to prove of lasting benefit in settling the race problem in the South. In October a meeting was called at Huntsville, which had for its object the discussion of all matters relating to the upbuilding of the South. It was well attended by representatives from nearly every Southern State, and was a strong body of men. Among the other subjects discussed was the Negro problem in its relation to the industrial progress of the South.

In connection with others, I was invited to deliver an address. The audience was composed mainly of Southern white men, but in it was a large number of Southern white women, together with quite an attendance of colored men and women. The address which I delivered on that occasion attracted a great deal of attention throughout the country, and for that reason I have taken the liberty of giving it in full:

"In all discussion and legislation bearing upon the presence of the Negro in America, it should be borne in mind that we are dealing with a people who were forced to come here without their consent and in the face of a most earnest protest. This gives the Negro a claim upon your sympathy and generosity that no other race can possess. Besides, though forced from his native land into residence in a country that was not of his choosing, he has earned his right to the title of American citizen by obedience to the law, by patriotism and fidelity, and by the millions which his brawny arms and willing hands have added to the wealth of this country.

"In saying what I have to-day, although a Negro and an ex-slave myself, there is no white man whose heart is more wrapped up in every interest of the South and who loves it more dearly than is true of myself. She can have no sorrow that I do not share; she can have no prosperity that I do not rejoice in. She can commit no error that I do not deplore. She can take no step forward that I do not approve.

"Different in race, in color, in history, we can teach the world that, although thus differing, it is possible for us to dwell side by side in love, in peace, and in material prosperity. We can be one, as I believe we will be in a larger degree in the future, in sympathy, purpose, forbearance and mutual helpfulness. Let him who would embitter, who would bring strife between your race and mine, be accursed in his basket and in his store, accursed in the fruit of his body and the fruit of his land. No man can plan the degradation of another race without being himself degraded. The highest test of the civilization of any race is its willingness to extend a helping hand to the less fortunate.

"The South extends a protecting arm and a welcome voice to the foreigner, of all nationalities, languages and conditions, but in this I pray that you will not forget the black man at your door, whose habits you know, whose fidelity you have tested. You may make of others larger gatherers of wealth, but you cannot make of them more law-abiding, useful and God-fearing people than the Negro who has been by your side for three centuries, and whose toil in forest, field and mine has helped to make the South the land of promise and glorious possibility.

"Before we can make much progress we must decide whether or not the Negro is to be a permanent part of the South. With the light that is before us, I have no hesitation in declaring that the great bulk of the Negro population will reside among you. Any hesitation or doubting as to the permanent residence of the race will work infinite harm to the industrial and economic interests of both races. Here, in His wisdom, Providence has placed the Negro. Here he will remain. Here he came without a language; here he found the Anglo-Saxon tongue. Here he came in paganism; here he found the religion of Christ. Here he came in barbarism; here he found civilization. Here he came with untrained hands; here he found industry. If these centuries of contact with the American has done this, can you not trust to the wise Creator, aided by the efforts of the Negro himself, and your guidance, to do the remainder? At this point, are you willing to cease your efforts and turn the work over to others for completion? Your duty to the Negro will not be fulfilled until you have made of him the highest type of American citizen, in intelligence, usefulness and morality.

"The South has within itself the forces that are to solve this tremendous problem. You have the climate, the soil and the material wealth. You have the labor to be performed that will occupy many times our present Negro population. While the calls come daily from South Africa, from the Hawaiian Islands, from the North and the West for the strong and willing arm of the Negro in the field of industry, you, at your very door, have that which others are energetically seeking. Not only are you in possession of that which others are seeking, but more important than all, custom and contact have so knit the two races together that the black man finds in these Southern States an open sesame in labor, industry and business that is not surpassed anywhere. It is here alone, by reason of the presence of the Negro, that capital is free from tyranny and despotism that prevents you from employing whom you please and for that wage that is mutually agreeable and profitable. It is here that that form of slavery which prevents a man from selling his labor to whom he pleases on account of his color is almost unknown. We have had slavery, now dead, that forced an individual to labor without a recompense, but none that compelled a man to remain in idleness while his family starved.

"The Negro in all parts of the country is beginning to appreciate the advantage which the South affords for earning a living, for commercial development, and in proportion as this is true, it will constitute the basis for the settlement of other difficulties. The colored man is beginning to learn that the bed rock upon which every individual rests his chances for success in life is securing in every manly way—never at the sacrifice of principle—the friendship, the confidence, the respect of his next-door neighbor in the little community in which he lives. Almost the whole problem of the Negro in the South rests itself upon the question as to whether he makes himself of such indispensable service to his neighbor, to the community, that no one can fill his place better in the body politic. There is no other safe course for the Negro to pursue. If the black man in the South has a friend in his white neighbor, and a still larger number of friends in his own community, he has a protection and a guarantee of his rights that will be more potent and more lasting than any Federal Congress or any outside power can confer. While the Negro is grateful for the opportunities which he enjoys in the business of the South, you should remember that you are in debt to the black man for furnishing you with labor that is almost a stranger to strikes, lock-outs and labor wars; labor that is law-abiding, peaceful, teachable; labor that is one with you in language, sympathy, religion and patriotism; labor that has never been tempted to follow the red flag of anarchy, but always the safe flag of his country and the spotless banner of the cross.

"But if the South is to go forward and not stand still, if she is to reach the highest reward from her wonderful resources and keep abreast of the progress of the world, she must reach that point, without needless delay, where she will not be continually advertising to the world that she has a race question to settle. We must reach that point where, at every election, from the choice of a magistrate to that of a governor, the decision will not hinge upon a discussion or a revival of the race question. We must arrive at that period where the great fundamental question of good roads, education of farmers, agricultural and mineral development, manufacturing and industrial and public school education will be, in a large degree, the absorbing topics in our political campaign. But that we may get this question from among us, the white man has a duty to perform, the black man has a duty. No question is ever permanently settled until it is settled in the principles of the highest justice. Capital and lawlessness will not dwell together. The white man who learns to disregard law when a Negro is concerned will soon disregard it when a white man is concerned.

"In the evolution of the South it seems to me that we have reached that period where private philanthropy and the Christian church of the white South should, in a large degree, share directly in the elevation of the Negro. In saying this I am not unmindful of or ungrateful for what has already been done by individuals and through public schools. When we consider the past, the wonder is that so much has been done by our brothers in white. All great reforms and improvements rest, in a large measure, upon the church for success. You acknowledge that Christianity and education make a man more valuable as a citizen, make him more industrious, make him earn more, make him more upright. In this respect let me see how the three largest white denominations in the South regard the Negro.

"To elevate the ignorant and degraded in Africa, China, Japan, India, these three denominations in the South give annually about $544,000, but to elevate the ignorant, the degraded at your doors, to protect your families, to lessen your taxes, to increase their earning power; in a word, to Christianize and elevate the people at your very side, upon whom, in a large measure, your safety and property depend, these same denominations give $21,000—$21,000 for the benighted at your doors, $544,000 for the benighted abroad. That thirty-five years after slavery and a fratricidal war the master should give even $21,000 through the medium of the church for the elevation of his former slave means much. Nor would I have one dollar less go to the foreign fields, but I would plead with all the earnestness of my soul that the Christian South give increased attention to the 8,000,000 of Negroes by whom it is surrounded. All this has a most vital and direct relation to the work of this Industrial convention. Every dollar that goes into the education of the Negro is an interest-bearing dollar.

"For years all acknowlege that the South has suffered from the low price of cotton because of over-production. The economic history of the world teaches that an ignorant farming class means a single crop, and that a single crop means, too often, low prices from over-production or famine from under-production. The Negro constitutes the principal farming class of the South. So long as the Negro is ignorant in head, unskilled in hand, unacquainted with labor-saving machinery, so long will he confine himself to a single crop, and over-production of cotton will result. So long as this is true, you will be bound in economic fetters; you will be hugging the bear, while crying for some one to help you let go. Every man, black and white, in the South, with his crop mortgaged, in debt at the end of the year, buying his meat from Iowa, his corn from Illinois, his shoes from New York, his clothing from Pennsylvania, his wagon from Indiana, his plow from Massachusetts, his mule from Missouri, and his coffin from Ohio, everyone who is thus situated, is a citizen who is not producing the highest results for his state. It is argued that the South is too poor to educate such an individual so as to make him an intelligent producer. I reply that the South is too poor not to educate such an individual.

"Ignorance is many fold more costly to taxpayers than intelligence. Every black youth that is given this training of hand and strength of mind, so that he is able to grasp the full meaning and responsibility of life, so that he can go into some forest and turn the raw material into wagons and buggies, becomes a citizen who is able to add to the wealth of the state and to bear his share of the expenses of educational government. Do you suggest that this cannot be done? I answer that it is being done every day at Tuskegee, and should be duplicated in a hundred places in every Southern state. This I take to be the white man's burden just now—no, no, not his burden, but his privilege, his opportunity, to give the black man sight, to give him strength, skill of hand, light of mind and honesty of heart. Do this, my white friends, and I will paint you a picture that shall represent the future, partly as the outcome of this Industrial Convention, and will represent the land where your race and mine dwell:

"Fourteen slaves brought into the South a few centuries ago, in ignorance, superstition and weakness, are now a free people, multiplied into 8,000,000. They are surrounded, protected, encouraged, educated in hand, heart and head, given the full protection of the law, the highest justice meted out to them through courts and legislative enactment, they are stimulated and not oppressed, made citizens, and not aliens, made to understand by word and act that in proportion as they show themselves worthy to bear responsibilities, the greater opportunities will be given them. I see them loving you, trusting you, adding to the wealth, the intelligence, the renown of each Southern commonwealth. In turn, I see you confiding in them, ennobling them, beckoning them on to the highest success, and we have all been made to appreciate in full that,

'The slave's chain and the master's alike are broken,
  The one curse of the race held both in tether;
They are rising, all are rising,
  The black and white together.'"

The most encouraging thing that happened in connection with this convention was an address delivered by ex-Governor MacCorkle, of West Virginia, in which he took the position that the time had come when the Southern States must face

ADMIRAL EVANS PRESENTING BOOKER T. WASHINGTON TO PRINCE HENRY AT THE WALDORF-ASTORIA.

THOMPKIN'S DINING HALL. ERECTED AT A COST OF $160,000. COMPLETED IN 1910.

the race problem bravely and honestly; that the South could not any longer afford to get rid of the Negro's ballot by questionable methods, and that the Southern States ought to pass a law which would require an educational or property test, or both, for voting, and that this law ought to be made to apply alike to both races honestly and fairly, and that there should be no evasion permitted or attempted.

Governor MacCorkle is a Southern man, a democrat. The words which he spoke on this occasion received the most hearty cheering, and the convention on the next day passed a resolution without a dissenting vote recommending Governor MacCorkle's suggestion in the settlement of the franchise question in the Southern States. The influence of this convention was most beneficial on the minds of the Southern white people, and gave encouragement to the Negro and to his friends throughout the country.

As I write this chapter a conference is being arranged for by the leading white citizens of Montgomery, Ala., which it is intended shall be there during May of each year. The object of this conference is to afford an opportunity for free and generous discussion of the race problem from every point of view. This movement, organized as it has been at the seat of the Confederate government, is most remarkable. It seems fitting that Montgomery should be the place where from year to year the best thought of the nation can assemble and assist in working out our national problem.

In closing this chapter I simply wish to add that I see no reason why the race should not feel encouraged. Every individual or race that has succeeded has done so only by paying the price which success demands. We cannot expect to get something for nothing. We shall continue to prosper in proportion as each individual proves his usefulness in the community, as each individual makes himself such a pillar in property and character that his community will feel that he cannot be spared.

CHAPTER XX.

NATIONAL NEGRO BUSINESS LEAGUE
ORIGIN AND WORK.

After advising carefully with some of the most successful colored men throughout the country, it was deemed by us that there ought to be in the United States some organization that would bring together annually the most substantial and successful colored men and women who are engaged in business and industrial enterprises, for the purpose of consultation and receiving inspiration and encouragement from each other, as well as for the purpose of arranging for the organization of local business leagues that would co-operate with the national organization. Accordingly, the first meeting was called to meet in Boston, in August, 1900. The meeting was in session three days. The following is a copy of the call sent out for the meeting:

"After careful consideration and consultation with prominent colored people throughout the country, it has been decided to organize what will be known as the National Negro Business League.

"The need of an organization that will bring the colored people who are engaged in business together for consultation, and to secure information and inspiration from each other, has long been felt. Out of this national organization it is expected will grow local business leagues that will tend to improve the Negro as a business factor.

"Boston has been selected as the place of meeting, because of its historic importance, its cool summer climate and general favorable condition. It is felt that the rest, recreation and new ideas which business men and women will secure from a trip to Boston will more than repay them for the time and money spent.

"The date of the meeting will be Thursday and Friday, August 23rd and 24th, because it is felt that this is the season when business can be left with least loss. Then, too, nearly all the steamship lines and railroads have reduced their rates to Boston to one fare for the round trip for the entire summer.

"Every individual engaged in business will be entitled to membership, but as far as possible the colored people in all the cities and towns of the country should take steps at once to organize local business leagues, where no such organizations already exist, and should see that these organizations send one or more delegates to represent them.

"It is very important that every line of business that any Negro man or woman is engaged in be represented. This meeting will present a great opportunity for us to show the world what progress we have made in business lines since our freedom.

"This organization is not in opposition to any other now in existence, but is expected to do a distinct work that no other organization now in existence can do as well.

"Another circular, giving further information as to programme and other details of the meeting, will be issued in a few weeks. All persons, whether men or women, interested in the movement, are invited to correspond with

"Yours very truly,
"BOOKER T. WASHINGTON,
"Tuskegee, Alabama, June 15, 1900."

The number and character of the men and women who responded to this call was a surprise and a source of gratification to everyone. Representatives came from two-thirds of the States in the Union, the greater proportion coming from the South. Many of them had been in slavery during a large portion of their lives and had started in a most humble way, and in most cases in poverty, and had struggled up through the greatest disadvantages to the point where they could be classed in the world of commerce. They represented many of the commercial enterprises in which white men are engaged. There were among them bankers, real estate dealers, grocers, dry goods merchants, caterers, manufacturers, contractors, druggists, undertakers, bakers, restaurant keepers, barbers, printers, plumbers, milliners, dressmakers, jewelers, publishers and farmers.

Perhaps the most gratifying feature in connection with the first session of the League was the entire absence of anything even bordering on bickering, greed for office, and "point of order." In fact, during the whole meeting, there was not a single point of order raised. The men and women composing the organization came together with an earnest purpose—that of doing something—something that would permanently benefit themselves and the race; and they would not permit anything to turn them aside from this purpose. While the League did not by any means underestimate the outrages inflicted upon the race, it was firmly of our opinion that one way to eventually end these outrages, would be to help make the Negro such a potent factor in the commercial and industrial enterprises of the community in which he lives that he would demand respect and confidence by reason of his usefulness.

It is not the object of the League to, in any way, place mere national success above the high religious character and thorough mental culture, but to make commercial success a means to the promotion of these ends.

The choice of officers for the League resulted in the following being elected:

Booker T. Washington, President, Tuskegee, Ala.; Giles B. Jackson, Vice President, Richmond, Va.; Mrs. Albreta Moore Smith, Vice President, Chicago, Ill.; Gilbert C. Harris, Treasurer, Boston, Mass.; Edward E. Cooper, Secretary, Washington, D. C.; E. A. Johnson, Compiler, Raleigh, N. C.

EXECUTIVE COMMITTEE.

T. Thomas Fortune, New York, Chairman; T. W. Jones, Chicago, Ill.; Isaiah T. Montgomery, Mound Bayou, Miss.; Booker T. Washington, Tuskegee, Ala.; E. E. Cooper, Washington, D. C.; George E. Jones, Little Rock, Ark.; W. R. Pettiford, Birmingham, Ala.; Gilbert C. Harris, Boston, Mass; Louis F. Baldwin, Boston, Mass.

Another very encouraging phase of the Boston meeting was the surprising number of highly successful men and women who appeared from different parts of the country, and who before had not been heard from. Many expressed the idea that the Business League had been long wanted and had in its power to do a work which no other organization could perform. The following editorials from various influential newspapers will give some of the value that was placed upon the Business League meeting:

From The Outlook, New York City: "The

Convention of the National Negro Business League, held in Boston last week, brought together upwards of a hundred delegates, representing over twenty different states. The members of the convention made an excellent impression upon the representatives of the Boston press, both by their appearance and the intellectual quality of their speeches. The League was organized upon the initiative of Booker T. Washington, and his common-sense philosophy permeated most of the addresses. Had these been made at a gathering of white leaders, they might justly be condemned as materialistic. Indeed, one of them, glorifying the 'almighty dollar' as the 'new king that has been born,' should be so condemned. But in the main the emphasis put upon the acquiring of property sprang from the desire to lift up the manhood of the Negro race; for there is a moral difference between the advocacy of money-getting to secure independence and advocacy of money-getting to secure power. Economic independence is to-day as much needed for the further advancement of the Negro race as was emancipation from slavery for the advance which the present generation has witnessed. Even so uncompromising an opponent of materialism as Mr. William Lloyd Garrison, Jr., recognized this and emphasized it in his address to the convention: 'The particular word I wish to leave with you,' he said, 'is this: Aim to be your own employers as speedily as possible. If you are farmers, do not rest until you control the land from which you gain your living. If you are mechanics, or traders, seek first to gain a home without a mortgage, foregoing many desirable things until you are free from debt. Independence and debt cannot long keep company. But, in the South, as in the North, possession of honestly earned property will surely bring respect and increase personal security.' Among the Negro speakers were several men who have been remarkably successful; among others, a slave of Jefferson Davis who is now mayor of his little town in Mississippi. The speeches of some of these men telling of early struggles were full of encouragement to Negroes everywhere. The fact that some Negroes have succeeded in business, as well as the fact that some have succeeded in literature and art, forces all men to distinguish between Negroes and Negroes, and opens the door of opportunity to all Negroes who aspire."

From Buffalo Express: "The recent meeting of the National Negro Business League in Boston brought to public notice a new line of endeavor advocated by the leading Negroes of the country for the betterment of their race's commercial and social position. The call for the formation of the League was issued by President

Booker T. Washington of the Tuskegee Institute, and that it was heartily responded to by Negro business men in all parts of the country, was shown by the assembling of delegates from no less than twenty-five states. The key to the discussion during this interesting conference is to be found in the address of Prof. Booker T. Washington, who said in part: 'I have faith in the timeliness of this organization. As I have noted the conditions of our people in nearly every part of our country, I have always been encouraged by the fact that almost without exception, whether in the North or South, wherever I have seen a black man who was succeeding in business, who was a tax-payer, and who possessed intelligence and high character, that individual was treated with highest respect by the members of the white race. In proportion as we can multiply those examples North and South will our problem be solved. Let every man strive to become the most useful and indispensable man in his community. A useless, idle class is a menace and a danger. We must not in any part of our country, become discouraged, notwithstanding the way often seems dark and desolate. We must maintain faith in ourselves and in our country.'

"This opens the line of work, the possibilities of which are most promising. The development of industrial life among the Negroes in the South by schools is essential to the growth of one element and is remedying the evil of idleness. The new plan goes farther and aids in developing the business instincts of the race, establishing Negroes in mercantile pursuits and in other ways making them important factors in the commercial circles of the country. Already there are many examples of the progress of the Negro in this direction. In Chicago is a large co-operative store, where groceries and meats are sold, while Philadelphia and Richmond each have a large department store conducted by Negroes. Nearly two hundred Negroes in Chicago alone are engaged in various lines of business. Still another example is found in the corporation of New Jersey of an investment and supply company in which the corporators are Negroes. This company is authorized to furnish supplies to families, establish stores, deal in real estate without limit and engage generally in commercial pursuits. It is stated in the papers that the company will carry on a portion of its business in the cities of New York, Philadelphia, Baltimore, Washington, Chicago, Cincinnati, St. Louis, Wilmington, Del., and Richmond and Norfolk, Va., as well as in other places. The capitalization of this company is $75,000."

From Springfield Republican: "The organization of the National Negro Business League by the great convention at Boston, last week, was one of the most important steps yet taken in the lifting of the Negro race to that equality proclaimed implicitly by the Declaration of Independence and explicitly by the constitutional amendments which followed the war. Between one and two hundred delegates were present; the South that made the civil war for Negro slavery was well represented; New England, New York, Pennsylvania, were now the ruling factors in this congress of men opening a new stage in the progress of the race. They came as Americans,— and who has a better right than the Negro to that title? A few days ago a Southern white said that the Negroes had no country, no birthright —not reflecting that he has been given a country by arbitrament of war, and that his birthright, in a majority of cases, was quite as clearly traceable to white ancestry as his traducer's own. But the Negro race has been compelled to a solidarity which is rare in mixed races; the man or woman so white that no one could guess from his hair or complexion the stain of black blood, perforce casts in his lot with the blackest 'Afro-American'—and be it acknowledged that he does it proudly, for the warmest advocates of the Negro race feeling are these very persons; they rightly feel that the African descent is the more honorable.

"The convention was one of such dignity and

such seriousness, such clear-headed consideration of the situation—views being taken in broader horizons than those of the 'nigger' haters,—as to win respect on all sides. And it will not be strange, indeed, it is to be expected, that the effect all over the country will be of the most valuable sort. It is scarcely possible to underrate or condemn a class of people who have so evinced their equality in what the white man especially prides himself on,—the faculty of concentrated effort, the power of organization. This has been attained by the Negro under the most adverse conditions, as we know; even when he has been most favored he has been scantily helped; he has helped himself; and his small advantages he has made the most of, proving that he has the self-same spirit and purpose that has made America, and is just as much an American and as entitled to the blessings and honors of life, as a descendant of the English Puritan or the French Huguenots, the Hollanders, the Irish, the Scandinavian and the German. And when we reflect upon the motley crowds from southern Europe that have entered our country of late years, the comparison becomes absurd.

"The most interesting address was that of A. I. Hillyer, a graduate of the University of Minnesota, a prominent citizen of the National capital, who has compiled and published three editions of a directory of the 'colored business men and women of Washington,' and founded, and was first president of the 'Union League' so described. Mr. Hillyer was appointed by the United States Commission to make up the figures of the Negro exhibit at the Paris exposition, and thus he spoke with knowledge. By the census of 1890 it appears that, twenty-five years after Emancipation, the race had a representative in every business listed in the census schedules. The numbers engaged and the capital invested in many branches were not imposing, but the beginning had been made. That census showed 20,020 persons of Negro descent in business. There were agents and collectors, auctioneers, bankers and brokers (114), druggists, dairymen, dry-goods dealers, grocers, hotel-keepers, liquor dealers, undertakers, officials of banks and insurance companies, journalists and publishers, builders and contractors, photographers, market-men, printers, blacksmiths, watch and clock-makers and of course, barbers. Outside of the business list over 20,000 are to be numbered: Over 1,700 barbers; next to these in numbers caterers, hotel and restaurant men. Mr. Hillyer noted a stove foundry in Tennessee, a cotton mill in North Carolina, a carriage factory in Ohio, and several brick-making plants with large capital. He mentioned four banks, one in Birmingham, Ala., one in Washington, D. C., and one in Richmond, Va. Nor is it true that the business patronage of these and other institutions is confined to the Negro. Giles B. Jackson of Richmond, who spoke concerning the Negroes as real estate owners in that region, said that when the city of Richmond was unable, because of its poverty, to keep its white schools open, it applied to all of the white banks for money in vain. Then an appeal was made to the colored bank. 'How much do you want?' was asked. The reply was, 'Fifty thousand dollars.' 'You can have a hundred thousand,' said the cashier, and this was the sum loaned. Mr. Jackson also said that one-twentieth of the real estate in Virginia is owned by the colored people. The doings of the convention have been fair, measured by the dispatches we have published. They show an undaunted spirit in the face of all discouragements and a ready hopefulness in their achievements. It was a great project to form this League, and its principal pusher, if not its originator, was Mr. Washington of Tuskegee, the great statesman of the Negro race, and not the less great because he is working without the help of the state, and directly for his people. Not, however, solely for them; for Mr. Washington knows, as all thoughtful men ought to see, that the white races are on their trial in this matter. They have to determine whether barbarism or civilization shall rule. Much for the future of the United States depends upon the wise counsel of Booker T. Washington, who is elevating his race, and also elevating the human family itself. He is fitly chosen the first President of the National Negro Business League."

One of the most interesting articles about the first session of the League was contributed by Mr. Henry J. Barrymore, to the Boston Transcript. It seems quite fairly the conclusion reached by most persons who attended the session of the League:

"New Orleans, New York and Akron on the one hand; the Negro business convention on the other! It is a round-about logic—but nevertheless a good one—that answers race antipathy with commercial success. Mr. J. H. Lewis got close to the root of things when he told that convention that the Negro problem was at bottom a mercantile problem; that the business world knows nothing of color, that human selfishness, the desire of every man to get money, would eventually banish prejudice. The almighty dollar is thoroughly color-blind. Money commands respect. Rare is the merchant or manufacturer who will refuse to shake hands with a hundred thousand dollars.

"'But what hope has the Negro to succeed in business?' said Mr. Lewis. 'If you can make a better article than anybody else, and sell it cheaper than anybody else, you can command the markets of the world. Produce something that somebody else wants, whether it be a shoestring or a savings bank, and the purchaser or patron will not trouble himself to ask who the seller is. This same great economic law runs through every line of industry, whether it be farming, manufacturing, mercantile or professional pursuits. Recognize this fundamental law of trade; add to it tact, good manners, a resolute will, a tireless capacity for work, and you will succeed in business. I have found in my own experience of thirty years in business, that success and its conditions lie all around us, regardless of race or color. I believe that it is possible for any man with the proper stuff in him to make a success in business wherever he may be. The best and only capital necessary to begin with is simply honesty, industry and common sense.' This is good reasoning.

"It is also both practical and practicable. Results prove it. Mr. Booker T. Washington, in his travels through widely separated regions of the United States, found so many Negroes engaged in profitable commercial pursuits that he thought the time had come to put the Negro business men on terms of mutual acquaintanceship and mutual helpfulness. Then, with that rare insight which characterizes the man's really indisputable genius, he conceived a big convention, where the Negro business world should take to itself a voice that must at once impress the white man and encourage the black man. The plan worked as per specification. Newspapers saw space in it—space, and timeliness and vital human interest, with here and there a touch of the sensational. The business Negro is, therefore, getting the public notice he so genuinely deserves. It will do us all good.

"For one, it did me good. I confess I went to the Parker Memorial with ill-stifled chuckles of expectant amusement. My chuckles ceased as I entered, for there was something impressive in the splendid show of bunting, something impressive, too, in the gravity of the colored audience, and something wonderfully earnest about the big banner at the back of the stage. That banner made plain, blunt use of the word Negro. So did the speakers. Racial pride is beginning to assert itself. These men have little to say of the 'colored' people or of the 'Afro-American.' They are outgrowing all that sort of affectation. They do, however, insist that the word Negro shall be written with a capital N. And why should they not? We capitalize the Indian, the Chinaman, the Filipino; shame to withhold so small an honor from the Negro!

ored.' In fact, I began to wonder whether I was white myself.

"The ear was as often deceived as the eye. Had I been blind, I should have said the speakers were white Southerners. With hardly an exception, their grammar was perfect and their pronunciation excellent. I had expected some marvelous Negro malapropisms. I heard none. I came with the writer's usual hunger for 'color,' but nothing could have been more hopelessly devoid of color than the colored congress. Those black men had even to a considerable degree, the common Caucasian foibles; uniformly, when told they had only five minutes left, they consumed four minutes at least in explaining how sorry they were that there remained but five minutes; uniformly, they wasted precious time in introducing their speeches with irrelevant stories; uniformly they put themselves at altogether unnecessary pains to explain that Boston was the grandest city in North America or anywhere else.

"It pleased me to see how brave the Negro could be and how patient. I waited for outbreaks of protest against white oppression, and especially against recent white cruelty. I heard none. No one 'cried baby.' The spirit of the whole occasion was distinctly hopeful. Regarding material advancement as the basis of every other sort of progress, the convention listened eagerly to every account of Negroes, once poor, who had built houses, bought land, opened places of independent business and established solid bank accounts. Repeatedly it was pointed out that men born slaves had actually become rich; also that the total material progress of the Negro race had been accomplished in only thirty-five years—a happy augury for the future! Such utterances called out tumultuous cheers, mingled with the shrill 'rebel yell' of the Southerners. Yet there was scarcely any tendency to indulge in racial self-laudation. More than once the speakers insisted that the commercial superiority of the white man must be frankly recognized and that the Negro must learn to copy the white man's methods. In general, the convention depreciated the Negro's desire to flatter the Negro. 'Far from that, let us look the conditions honestly and courageously in the face. Let us say the things that will help our people, whether those things are pleasant or otherwise.' To be sure, a good many of those beneficial deliverances were sheer platitudes, but the Negro race is in need of platitudes. It is fortunately developing a relish for platitudes. It has reached that stage of moral and intellectual evolution where it has come to realize the vital importance of plain, home-spun, brown-colored truths. It is laying the basis for its social philosophy by making sure of its axioms.

"Supposably, an enormous fund of emotional dynamics was walled in and roofed over at the Negro convention. Nevertheless the convention left the impression of a deliberative council seriously at work. Somebody says the best test of the earnestness and intelligence of an audience is to see how the audience acts when a little interruption occurs. The convention was put to that test. In the midst of Mr. William Lloyd Garrison's stirring address, the fire company, stationed just across the way, responded to an alarm. There was pandemonium in the street below, but not an eye left the speaker. Just once the convention lost complete control of itself. A tall, slender youth had spoken some moments in a vein so modest that the chairman interrupted: 'Gentlemen,' said he, 'the speaker hasn't much to say for himself, so I'm going to put in a word of my own. I can't help it. That man, gentlemen—that man there was in the front of the charge at San Juan!' At that the air seemed suddenly to be composed of equally active parts of handkerchiefs, hats and hilarious cheers. The slender youth bowed acknowledgments and said his speech ought to take a military turn, but that he hesitated to say the thing he had in mind. 'It was not a pleasant thing.'

"'Say it out!' yelled twenty voices.

"So he said it out. He was disappointed in

Theodore Roosevelt. Roosevelt, said he, had slandered the Negro soldier; and there was really no braver soldier in the world. The Negro never flinched, never retreated. 'Why, gentlemen, way back in the old days there was a Negro in the fight. And as for what Col. Roosevelt says about Negro soldiers being dependent upon white officers, I'll tell you the truth. There wasn't any officer in control on San Juan Hill—or rather, every Negro private was a Negro captain!'

"Then I knew what Stephen Crane meant by 'red yells.' But this, as I say, was an isolated instance of rampant emotionalism. The uproar was not repeated. And think what the orderly, decorous, well dressed, educated assemblage represents? Think of the change brought by thirty-five years of Negro progress — slaves, freedmen, laborers, capitalists, reformers, leaders of a struggling race, and all in scarcely more than a generation of time! Think of the millions who are still coming up, the millions who have in them the possibilities of success, the millions whom we must judge by the standards of the business convention, and not by the standards of the criminal courts. The convention, now that it has come and gone, leaves a memory of heroic hopefulness and patience, not unmingled with pathos. It was significant and altogether appropriate, that a Negro singer (on Thursday evening) should have sung the 'Recessional' with its double refrain, 'Lord God of hosts, be with us yet!'"

After considering the matter carefully it was decided to make the League a permanent organization that should meet annually.

The second session was held in Chicago, Illinois, August 21, 22 and 23, 1901, and was even more largely attended than was the first meeting. This meeting was made noteworthy in one respect by the result of the following telegram of congratulation from the late President of the United States:

"CANTON, OHIO, August 22, 1901.
"PRESIDENT BOOKER T. WASHINGTON,
"Convention of the National Negro Business League:

"I have received your recent letter, but regret that I will be unable to accept your kind invitation to attend the meeting of the National Negro Business League, to be held in Chicago this week. Please accept for yourself and those assembled my best wishes for the advancement and prosperity of your race.
"WILLIAM MCKINLEY."

The second meeting was free, as was the first one, from those unseemly and useless parliamentary wrangles which too often mar the character of public meetings among our people. The second meeting was composed, as was the first, of hard-headed, earnest men and women who met for a purpose and were determined that success should crown their efforts.

The following programme will give some idea of the scope and character of the Chicago meeting:

Wednesday, August 21, 10 A. M.

Meeting Called to Order.
Invocation.
Address of Welcome, on behalf of the State,
His Excellency, Governor Richard Yates.
Address of Welcome, on behalf of the City of Chicago,
His Honor, Mayor Carter H. Harrison.
Address of Welcome, on behalf of the Colored Business Men and Women of Chicago, - - - Mr. W. F. Taylor.
The President's Address.
Appointment of Committees,
    (a) Credentials.
    (b) Resolutions and Organization.
The Business League of Virginia,
Giles B. Jackson, Richmond, Va.
Business Features of the Order of True Reformers,
W. L. Taylor, Richmond, Va.
What the Twin-City Business Association is Accomplishing,
J. A. Wilson, Kansas City, Mo.
Can the Negro Succeed as a Business Man?
Theodore W. Jones, Chicago, Ill.

Evening Session, 8 P. M.

The Negro Women's Business Club of Chicago and its Achievements, - - Mrs. Albreta M. Smith, Chicago, Ill.
Merchandising, - - Charles Banks, Clarksdale, Miss.
The Grocery Business, William Oscar Murphy, Atlanta, Ga.
The Hampton Building and Loan Association,
Harris Barrett, Hampton, Va.
Negro Business Enterprises, of Mobile,
A. N. Johnson, Mobile, Ala.

Thursday, August 22, 10 A. M.

The Drug Business, - Dr. Willis S. Sterrs, Decatur, Ala.
Mistakes to be Avoided, - S. R. Scottron, Brooklyn, N. Y.
Merchant Tailoring, - - L. G. Wheeler, Chicago, Ill.
Colored Business Women of the East,
 Mrs. Dora A. Millar, Brooklyn, N. Y.
The Game and Poultry Business,
 Walter P. Hall, Philadelphia, Penn.
Dress-making and Millinery, Mrs. Emma L. Pitts, Macon, Ga.
Representing the Kansas City Coal and Feed Company, and The Wyandotte Drug Company,
 I. F. Bradley, Kansas City, Kan.
NO NIGHT SESSION.—A banquet was tendered the officers and delegates of the National Negro Business League by the citizens of Chicago, Thursday evening, August 22d, at First Regiment Armory, Sixteenth and Michigan Boulevard.

Friday, August 23, 10 A. M.

Carriage Manufacturing, - F. D. Patterson, Greenfield, Ohio.
Real Estate, - - - - J. C. Napier, Nashville, Tenn.
The Negro in Insurance, - W. F. Graham, Richmond, Va.
The Negro as a Silk Operative,
 T. W. Thurston, Fayetteville, N. C.
The Negro Publishing House, - R. H. Boyd, Nashville, Tenn.
Catering, - - - { C. H. Smiley, Chicago, Ill.
 { Jno. S. Trower, Philadelphia, Pa.
Report of Officers.
Report of Committee,
 (a) Resolutions.
 (b) Organization.

Evening Session, 8 P. M.

The Negro as a Manufacturer and Jobber,
 Anthony Overton, Kansas City, Kan.
The Logic of Business Development,
 T. Thomas Fortune, New York, N. Y.
The Founding of a Negro City, { S. L. Davis, Hobson City, Ala.
 { Isaiah T. Montgomery, Mound Bayou, Miss.

The reception tendered the members of the League by the citizens of Chicago at Armory

Hall brought 2,500 of the most intelligent and cultured colored people that it has ever been my privilege to meet in any part of the country. I am sure that no one could have come in contact with those attending the reception and have sat for three days' session of the League without being convinced that the race has made tremendous progress since the days of slavery.

The present officers of the National Negro Business League elected at Chicago, August 23d, are as follows:

President—Booker T. Washington, Tuskegee, Alabama; First Vice-President—Giles B. Jackson, Richmond, Virginia; Second Vice-President—Mrs. D. R. Robinson, St. Louis, Missouri; Third Vice-President—Charles Banks, Clarksdale, Mississippi; Recording Secretary—Edward E. Cooper; Corresponding Secretary—Emmett J. Scott, Tuskegee, Alabama; Treasurer—Gilbert C. Harris, Boston, Massachusetts; Compiler—S. Laing Williams, Chicago, Illinois; Registrar—P. J. Smith, Jr., Boston, Massachusetts; Executive Committee—T. Thomas Fortune, Chairman, New York; Dr. S. B. Courtney, Boston, Mass.; T. W. Jones, Chicago; George E. Jones, Little Rock, Ark.; N. T. Veler, Brinton, Pa.; W. L. Taylor, Richmond, Va.; T. A. Brown, San Francisco, Cal.; J. C. Napier, Nashville, Tenn.; M. M. Lewey, Pensacola, Fla.

CHAPTER XXI.

THE MOVEMENT FOR A PERMANENT ENDOWMENT

Having, through nearly twenty years of incessant toil, succeeded in securing for Tuskegee the annual expenses for running the school and the money with which to purchase its present plant and equipment, valued at about $300,000, it has been for several years clearly seen by the trustees and myself that the thing needed to secure Tuskegee in the future was a permanent endowment fund. Not only is an endowment fund necessary as an assurance that the work of Tuskegee shall go on in the future, but it is necessary in order to relieve the Principal of the hard work of remaining in the North the greater portion of his time begging and speaking in order to raise the amount annually necessary to carry on the work. An endowment fund, the interest from which would be sufficient to meet, partially, the current expenses of the institution, would enable the Principal to devote his time to the executive work of the school, and this would obviously lead to greater perfection in the work there, both in the academic and industrial branches. Improved methods and facilities would redound to the benefit of each person educated at the institution. Various appeals, for the last year or two, have been made to the friends of Tuskegee for an endowment fund, and within the past year we have received by gifts and bequests $38,848.93 for this purpose. The United States Congress, in the winter of 1899, donated to Tuskegee 25,000 acres of land out of the public domain of Alabama, the proceeds of this grant to be added to the endowment fund.

No organized effort, however, was made to interest the friends of Tuskegee in the matter of raising a permanent endowment until the fall of 1899. It was then thought by the trustees and myself that the time was ripe for putting forth specific effort in this direction. Accordingly, it was decided to hold a public meeting in December, 1899, in the city of New York, at which the work of Tuskegee might be set forth by capable speakers, and the good the school was accomplishing, not only among the Negroes of the "black belt" but for the whole country, might be brought forcibly to the ears of the public. This meeting was held in the concert hall of Madison Square Garden, in the City of New York, on the evening of December 4, 1899. I take pleasure in giving a description of this meeting and in mentioning some of its immediate results, because it proved to be a magnificent tribute to the cause for which Tuskegee stands.

Ex-President Grover Cleveland had very kindly consented to be present and to preside at this meeting. The beautiful concert hall, which holds about 2,000 people, was packed that night so that it was difficult to procure even standing room. Many prominent people occupied seats upon the platform and in the boxes. Among the former I might mention Mr. Morris K. Jesup, Mr. Wm. E. Dodge, Mr. Alexander Orr, Mr. Robert C. Ogden, Mr. George Foster Peabody, Rev. Dr. C. H. Parkhurst, Rev. Dr. D. H. Greer, Mr. Charles E. Bigelow, Mr. Arthur Curtiss James, Mr. John A. Stewart, Mr. A. S. Frissell, Mr. George McAneny, Mr. Horace White, Hon. John M. Barrett, Mr. Walter H. Page, Hon. Seth Low, Hon. E. M. Shepard, Hon. Levi P. Morton, Dr. N. M. Butler, Mr. J. G. Phelps Stokes, Mr. John E. Parsons, Hon. Carl Schurz, Rev. P. B. Tompkins, Mr. Samuel P. Avery, Mr. R. F. Cutting, Mr. J. S. Kennedy, Mr. C. P. Huntington, Mr. C. S. Smith, Mr. R. W. Gilder, Chancellor H. K. McCracken, Mr. William G. Low, Mr. W. P. Ware, Prof. Chas. Sprague Smith, Mr. Wm. Jay Schieffelin, Mr. Charles Lanier, Mr. J. Hampden Robb, Mr. Dorman B. Eaton, Mr. Horace E. Deming, Mr. Joseph Lorocque, Mr. J. Kennedy Todd, Mr. LeGrand B. Cannon, Mr. Charles S.

Fairchild, Mr. August Belmont, Mr. Jacob H. Schiff, Mr. Gustav Schwab, Mr. James C. Carter, Mr. John L. Cadwallader, Mr. Cleveland H. Dodge, Rev. Dr. H. Heber Newton, Mr. Edward Hewitt, Dr. Hamilton W. Mabie, Mr. Wheeler H. Peckham, Mr. Everett P. Wheeler, Mr. I. Fredk. Kernochan, Col. Wm. Jay, Mr. Chas. C. Beaman, Rev. Dr. Wm. R. Huntington, Rev. Dr. Morgan Dix, Rev. Dr. Lyman Abbott, Mr. William Dean Howells, Gen. Wager Swayne, Hon. W. L. Strong, Mr. Charles H. Marshall, Mr. Henry Holt, Mr. J. Pierpont Morgan. Among those who occupied boxes were Mr. Robert C. Ogden, Mr. and Mrs. W. E. Dodge, Mrs. C. R. Lowell, Mr. Henry Villard, Mr. C. D. Smith, Miss Putnam, Mr. George Foster Peabody, Mr. and Mrs. John D. Rockefeller, Mrs. Fredk. Billings, Miss Olivia Stokes, Mrs. C. A. Runkle, Miss Matilda W. Bruce, Miss Mary Parsons, Mr. W. H. Baldwin, Jr., Mr. and Mrs. Morris K. Jesup, Mr. and Mrs. Theodore K. Gibbs, Mrs. W. H. Harkness, Mrs. C. B. Hackley, Miss Bryce, Mrs. F. C. Barlow, Mr. and Mrs. A. T. White, Mr. and Mrs. C. M. Pratt, Mr. C. E. Bigelow.

The day before the meeting was to be held Mr. Cleveland found himself confined to his house by illness, and wrote me of his inability to be present. The letter proved to be almost, if not quite, as

GIRLS' OUT OF DOOR WORK—BEE KEEPING, TUSKEGEE INSTITUTE.

DR. WASHINGTON SPEAKING AT NEW IBERIA, LA., ON HIS LAST STATE EDUCATIONAL TOUR.

great an encouragement to the object of the meeting as Mr. Cleveland's presence would have been. The letter was read at the meeting, and I think the reader will not complain if I quote it here. It is as follows:

PRINCETON, N. J., Dec. 3, 1899.

"MY DEAR MR. WASHINGTON:

"My inability to attend the meeting to-morrow evening, in the interest of Tuskegee Institute, is a very great disappointment to me. If my participation could have, in the slightest degree, aided the cause you represent, or in the least encouraged you in your noble efforts, I would have felt that my highest duty was in close company with my greatest personal gratification.

"It has frequently occurred to me that in the present condition of our free Negro population in the South, and the incidents often surrounding them, we cannot absolutely calculate that the future of our nation will always be free from dangers and convulsions, perhaps not less lamentable than those which resulted from the enslaved Negros, less than forty years ago. Then the cause of trouble was the injustice of the enslavement of four millions; but now we have to deal with eight millions, who, though free, and invested with all the rights of citizenship, still constitute, in the body politic, a mass largely affected with ignorance, slothfulness and a resulting lack of appreciation of the obligations of that citizenship.

"I am so certain that these conditions cannot be neglected, and so convinced that the mission marked out by the Tuskegee Institute presents the best hope of their amelioration, and that every consideration makes immediate action important, whether based upon Christian benevolence, a love of country, or selfish material interests, that I am profoundly impressed with the necessity of such prompt aid to your efforts as will best insure their success.

"I cannot believe that your appeal to the good people of our country will be unsuccessful. Such disinterested devotion as you have exhibited, and the results already accomplished by your unselfish work, ought to be sufficient guarantee of the far-reaching and beneficent results that must follow such a manifestation of Christian charity and good citizenship, as would be apparent in a cordial and effective support of your endeavor.

"I need not say how gratified I am to be able to indicate to you that such support is forthcoming. It will be seen by the letters which I enclose, that already an offer has been made through me, by a benevolent lady in a Western city, to contribute twenty-five thousand dollars toward the Endowment Fund, upon condition that other subscriptions to this fund aggregate the amount required. With so good a beginning I cannot believe it possible that there will be a failure in securing the endowment which Tuskegee so much needs.

"Yours very truly,
"GROVER CLEVELAND."
"BOOKER T. WASHINGTON, ESQ."

In the absence of Mr. Cleveland, the Hon. Carl Schurz consented to preside at the meeting; and, as might be expected of one so ripe in experiences, he proved to be all that could be desired of a presiding officer. His short speech on taking the chair showed a hearty sympathy with the work that is being done at Hampton and Tuskegee Mr. Schurz is a well-known German-American, who has been a general in the war of the Rebellion, a Senator in Congress and a member of the Cabinet of President Hayes. He has been for years a foremost worker in the Civil Service Reform movement. He is a writer of ability and a man who needs no introduction in the United States.

The Tuskegee Male Quartette was present and rendered plantation melodies, to the great delight of the audience.

The first speaker of the evening was Mr. Walter H. Page, a native of North Carolina, but for several years the editor of the Atlantic

Monthly, in Boston. The effort of Mr. Page was truly wonderful. He is a native Southerner, who has studied the Negro question for more than twenty years, from every point of view, as he alleged. He was well prepared to speak, and with irresistible logic and unusual eloquence, pointed out the benefits of the Tuskegee plan for the solution of the race problem. He claimed it to be the only solution that had been discovered. He pointed out how hopeless was the condition of the race, unless the problem was solved by industrial and moral training, and how hopeful would be its condition if the problem were settled in this way.

At the conclusion of Mr. Page's address, Mr. William H. Baldwin, Jr., one of our trustees, and a member of the Committee on the Investment of the Endowment Fund, spoke in behalf of the trustees, as follows:

"It is my privilege to speak to you as a trustee of Tuskegee Institute on the subject of its finances. The generous friends who have made Tuskegee possible should know its exact business condition. It has been a hard but beneficial struggle for Mr. Washington to raise the funds necessary to pay the current expenses of the Institution, to acquire the 2,267 acres of land, and to erect the forty-two buildings now comprising the school.

"During the eighteen years of development, there have been imperative demands from time to time for buildings for which no specific funds were available. The rapid growth of the work, the constantly increasing number of students, with applications for admission far beyond the capacity of the buildings, put a burden on the trustees which compelled them in their positions as trustees, to advance some of the unrestricted contributions for the construction of buildings to protect the general welfare of the Institution.

"During this period, enough money has been collected to pay the current expenses, and to accumulate $300,000 in plant and equipment, and an endowment fund of $62,253.39.

"No mortgage has ever been placed upon the property, and the trustees desire to pay any and all indebtedness without mortgaging the property, and without using other resources which should be used for endowment, or for increased plant.

"The grant of 25,000 acres of land from the United States Government in 1897, is valued at a minimum of $100,000, and that land, together with unrestricted legacies to be received, are obviously full security for the advances made by the trustees. But these resources should be kept for permanent uses, and to care for the constantly increasing demands of the School.

"The income for the fiscal year ending May

31, 1899, amounted to $110,161.59. The current expenses for running the Institution were $64,386.70, showing very economical administration for the care of nearly 1,200 people. The balance of income was used in the construction and completion of buildings, and in reducing a part of the indebtedness. The endowment fund received $38,848.93 last year.

"In order that the accounts of the School should be kept on a strictly business basis, the trustees, in 1897, appointed an auditor, a certified public accountant of New York, to direct and supervise all the accounts. The trustees are in position to assure you that any contributions made, are properly and rigidly accounted for; and furthermore, that all expenditures are made with great economy and wise discretion.

"In short, Tuskegee has a good business organization, and warrants the entire confidence of its friends. Its endowment fund will be strictly preserved. Special contributions for buildings or other specific purposes will be kept separate for their particular uses, and the contributions for current expenses will be expended economically and effectively.

"Though the School is still in need of simple buildings for dormitories, classrooms and shops, the trustees determined in 1898 that a point of development had been reached when the Institute should not go into debt for any new buildings, and that in future no buildings should be erected until all the necessary funds are guaranteed for the purpose.

"There are two interests to be served by the upbuilding and strengthening of Tuskegee—the whole Negro race, and the country as a whole. The industrial education of the Negro—the education from the foundation up, as practiced at Tuskegee, is of vast business importance to all of us. The difference between ten million ignorant Blacks and ten million reasonably educated industrial workers, means more than sympathy, more than sentiment, more than our duty—it means wealth to the community.

"There is no longer the old problem of what to do with the Negro. That question has been settled. The problem now is one of co-operation and help and work.

"Booker Washington represents the evolution of this problem. His untiring devotion to the cause of the Blacks, his modesty, integrity, ability, in short, his greatness in dealing with this question, has brought about such a complete change in the understanding of the problem within the last few years that we can hardly repay the debt.

"Can we stand by and see a man who has such power to lead and educate his people, begging from door to door for the funds necessary to carry on his work? Is it not our duty to raise such a fund as will enable him to spend most of his time in the South, where he is needed, and where he can serve his people, and all of us, as no other man can do?

"Now is the time and the opportunity to show our recognition of the wonderful service he has done his people and his country, and to make the opportunity for him to be free to work to the best advantage. He asks an endowment fund of $500,000—a very modest request. Now that the White and the Negro of both the North and the South, and the authorities of the State of Alabama, and the President and Congress of the United States, have all agreed that Tuskegee and Booker Washington show the true way, we feel confident that there will be a quick response to the appeal to place Tuskegee on a firm financial standing.

"The friends of Tuskegee, in the past, have contributed generously to work out a problem. The problem is now solved—and it should be a privilege to us all to aid in this work, with the full knowledge that every dollar expended by Tuskegee will aid the Negro race in the only effective way, and that our whole country will profit by the investment."

At the conclusion of Mr. Baldwin's address I

was introduced to the audience by the presiding officer. In my speech I told the audience, among other things, that the White people North and South, and the Negroes as well, had practically agreed that the methods of Tuskegee and Hampton offered the best solution of the perplexing Negro problem that had been put forth. In other words, that the whole country had agreed upon this solution of so important an economic, political and social problem. It was the duty, therefore, of those who could, to supply the means for an effective solution in this way. I will not burden the reader with extracts from that speech.

After I had concluded, Rev. Dr. W. S. Rainsford, Rector of St. George's Church, New York, made a few extemporaneous remarks which were regarded as a strong appeal in behalf of the purpose of the meeting. I only wish I could lay before the reader the remarks of this gentleman in full. He said, among other things, that Tuskegee was doing a work for humanity—not only for the "Black Belt," but for the whole country. Pointing to me, he said, "It is our duty to do for that man, engaged in that noble work, what we failed to do for General Armstrong. We allowed General Armstrong to go around begging, begging from door to door, to carry on the work at Hampton, until it killed him. It is our duty to save Mr. Washington from an untimely death, brought on in this way. It is our duty to save him for useful service by endowing Tuskegee."

As may be partly gleaned from Mr. Cleveland's letter, the results of this meeting began to be felt immediately.

A few days after the lady in the West, mentioned in Mr. Cleveland's letter, gave notice that she would give us $25,000 on condition that the whole amount sought for was raised, we were very pleasantly surprised to receive her check for the $25,000, she having decided to remove the condition. Counting this $25,000 with the $50,000 given by Mr. Huntington and $10,000 by Mr. John D. Rockefeller, the result of the meeting was $85,000; Mr. Rockefeller's $10,000, however, being given for current expenses. Adding what was received as a result of this meeting to our previous endowment fund, we have now (1901) in the hands of our endowment committee about $290,000 from which the school is receiving interest. This does not, of course, include the value of the unsold 25,000 acres of public land.

CHAPTER XXII.

A DESCRIPTION OF THE WORK OF THE TUSKEGEE INSTITUTE.

The reader has doubtless noted that much space has been occupied in this volume in detailing the history of the Tuskegee Institute, and to the casual reader this may have appeared out of place in an autobiography. When it is borne in mind, however, that the whole of my time, thought and energy, for the past eighteen years, have been devoted to the building up of this Institute, it will be conceded that in any autobiography of mine, a history of the Tuskegee Institute is unavoidable and necessary. When the history of Tuskegee Institute, since its founding until now, shall be completely written, you will have also a history of my life for the same space of time. It shall be my purpose in this chapter, therefore, to give some definite idea of the extent to which the Institute has grown, and also to describe with some degree of accuracy the work that is being accomplished there in its various departments, agricultural, mechanical, domestic science, nurse training, musical, Bible training, and academic.

As has been said many times before, the

school began in 1881 with only the State appropriation of $2,000 per annum, specifically for the payment of teachers' salaries, and for no other purpose. The method by which we have succeeded in securing the 2,500 acres of land which the school now owns has heretofore been described. This land is mainly comprised in two tracts. The tract that forms the site of the Institute is composed of 835 acres, and is known as the "home farm." The other large tract, which is about four miles southeast of the Institute, composed of 800 acres, is known as "Marshall farm."

Upon the home farm are located the fifty-two buildings, counting large and small, which make up the Tuskegee Institute. Of these fifty-two buildings, Alabama, Davidson, Huntington, Cassedy and Science Halls, the Agricultural, Trades and Laundry Buildings, Carnegie Library, Rockefeller Hall, Dorothy Hall and the Chapel are built of brick. There are also two large frame halls—Porter Hall, which was the first building built of the Tuskegee group, and Phelps Hall, a commodious and well appointed structure dedicated to the Bible Training department. The other buildings are smaller frame buildings and various cottages used for commissary, store rooms, recitation rooms, dormitories and teachers' residences. There are also the shop and saw mill, with engine rooms and dynamo in conjunction.

The brickyard, where all the bricks that have been used in building our brick buildings were made, is also situated near the school. Last year alone the brickyard made 1,500,000 bricks. It is equipped with excellent and improved machinery for brickmaking, and is under the immediate supervision of Mr. William Gregory, a graduate of Tuskegee. The total valuation of the property, including the yards and all buildings, the home and the Marshall farms is placed at $300,000. This does not include the endowment fund.

The Agricultural Department of the school has at its head Prof. G. W. Carver, a graduate of the Iowa State University, and a man of experience as a scientific farmer and a scientist of no mean acquirements. He has eight assistants who help in looking after the divisions of dairying, stock-raising, horticulture and truck farming embraced in this department. The State of Alabama appropriates annually the sum of $1,500 for the maintenance of an agricultural experiment station in connection with our agricultural department. Some of the experiments of Prof. Carver have attracted much attention, and it is recognized that his conduct of the station is doing much to show what improvements upon the old methods of farming may be wrought by scientific agriculture. This department is well housed in a beautiful brick building, containing a well equipped chemical laboratory, erected at a cost of $10,000, adapted to the purposes of agricultural experiment, and other apparatus necessary for the dairy and other divisions.

It is through the direction of the Agricultural department that the vast amount of farm and garden products, used by the 1,200 people constituting the population of the school when in session, is grown. About 135 acres of the home farm are devoted to the raising of vegetables, strawberries, grapes, and other fruits. The Marshall farm, with 350 acres in cultivation, is utilized for the growing of corn, sugar cane (from which syrup is made), potatoes, grain, hay and other farm products.

Mr. J. N. Calloway is the manager of the Marshall farm. It is worked by student labor, from thirty to forty-five boys being employed on it constantly. There is also a night school upon this farm, for the accommodation of students who work there, which is a branch of the main night school at the Institute. At present the farm night school requires the services of two teachers.

The Marshall farm not only produces a large amount of the farm products that are used by the school and its 800 head of live stock, counting horses, mules, cows, oxen, sheep and hogs, but also furnishes opportunity for students to learn the art and science of farming, at the same time attending night school and making something above expenses to be used when the student enters day school.

A large portion of the Marshall farm, about 400 acres, is utilized as pasture for the dry cows and beef cattle. Everything grown upon the farm is sold to the school at market prices. The expenses of running the farm are also accurately kept. At the end of the year a balance is struck. Last year the Marshall farm come out over $500 ahead, including in the expense account the salary of the manager.

The mechanical department of the institution is now housed in the well equipped trades building, recently completed at a cost of $36,000. This is known as the Slater-Armstrong Memorial Trades Building. It was dedicated and formally opened on Wednesday, January 10, 1900, and is the largest building on the Tuskegee Institute grounds. It stands between the Agricultural Building and the new chapel. The shape is that of a double Greek cross, having an open court 85x112 feet in the center. When completed, it will measure 283x300 feet, the main or central portion being two stories high, the wings one story. This measurement does not include a room for the sawmill, which is to come at the extreme rear end. Owing to the fact that sufficient money has not yet been obtained, the rear portion of the building, consisting of seven rooms, has not been completed. It is built entirely of brick, and contains twenty-seven rooms. In round numbers, it took ten hundred thousand bricks to construct the building thus far, and every one of these bricks was made by students under the instructor in brickmaking, and laid in the wall by students under the instructor of bricklaying. The plans and specifications of the building were drawn by Mr. R. R. Taylor, formerly in charge of the architectural and mechanical drawing department of the Institute. The general oversight of both the planning and construction was, of course, exercised by Mr. J. H. Washington, Director of Industries.

The interior arrangements of the building are well suited to the teaching of the trades. The rooms, while varying in size from 37x42, the smallest, to 37x85, the largest, will average 37x55, the ceiling being 13 feet high. On the first floor there are the director's office, reading room, exhibit room, wheelwright shop, blacksmith shop, tin shop, printing office, carpenter shop, repair shop, woodworking machine room, ironworking machine room, foundry, brickmaking and plastering rooms, general stock and supply room, and a boiler and engine room. The second floor contains the mechanical drawing room, harness shop.

one or two days of each week are devoted to hospital work. There are special provisions for those who apply for this department only. The school is open also to those who do not wish to follow the work as a profession, but desire to know how to intelligently care for the sick.

The division of music is under the supervision of the Director of the Academic Department, and like the nurse training department it has not been constituted an independent department. While the study of music has always been encouraged at Tuskegee, and considerable work has been done, we have been able only within the last few years to furnish a systematic and thorough course of study. The course in pianoforte embraces four years. The institution owns eight pianos, two cabinet organs and a library of music. Vocal music is taught to the classes in the academic department throughout the entire course.

Tuskegee students are famous for their fine singing of plantation melodies, and it is the object of the Institute to make these old, sweet, slave songs a source of pride and pleasure to the students.

There are at Tuskegee the following musical organizations: A choir, consisting of seventy-five voices; a choral society, consisting of one hundred and fifty voices, organized for the study of music from the masters; glee club, consisting of forty male voices; glee club, consisting of twenty female voices; and a male quartette, whose work is to travel in the North. The institution maintains an excellent brass band of thirty pieces, which is instructed by a competent director, employed by the school. Any student possessing knowledge of wind instruments, will be given a chance to enter the band; but this knowledge is not essential to membership. The band plays every school day morning for inspection and drill.

One of the most important branches of the Music Department is the orchestra, which consists of fourteen pieces. The same rule regarding membership in the band holds good for the orchestra. The orchestra plays every week night at evening devotions. Many students who have played in the orchestra have developed into competent musicians. The director of the band has charge of the orchestra. All students belonging to the orchestra are subject to certain rules governing this organization.

The Bible Training Department was established in 1893. The desire for increased opportunities for those who wish to fit themselves for the ministry, or other forms of Christian work in the South, had been long felt. To meet this need, a generous lady in New York erected at Tuskegee a building called Phelps Hall, a picture of which is herewith given, containing a chapel, library, reading room, office, three recitation rooms and forty sleeping rooms, to be used as a Bible School. The donor of this building furnished each room in a comfortable and convenient manner, making it one of the most beautiful and desirable buildings on the school grounds. The instruction is wholly undenominational. It is the aim of this new department to help all denominations, and not to antagonize any. The Bible School is not in opposition to any other theological work now being done, but it is simply a means of helping. The faculty is composed of some of the strongest men in the country. Rev. Edgar J. Penney is in charge of the work, assisted by Rev. B. H. Peterson. Rt. Rev. B. T. Tanner, Rev. C. O. Boothe, D. D., and Rt. Rev. George W. Clinton have been engaged to give a regular course of lectures during each term.

The members of the Bible School are required to do mission work on the Sabbath in the neighboring churches—preaching and teaching in the Sunday Schools whenever their services are needed—and to make weekly reports in writing of the work done.

It is not necessary to have a special call to the ministry to enter the Bible School at Tuskegee. Many who desire to do only missionary work or to become intelligent teachers of the Bible in the

Sunday Schools, will be greatly benefited and helped; indeed, quite a few of those who are now members of this department are fitting themselves for this kind of work.

The demand for an educated ministry is growing throughout the South, and those who expect to preach must prepare themselves for the work.

This department was established for the express purpose of giving colored men and women a knowledge of the English Bible; implanting in their hearts a noble ambition to go out into the dark and benighted districts of the South and give their lives for the elevation and Christianizing of the South. Last year eighty-three students attended this department. This was the largest attendance since the department was founded.

Last, but not least, I mention the Academic Department, which offers a thorough course of instruction, nearly, if not quite, equal to the high school courses of the Northern and Western States. No language, however, except English, is taught. It is our aim to correlate the work of the Academic Department with the Industrial Departments, and it is the policy of the school not to give any student a diploma of graduation who has not completed the course in at least one division of one or another of the industrial departments.

Last year, of the 1,164 students who attended the Institute, except a part of those in the Bible Training School, all were taking studies in this department, either in the night or day school, they being about equally divided between the night and the day school.

The night school course is so arranged that a student is enabled to do just half the amount of work in night school as in day school. A student in night school will therefore cover a year's work, as laid out for day school students, in two years.

In 1899 there were seventy-seven graduates from all of the departments.

We received twenty thousand dollars from Mr. Andrew Carnegie for a new library building. Our first library and reading-room were in a corner of a shanty, occupying a space of about five by twelve feet. It was ten years from my first effort before I was able to secure Mr. Carnegie's interest and help. The first time I saw him, ten years before, he seemed to take but little interest in our school, but I was determined to show him that we were worthy of his help. The following letter will explain itself:

December 15, 1900.

MR. ANDREW CARNEGIE,
5 W. Fifty-first Street, New York.

DEAR SIR: Complying with the request which you made of me when I saw you at your residence a few days ago, I now submit in writing an appeal for a library building for our institution.

We have 1,100 students, 86 officers and instructors, together with their families, and about 200 colored people living near the school, all of whom would make use of the library building.

We have over 12,000 books, periodicals, etc., gifts from our friends, but we have no suitable place for them, and we have no suitable reading-room.

Our graduates go to work in every section of the South, and whatever knowledge might be obtained in the library would serve to assist in the elevation of the Negro race.

Such a building as we need could be erected for about $20,000. All of the work for the building, such as brickmaking, brick masonry, carpentry, blacksmithing, etc., would be done by the students. The money which you would give would not only supply the building, but the erection of the building would give a large number of students an opportunity to learn the building trades, and the students would use the money paid to them to keep themselves in school. I do not believe that a similar amount of money often could be made to go so far in uplifting a whole race.

If you wish further information, I shall be glad to furnish it. Yours truly,

BOOKER T. WASHINGTON, Principal.

The next mail brought the following reply: "I will be very glad to pay the bills for the library building as they are incurred, to the extent of twenty thousand dollars, and I am glad of the opportunity to show the interest I have in your noble work."

As illustrating the value of the work which we are doing at Tuskegee, I am glad to add that I was agreeably surprised during the summer of 1900 to receive a letter from the German Consul at Washington, asking me to meet him for a conference. In the conference it developed that his government had heard of the value of the agricultural work being done at Tuskegee, and that he was commissioned by the Committee of Agriculture of the German Government to secure four persons from Tuskegee to go to Africa to introduce cotton raising into the German colony of Togo. After considering the matter in all its details, Messrs. John W. Robinson, Allen L. Burks, Shepard L. Harris as graduates of the institution were selected, and with them Mr. J. N. Calloway, who for a number of years, had been in charge of one of the school farms, went to serve as superintendent and executive manager of the enterprise. This experiment is being watched with the greatest interest throughout this country. Germany has an African dominion amounting to 925,000 square miles, which is a third larger than the total area of the American cotton producing states. It has been found that this territory is fertile, fairly well watered, and not too hot for cotton. Togo, in which the experiment is being tried, is north of the Gulf of Guinea and four hundred miles north of the Equator. It is a little larger than South Carolina and has an estimated Negro population of two and one-half millions.

The party sailed from New York, November 3, 1900, carrying with them plows, hoes, cotton gin and press, ties and several varieties of cotton seed.

The German government has enjoined secrecy upon those interested in the experiment and so no detailed information can be published aside from the fact that the experiment is succeeding admirably.

Messrs. Robinson and Burks are graduates of the academic and agricultural departments of the school; Mr. Harris is a graduate of the academic and mechanical departments. The latter has charge of the matter of building gin houses and such other structures as may be needed.

It is true that the action is experimental, but those engaged in it are most hopeful. The young men under the careful guidance of Mr. Calloway are perhaps the pioneers in a movement which may mean much in the economic history of the world. The German government in committing this experiment to the hands of graduates of Tuskegee has shown a breadth of view which is appreciated. If any people can make a success in cotton raising in West Africa, we believe that the graduates sent out from Tuskegee will do it.

I cannot close this chapter without making some special reference to the chapel at Tuskegee, since this is regarded as the architectural gem of the Tuskegee group of buildings. It was planned by Mr. R. R. Taylor, who was then our teacher in architecture and mechanical drawing. The work of construction, even to the making of the bricks, was done wholly by students. The cost of erection of the building was valued at $30,000.

The following is a description of the building, a cut of which is also given in this volume: The plan of the chapel is that of a Greek cross, the main axis extending from northeast to southwest. The extreme dimension from northeast to southwest, extending through nave and choir, is one hundred and fifty-four feet six inches. The dimension from northwest to southeast, through transepts, is one hundred and six feet. The roof is of the hammer beam construction. The clear span of the main trusses is sixty-three feet, which is the width of the nave and transept. The angle trusses have a clear span of eighty-seven feet, projections from the walls under trusses slightly decreasing the span. The gallery on back is thirty feet wide, extending over girls' cloak room and twelve feet into main auditorium.

In the rear are choir room, study for minister, and two small vestibules, one on either side of chapel, giving entrance to choir room, study and main auditorium. A large basement is provided, and in this the steam heating plant is located. At the northeast end of the auditorium is the pulpit platform, which is large enough to seat the entire faculty of eighty-eight members. This platform is two feet six inches above the main floor. Immediately behind this and elevated three feet above it, is the choir stand, with seating capacity for one hundred and fifty persons. The chapel is sufficiently supplied with windows to give abundant light and ventilation, a very pretty effect being secured by the use of delicately tinted colored glass.

The woodwork is all of yellow pine with hard oil finish, except the floor, which is of oak. The seating capacity of the auditorium is 2,400. One million two hundred thousand bricks were used in the construction, all made and laid by students. All the mouldings, casings and caps used were made by students. The floor is bowled. The height of the walls from top of floor is twenty-four feet six inches; from floor line to highest point of ceiling, forty-eight feet six inches. The height of tower from line of ground to top of cross which terminates it, is one hundred and five feet. The electric lighting is from three main chandeliers, with thirty lights each, ten of two lights each, twelve of one light each, and from a reflecting disc of forty lights over the choir stand.

Gradually, by patience and hard work, we have brought order out of chaos, just as will be true of any problem if we stick to it with patience and wisdom and earnest effort.

As I look back now over our struggle, I am glad that we had it. I am glad that we endured all those discomforts and inconveniences. I am glad that our students had to dig out the place for their kitchen and dining-room. I am glad that our first boarding place was in that dismal, ill-lighted, and damp basement. Had we started in a fine, attractive, convenient room, I fear we would have "lost our heads" and become "stuck up." It means a great deal, I think, to build on a foundation which one has made for himself.

When our students return to Tuskegee now, as they often do, and go into our large, beautiful, well ventilated, and well lighted dining-room, and see tempting, well-cooked food—largely grown by the students themselves—and see tables, neat tablecloths and napkins, and vases of flowers upon the tables, and hear singing birds, and note that each meal is served exactly upon the minute, with no disorder and with almost no complaint coming from the hundreds that now fill our dining-room, they, too, often say to me that they are glad that we started as we did, and built ourselves up, year by year, by a slow and natural process of growth.

The school is regularly incorporated under the name of "The Tuskegee Normal and Industrial Institute." The charter was granted by special act of the Legislature of Alabama. It provides for a board of nineteen trustees. As now constituted (October, 1901), their names are:

George W. Campbell, President, Tuskegee, Ala.; Rev. G. L. Chaney, Vice-President, Leominster, Mass.; Rev. R. C. Bedford, Secretary, Beloit, Wis.; Warren Logan, Treasurer, Tuskegee, Ala.; Lewis Adams, Tuskegee, Ala.; Charles W. Hare, Tuskegee, Ala.; Booker T. Washington, Tuskegee, Ala.; George Foster Peabody, New York; Robert C. Ogden, New York; John C. Grant, LL. D., Chicago, Ill.; J. W. Adams, Montgomery, Ala.; Rev. George A. Gordon, D. D., Boston, Mass.; Rev. Charles F. Dole, Boston, Mass.; J. G. Phelps Stokes, New York; S. C. Dizer, Boston, Mass.; Wm. H. Baldwin, Jr., New York; R. O. Simpson, Furman, Ala.; Hugh H. Hanna, Indianapolis, Ind.

Mr. Campbell has been president of the board from the beginning and, in the twenty years of its history, has never missed a meeting.

CHAPTER XXIII.
LOOKING BACKWARD.

My work at Tuskegee has always been of a three fold nature. First, the executive work of the institution proper; second, the securing of money with which to carry on the institution; and, third, the education through the public press and through public addresses of the white people North and South as to the condition and needs of the race. On the grounds, in addition to the ordinary task involved in educating and disoiplining over a thousand students, is added the responsibility of training them in parental directions, involving systematic regulations for bathing, eating, sleeping, the use of the tooth brush and care of health. In performing these duties, especially in collecting money in the early years, I have often met with many discouragements, but I early resolved to let nothing cause me to despair completely.

The first time I went North to secure money for the Tuskegee Institute, I remember that on my way I called to see one of the secretaries of an organization which for years had been deeply interested in the education of our people in the

South. I supposed, of course, that I should receive a most cordial and encouraging reception at his hands. To my surprise he received me most coldly and proceeded to tell me in the most discouraging tones possible that I had made a mistake by coming North to secure aid for our school, and he advised me to take the first train South. He said that I could not possibly succeed in securing any funds for Tuskegee. In fact, he told me very frankly that I would not secure enough money to pay my traveling expenses. I confess that this bucket of cold water thrown upon me at a time when I needed encouraging and sympathetic words more than anything else, rather tended to take the heart out of me, but I determined not to give up, but to keep pressing forward, until I had thoroughly demonstrated whether or not it was possible for me to secure funds in the North. I will not prolong this story except to say that within a period of four years after I was so coldly received by this secretary, he introduced me where I was to speak at a large public meeting in New York City in the interest of Tuskegee; and, in introducing me to the large audience, he used the most flattering language and praised me without stint for the successful work that I was engaged in doing. I do not know whether he remembered, while he

CROWD LISTENING TO DR. WASHINGTON'S ADDRESS, BATON ROUGE, LA.

NEW RESIDENCE OF PRINCIPAL BOOKER T. WASHINGTON.

was introducing me, that I was the young man he had discouraged only four years before.

I shall never forget my first experience in speaking before a Northern audience. Before I went North Gen. Armstrong had talked to me a good deal about what to say and how to say it. I shall always remember one of his injunctions, which was, "Give them an idea for every word." When I first went into the North to get money I began work in one or two of the small towns in the Western part of Massachusetts. As I remember it, the first town that I reached was Northampton. As I expected to remain in the town several days, my first effort was to find a colored family with whom I could board, but as very few colored families lived in that town I found this not an easy job. It did not once occur to me that I could find accommodation at any of the hotels in Northampton.

As an indication of Gen. Armstrong's deep interest and helpful influence in the establishment and progress of this institution, I insert a letter of recommendation he gave me to be used among people in the North. These letters were always given most freely, and the General was constantly in search of opportunities to serve the school:

"HAMPTON, VA., Oct. 26, 1891.

"This is to introduce Mr. Booker T. Washington, the head of the Tuskegee, Alabama, Colored Normal and Industrial School.

"It is a noble, notable work; the best product of Negro enterprise of the century. I make this statement advisedly. I beg a hearing for Mr. Washington, he is a true 'Moses.'

"As much as any man in the land, he is securing to the whole country the moral results which the Civil War meant to produce.

"Tuskegee is the bright spot in the Black Belt of the South. It is a proof that the Negro can raise the Negro.

"S. C. ARMSTRONG."

On the day before Gen. Armstrong was stricken with the paralysis which finally resulted in his death, I remember that I met him on Beacon Street, in Boston, and told him that some ladies in New York were discussing the matter of giving us a new building, but seemed somewhat undecided as to the wisdom of doing so. I was talking to the General about interceding in order to get these friends to decide to furnish the building. He seemed greatly interested in the matter and promised to either see or communicate with these New York ladies. Before we finished our conversation, however, we were interrupted by some one and we did not finish the talk about the building. The next day Gen. Armstrong was stricken with paralysis, and no one was permitted to see him for several days. After several days had passed by, the doctors seemed to be convinced that he could not live but for a few hours, and I, in company with several other persons, was allowed to see him in his room at the Parker House. To my surprise, the minute I entered the room, he took up the thread of our conversation concerning the building where it was broken off several days previously on Beacon Street, and began at once advising how to secure the building. The General did not recover from this stroke of paralysis, but lived about eight months after it. In January, 1893, that is, about four months before he died, he came to Tuskegee, or rather was brought to Tuskegee, because he was too weak to travel alone, and remained a guest at my home for three weeks. During these weeks he suffered intensely at times, but was always in good spirits and cheerful. His heart was so wrapped up in the elevation of the Negro that it seemed impossible to induce him to take any rest. Most of the time when he was not asleep he was planning or advising concerning the interest of the black man, and spent much time in writing articles for newspapers and to friends in the North. He was present during the session of our Negro Conference in February, 1893, and it was a memorable sight to see him carried by the strong arms of four students up the stairs of the chapel, and into the presence of the Conference. The impression that the sight of Gen. Armstrong made upon the members of the Conference is almost indescribable. All felt as though he was their most strong and helpful friend, and they had a confidence in him that they had in no other being on earth. It was at this Conference that Gen. Armstromg made his first attempt to speak in public after he was stricken with paralysis, and his success in being heard and understood was so encouraging that he spoke to audiences on several other occasions.

I must not neglect to mention the manner in which Gen. Armstrong and Mr. Howe, the farm manager at Hampton, were received at the school on the occasion of this visit, for this was the second visit that the General had made to the school. Both students and teachers were most anxious to do him all the honor possible, and for several weeks previous to his coming we were quite busily engaged in devising some plan to receive the General in a proper manner. At last it was decided to ask the authorities of the Tuskegee Railroad to run a special train from Tuskegee to Chehaw to meet the General. This request the railroad authorities very kindly granted. He arrived upon the school grounds at about nine o'clock at night. Each student and teacher had supplied himself with a long piece of light wood, or "litted," as the colored people are in the habit of calling it. A long line was formed, and when he came upon the school grounds, the General was driven between two rows of students, each one holding one of these lighted torches. The effect was most interesting and gratifying. I think I never saw anything done for the General which seemed to make him so happy and give him such satisfaction as this reception.

The first public address that I delivered in the North was in Chicopee, a town not far from Springfield. I spoke in the Congregational Church in the morning, but was careful to commit my entire address to memory. I was a little embarrassed after the morning meeting was over when several of the members of the congregation, in congratulating me over my success, stated that they had enjoyed my morning address so much that they had planned to go to Chicopee Falls, an adjoining town, to hear me speak in the evening. As I had only the one address to deliver one can easily see that I was in rather an embarrassing position.

While the greater portion of my speaking has been before Northern white audiences, I also improved every opportunity to speak to my own people, both in the North and in the South. In fact, during the earlier years of the institution I carried on a regular campaign of speaking among the colored people in the South, going to their churches, Sunday-schools, associations, institutes, camp-meetings, conferences, etc. They did not, as I have stated, take kindly to the idea of industrial education at first, and it was largely by reason of my efforts in these public meetings that I succeeded in converting them to the idea of favoring it. At one time I hired a team and took one of the older students with me, and we drove for many miles, stopping at the homes of individuals and at churches to explain to them the work of the school.

The first opportunity I had to speak to a Southern white audience was on the occasion of the gathering of the Christian Worker's Convention, which was held in Atlanta, in 1893. It seems that it was largely because of the impression that I made upon this audience in Atlanta that the authorities of the Atlanta Exposition were led to extend me an invitation to deliver an address at the opening of that exposition. I shall let an account given in the Christian World, published in New Haven, Conn., take the place of my own words in regard to this address before the Christian Worker's Convention:

"Booker T. Washington, principal of the

Tuskegee, Ala., Normal and Industrial Institute, was given a place on the program at the Convention of Christian Workers held at Atlanta, Ga., in 1893, for a five minutes report of progress, the time being thus brief on account of the fact that a full report with questions and answers covering three-quarters of an hour had been given at the Convention the year previous, held in Tremont Temple, Boston. When he made the engagement he doubtless expected to be either at Tuskegee, which is not far from Atlanta, or spending the Convention days with other Christian Workers in Atlanta. It came about, however, that he found it necessary to make engagements in the North immediately before and after the date on which he was announced to speak at Atlanta. To keep his Atlanta engagement it was necessary that he should leave Boston for that city, reaching there on the last train arriving before he was announced to speak, and to return North on the first train leaving Atlanta after his brief address. It was a great sacrifice for a five minutes' address. Mr. Washington said simply that it was his duty to keep his appointment. It does not appear that the fact that he would be compelled to travel about five hundred miles for every minute of his address, had much weight or even consideration. To do his duty was not small or unimportant. The results of this address were great, great beyond all human thought. Mr. Washington has since stated that he had never before made an address to the white people of the South. His audience of over 2,000 leading Christian people, ministers, business men, legislators, law makers, judges, officials, representatives of the press, from Atlanta, from Georgia and from other states of the South, were charmed by his personality and the passionate earnestness with which he set forth the magnificent scheme of Christian effort at Tuskegee, and pleaded for the upbuilding of his race under Southern skies. This representative audience saw before them a representative of his race such as they had not been wont to see. His address was flashed over the wires by sympathetic press agents through the South, and he probably never before spoke to a larger and more influential audience. But in the providence of God there were still greater results."

I have always made it a rule to keep engagements of a public nature when I have once made a promise to do so. On one occasion I had an appointment to speak in a small country church not far from Boston. Just before night a severe snow storm came up, and although I knew this storm would keep every one from the meeting, I made it a point to be present. When I got to the church there was no one present except the sexton. The minister himself did not come, and when I saw him later he was surprised to find that I had been at the church on the night appointed, and told me he felt sure I would not be present on account of the storm.

In the earlier days of the institution, of course, it was a difficult task to secure interviews with persons of prominence and wealth in the North, but Gen. Armstrong's recommendations, which he was always willing to give, in most cases served to secure me a hearing. It was equally difficult in our early history to secure opportunities from ministers and others to speak before their congregations. Such calls on ministers were, of course, very numerous, and one can hardly blame them for shutting out those with whom they were not well acquainted. I have often been surprised to note the number of irresponsible and unworthy colored men and women who spend their time in the North attempting to secure money for institutions that in many cases have no existence; or when they exist at all, are in such a feeble and unorganized condition as in no way to have a claim upon the generosity of the public. Many of these schools, of course, within a radius of a mile or two, do reasonably good work, but I am quite sure the time has come when the North should confine its gifts wholly to the larger and well organized institutions which are able to train teachers or industrial leaders who will go out and show these local communities how to build up schools for themselves. Three or four hundred dollars given to one local community may serve to help it for a time, but there are a hundred thousand other communities that need help just as much; scattering a few hundred dollars here and there among local communities amounts to little in putting the people upon their feet, but putting it into a teacher who will show the community how to help itself means much in the way of the solution of our problem.

The constant work of appealing to individuals, speaking before churches, Sunday-schools, etc., gradually served to make the institution known in most parts of the country. This was true to such an extent that in 1883 we received our first legacy of $500 through the will of Mr. Frederick Marquand of Southport, Conn. This was a most pleasant and gratifying surprise to us, as we had no thought of any one's remembering us in this way. Since then, however, hardly a year has passed that we have not been remembered by a legacy. The largest sum that we have received in this manner has been $30,000 through the will of Mr. Edward Austin, of Boston. Mr. Austin's case is another one which shows, as I have already mentioned, that one should try to cultivate the habit of doing his duty to the full extent each day and not worry over results.

I remember that the first time I saw Mr. Austin was about the year 1885 when the late Dr. W. I. Bowditch, of Boston, gave me a letter to him. At that time Mr. Austin gave me his check for $50, but gave nothing between 1885 and 1896 and seemed to take little interest in the school, in fact I had supposed that he had forgotten all about us. I tried on several occasions to get another audience with him but did not succeed. In 1896, while in Boston, I was very much surprised to receive an invitation from Mr. Austin to call at his home. He was then very feeble, being over ninety years of age, but he told me that he had remembered us in his will, and that as it would not be possible for him to live much longer, we would likely come into possession of the money within a reasonably short time, which proved to be true.

On another occasion, I walked a long distance out into the country during a cold winter day, to see a gentleman who lived near Stamford, Conn. More than once, I was rather inclined to blame myself for exposing my body to the cold on what might prove a fruitless journey. When I arrived at the gentleman's house rather late in the evening, he gave me, after considerable hesitation, a small check, but did not seem to take a great deal of interest in the school. The following year, however, I succeeded in obtaining from him a check for a somewhat larger amount. His interest, however, continued to grow from year to year, so that in 1891 he surprised us all by sending a check for $10,000. Up to that time this was the largest single gift in cash that the institution had ever received, and my readers can well imagine that the receipt of this large sum caused a day of general rejoicing on the grounds at Tuskegee.

I have referred already to the gift of $400 from a friend who helped us when we were in an embarrassing position. I might add that the following year this same friend sent us a check for $3,000, and since that time she and her sister have given regularly to us $3,000 each year. These two friends have done as much, if not more, to keep the institution on a firm footing than any one else that I know of.

I have had, in my eighteen years of experience in collecting money for the Tuskegee Institute, some very interesting episodes. On the whole, collecting money is hard, disagreeable, wearing work, but there are some compensations that come from it. In the first place, it brings one into contact with some of the best people in the world, as well as some of the meanest and most narrow ones. Very often, when I have been in the North seeking money, I have found myself completely without cash. I remember one time while in Providence, R. I., that when I had spent all the money I had and was still without breakfast, when, in crossing the streets, I found twenty-five cents near the sidewalk. With this I bought my breakfast, and with the added strength and courage which that breakfast gave me, I went in quest of donations for Tuskegee, and was soon rewarded by several large gifts.

As an example of the way in which I have used my time from year to year, there have been many occasions when I have slept in three different beds in one night, while traveling through different portions of the country. I give here a portion of a schedule which I followed on a recent lecture tour in the West. This will enable my readers to judge whether or not to speak from night to night is the easy job that many people take it to be:

I spoke at Mt. Vernon, Iowa, January 19, 1900, 8 P. M., then took the 11 o'clock train for Cedar Rapids, where I arrived in about twenty-five minutes. Laid over in Cedar Rapids until 3:15 o'clock, A. M., then took the Burlington, Cedar Rapids & Northern railway for Columbus Junction, where I arrived about 5 o'clock in the morning, remaining in Columbus Junction until about 8 o'clock, when I took the Chicago, Rock Island & Pacific railway for Centerville,

Iowa, where I arrived at 12:47, January 20, much fatigued and worn out from the long journey over three different railroads. At 8 o'clock I again spoke, and at 12:18 A. M. again took the train for Chicago, where I was billed to speak twice the same day, and on the following morning I took the train for a long journey westward, finally ending in Denver, and in returning stopped off at Omaha and other places.

During 1892 I was asked by Rev. Lyman Abbott, D. D., editor of the Outlook, to write an article for his paper which would let the country know the exact condition and needs of the Negro ministry in the South. In this article I told as fully and frankly as I could, just what the condition of the ministry was mentally, morally and religiously. A very large proportion of the colored ministers throughout the country became greatly incensed at what I said, feeling that I had injured the Negro ministry very materially by my plain language. For almost a year after this article was written scarcely a Negro conference or association assembled in any part of the country that did not proceed to pass resolutions condemning me and the article which I had written. This went on for some time, but I was determined not to in any way yield the position which I had taken, for the reason that I knew that I was right, and had spoken the truth. At the time when the discussion and condemnation of myself were at the highest pitch, the late Bishop D. A. Payne, of the A. M. E. Church, wrote a letter endorsing all the statements which I had made, and adding on his own account that I had not told the whole truth. This of course added fresh fuel to the flames and the Bishop for several months came in for his share of the condemnation.

At the present time, after the lapse of eight years, I feel that the institution at Tuskegee and myself personally have no warmer friends than we have in the Negro ministers. Almost without exception at the present time they acknowledge that the article which I wrote has done the whole body of ministers a great deal of good; that bishops and other church officers were made to realize the importance of not only purifying the ministry as far as possible, but demanding a higher standard in the pulpit, so far as mental education was concerned. I scarcely ever go anywhere without receiving the thanks of ministers for my plain talk. They feel that they are greatly indebted to me for much of the improvement that has taken place within recent years. Of course when it is considered that at the time I wrote this article a very small proportion of the colored ministers had had an opportunity to secure systematic training that would give them mental strength, and moral and religious stamina, it could not have been expected that any large proportion would have been fitted in the highest degree for the office of ministers. The improvement at the present time is constantly going on, and within a few years I believe that the Negro church is going to be quite a different thing from what it has had the reputation of being in the past.

At all times, during the discussion and condemnation of myself, there were not wanting strong and prominent persons in different parts of the country among our own race who stood valiantly and bravely by the position which I had taken. Among them, as leader, was Mr. T. Thomas Fortune, the editor of the New York Age. Mr. Fortune in this matter, as in all other matters where he has considered my position the correct one, has defended and supported me without regard to his personal popularity or unpopularity. While he and I differ and have differed on many important public questions, we have never allowed our differences to mar our personal friendship. In all matters pertaining to the welfare of our race in the South I

WHITE AND COLORED GATHERED TO HEAR DR. WASHINGTON SPEAK.

DR. WASHINGTON SPEAKING FROM REAR OF TRAIN.

have always consulted him most freely and frankly. For example, in the preparation of the open letter to the Louisiana State Constitutional Convention, Mr. Fortune and myself sat up nearly one whole night at Tuskegee preparing this letter. I have seldom ever given any public utterances to the country that have not had his criticism and approval. His help and friendship to me in many directions have been most potent in enabling me to accomplish whatever I have been able to do.

In the same class with Mr. Fortune I would put my private secretary, Mr. Emmet J. Scott, who, for a number of years, has been in the closest and most helpful relations to me in all my work. Without his constant and painstaking care it would be impossible for me to perform even a very small part of the labor that I now do. Mr. Scott understands so thoroughly my motives, plans and ambitions that he puts himself into my own position as nearly as it is possible for one individual to put himself into the place of another, and in this way makes himself invaluable not only to me personally but to the institution. Such a man as Mr. Scott I have found exceedingly rare, only once or twice in a lifetime are such people discovered.

There is only one way for an individual to

collect money for a worthy institution, as there is only one way for him to succeed in any line of work, and that is to make up his mind to do his duty to the fullest extent and let results take care of themselves.

In the earlier years of the institution I called to see a rich gentleman in New York, who did not even ask me to take a seat, but in a gruff and cold manner handed me two dollars, as if to say, I give you this to get rid of you. Since that time this same individual has given to Tuskegee as much as ten thousand dollars in cash, at one time. In other cases, where I found it impossible to secure an audience, in the early days of this work, I have since been sent for by these same individuals and asked to accept money for the institution. In many cases I have gone to individuals and presented our cause only to receive an insult or the coldest and most discouraging reception. Perhaps the next individual on whom I called would politely and earnestly thank me for calling and giving him an opportunity to make a gift to Tuskegee.

During the early struggles of our work, in many instances I went to ministers in the North to secure opportunity to speak in their churches, but received "No" for my answer. Often where I have received such answers, I have since received letters from these same ministers urging that I would deliver lectures in their churches; and naming large sums of money as compensation for my lectures.

The institution has now reached a point where it conducts all of its affairs on a more strictly cash basis than in its earlier years; in fact, the general policy of the school at present is to undertake no enterprise in the way of improvements until it has the money in hand for such improvements. This policy could not be carried out very well in the early years of the school, when we were so hard pressed for buildings. One thing which I have always thought has helped us a great deal is that we have always made it a point to have the strictest and most approved system of bookkeeping in connection with all of our financial transactions Our books have been at all times open to the inspection of the public. In accounting for our income and expenditures, Mr. Logan, our Treasurer, from the first has been of the highest service to the institution. We have never allowed any carelessness in the matter of bookkeeping.

I have often been asked by young men how they can succeed in this or that direction. My advice to them is to make up their minds carefully, in the first place, as to what they want to do, and then persistently devote themselves to accomplishing that end, letting nothing discourage them. If I may be allowed a little pardonable pride in connection with this statement, I would add, to show how mistaken that secretary was who attempted to discourage me by telling me that I would not secure enough funds to pay my traveling expenses, that since the institution at Tuskegee was started I have collected myself, or been instrumental in causing others to help me secure, all told, fully $1,000,000 for the permanent plant, endowment and the annual expenses of Tuskegee. Were I to attempt to give an account of all the ways and means by which individuals have tried to discourage me since I began at Tuskegee, this little book would contain little else than that. I have always found it easy to find people who could tell me how a thing could *not* be accomplished, but very hard to find those who could tell me how a thing could be accomplished. In my opinion the world is much more interested in finding people who know how to accomplish something than those who merely explain why it is impossible to accomplish certain results.

I have been asked many times how I have succeeded in this thing or in that thing. In almost every case I have replied that it has required constant, hard, conscientious work. I consider that there is no permanent success possible without hard and severe effort, coupled with the highest and most praiseworthy aims. Luck, as I have experienced it, is only another name for hard work. Almost any individual can succeed in any legitimate enterprise that he sets his heart upon, if he is willing to pay the price, but the price, in most cases, is being willing to toil when others are resting, being willing to work while others are sleeping, being willing to put forth the severest effort when there is no one to see or applaud. It is comparatively easy to find people who are willing to work when the world is looking on and ready to give applause, but very hard to find those who are willing to work in the corner or at midnight, when there is no watchful eye or anyone to give applause.

I end this volume as I began, with an apology for writing it. It is always highly distasteful to me to speak about myself, and in writing what I have, I have attempted in a small degree, at least, to subordinate my own personal feelings with a view to giving the public as much information as possible. I hope that some permanent good will result from my effort.

CHAPTER XXIV.

PRINCE HENRY'S EAGERNESS TO MEET BOOKER T. WASHINGTON.

This is best given in Rear Admiral Evans' own words as it appears in McClure's Magazine, May, 1902. He says in part:

"The first request made by Prince Henry after being received in New York was that I should arrange to give him some of the old Southern melodies, if possible, sung by the negroes; that he was passionately fond of them, and had been all his life—not the rag-time songs, but the old negro melodies. Several times during his trip I endeavored to carry out his wishes, with more or less success; but finally, at the Waldorf-Astoria, the Hampton singers presented themselves in one of the reception-rooms and gave him a recital of Indian and Negro melodies. He was charmed.

And while I was talking to him just after a Sioux Indian had sung a lullaby, he suddenly turned and said: 'Isn't that Booker T. Washington over there?' I recognized Washington and replied that it was, and he said: 'Evans, would you mind presenting him to me? I know how some of your people feel about Washington, but I have always had great sympathy with the African race, and I want to meet the man I regard as the leader of that race.' So I went at once to Washington and told him that the Prince wished him to be presented, and took him myself and presented him to the Prince. Booker Washington sat down and talked with him for fully ten minutes, and it was a most interesting conversation—one of the most interesting I ever heard in my life. The ease with which Washington conducted himself was very striking, and I only accounted for it afterwards when I remembered that he had dined with the Queen of England two or three times, so that this was not a new thing for him. Indeed, Booker Washington's manner was easier than that of almost any other man I saw meet the Prince in this country. The Prince afterwards referred to President Roosevelt's action in regard to Booker Washington, and applauded it very highly."

Among other things Prince Henry asked Mr. Washington whether the songs he had heard were in printed form. An affirmative answer being given, he requested that a copy be sent him. Turning to the students he said in part.

"I thank you very much for your beautiful songs, which I have enjoyed hearing. I believe music is a gift from heaven to men and women, and I do hope you will cherish your melodies, in order that they may be perpetuated."

The interview with Mr. Washington attracted the attention of the entire throng, and when the Associated Press gave the news to the country, the leading journals began to discuss the incident as an event of international importance.

Reaching Boston to look after some matters relating to Tuskegee Institute, Mr. Washington, in response to questions bearing upon his presentation to Prince Henry said:

"As I understand it the Prince asked Rear Admiral Evans to have me presented to him mainly for the reason that he wanted to talk with me concerning the work of the Tuskegee graduates who are introducing the raising of cotton in the German-African colony. The Prince also spoke of being deeply interested in the progress of the Negro in America, about which he asked many questions. He also asked me to send him a copy of my autobiography and a volume of the plantation songs. He said that few things had pleased him so much as the singing of the Hampton students, and expressed an earnest wish that the songs might not be permitted to die."

SUPPLEMENT

CHAPTER XXV.

GLIMPSES BACKWARD AND FORWARD.

Any attempt to chronicle briefly the activities of Dr. Booker T. Washington in the closing years of his life would hardly do justice to his memory, because so much was crowded into those years. So big, so important, and so effectively executed were his activities that they would more than fill the life of the average man.

To gather up the threads of his narrative and weave them into a suitable climax of his notable career, we must touch at some length upon the most important events and achievements which have been contributing influence upon the economic advancement of the race and factors in the upgrowth of the Tuskegee Institute.

The "Story of My Life and Work" deals with the lamented educator's activities up to, and including a part of the year 1902. It also describes the growth of the Tuskegee Normal and Industrial Institute from its inception up to that time. Therefore, in order to clearly understand the magnitude of his accomplishments during the last fourteen years of his life, we must make comparisons between the Tuskegee Institute of that period and the present Tuskegee.

In 1901 the property immediately belonging to the school consisted of 54 buildings, 2,000 acres of land which, together with equipment and live stock, was valued at $400,000.00. There were 106 teachers and officers employed and 1,310 students enrolled. In 1915 the school property consisted of 107 buildings, 2,345 acres of land, which together with equipment and live stock, is valued at $1,567,062. There are now employed 185 teachers and officers, and for the term ending May, 1915, 1,527 students were enrolled. In 1901 the Endowment Fund was about $200,000, and at the time of Dr. Washington's death it was approximately $2,000,000.

Thus it is clearly seen that most of the development of Tuskegee Institute has been intensive. There has been little increase in the number of acres owned and in average yearly enrollment of students, but the improvement has been in two directions: permanence and increased efficiency.

In 1901 the larger and more important buildings on the ground were Porter Hall, Olivia Davidson Hall, Science Hall, Cassidy Hall, Huntington Hall, Phelps Hall, Slater-Armstrong Memorial Trades Building, Slater-Armstrong Memorial Agricultural Building, the Hospital (now called Pinehurst), the Children's House, Carnegie Library and the Chapel.

Since that time Porter Hall and Alabama Hall have been torn down, Science Hall has been converted into a dormitory, and the Slater-Armstrong Memorial Agricultural Building converted into the Commissary and offices for the Business Agent and his corps of assistants. Of the new buildings completed within the past fourteen years, the important ones are:

Academic Building	$ 60,000.00
Tompkins' Hall (Dining Hall)	150,000.00
White Memorial Hall (Girls' Dormitory)	65,000.00
Huntington Hall (Girls' Dormitory)	20,000.00
Tantum Hall (Girls' Dormitory)	25,000.00
Milbank Building (Agricultural)	25,000.00
John A. Andrew Memorial Hospital	55,000.00
New Veterinary Hospital (In course of Erection)	5,000.00

Concerning these new buildings, Mr. William A. Hazel, Director of Mechanical Drawing, says: "With few exceptions the type of architecture adopted throughout the grounds might be described as modern Colonial.

Tompkins' Hall is the most imposing. It contains a students' dining room, seating capacity 2,000; a teachers' dining room, seating 300; a basement auditorium, seating 3,000; besides kitchens, storerooms, steward's offices, etc. Its principal entrance has a broad portico, with Doric columns 30 feet high, built of brick covered with concrete. All of the buildings are of red brick which were made by students from clays found at the Institute. All the wood used for framing, interior finish and much of the furniture was cut by students from the school's timber lands, sawed into lumber in its saw-mills by students, and finished and erected by students in the Carpentry Division.

"The slate and tin roofing, iron work, plastering, painting, tile setting; in fact, the buildings in their entirety, have been built by student labor, under the direction of the instructors in the several building trades.

"The plans, from the preliminary sketches to the working drawings and details, were made in the Architectural and Mechanical Drawing Divisions, under the direction of Mr. R. R. Taylor, as Supervising Architect and Director of the Department of Mechanical Industries."

In reference to the new Power Plant, which is by far the biggest achievement in connection with the physical development of the school, Mr. Taylor says:

"It is difficult to institute any comparison between this and any other plant in this country. Few, if any, perform such varied services or are so unceasingly in operation. Not only are the school grounds and buildings electrically lighted, but also the adjoining village of Greenwood and its colony of teachers' cottages. The lighting plant has also capacity for furnishing power to be sold on occasion to the town of Tuskegee. Thirty-one buildings are supplied with steam heat and hot water. 670,000 cubic feet of air per day is compressed for five artesian wells, and 265,000 gallons of water per day are pumped into the reservoir. Two engines of 287 horse power each, directly connected with 160 K. W. generators, furnish motor power for the shops and lighting.

"The plant is equipped with four boilers of combined 805 horse power; has modern coal bunkers with a storage capacity of twenty three cars—the daily average coal consumption being 13½ tons in the summer and 32 tons in the winter. Space is provided for the installation of an ice plant having a capacity of ten tons per day. The entire plant is of brick, steel and concrete. The chimney is 175 feet high, 7 feet inside diameter at the top."

CHAPTER XXVI.

AN APPEALING PERSONALITY MR. WASHINGTON'S STRONGEST ASSET.

Those who had an opportunity to study Mr. Washington know that his strongest and most valuable asset was his ability to make and hold good friends for the work to which he devoted his life. These friends who have stood by him and helped him to make possible the work of Tuskegee Institute have come from the ranks of the humblest and most exalted of both races. Frequently he has been in his private office talking to an old colored man whom, perhaps he had known since the early days of Tuskegee Institute and the office boy would carry in to him the card of some important business man. In a few moments the boy would return with the message: "Dr. Washington will see you in a few minutes." Finally Dr. Washington and the old colored man would come out together and if the person waiting happened to be one of his white friends from out of town he might say: "Mr. So-and-so, this is one of Macon County's successful farmers. He has been a friend to our work here since we started; I want you to meet him." Then the three of them would enjoy a good laugh over some incident related by Dr. Washington in which the old colored man had been a participant.

It is a remarkable fact that those who worked in Dr. Washington's outer offices—and there were more than a dozen—never saw anyone come from the private office with a frown on his face. Nearly every one came out with a smile. Of course, in some instances, students who had broken some rule of the school, which was beyond the disciplinary power of Mr. Palmer or Major Ramsey, would go in and they usually came out shamed and solemn faced. Other students, discouraged by reason of a lack of funds with which to remain in school, have gone in with serious faces and came out with faces wreathed in smiles.

Little wonder then that with such a personality friends of Tuskegee Institute were to be found in all parts of the country, and were numbered by the thousands.

The list of the members of the Board of Trustees of the Tuskegee Normal and Industrial Institute shows in a most conclusive way how he was able, by reason of his warm smile which radiated the sunshine of friendly fellowship, and his big open eyes which revealed strength and steadfastness of purpose, to surround himself with such an important group of representative Americans.

At the time of Mr. Washington's death the Board of Trustees consisted of the following:

Hon. Seth Low, Chairman, New York City, N. Y.
Mr. Wright W. Campbell, Vice-Chairman, Tuskegee, Ala.
Mr. William G. Willcox, New York, N. Y.
Mr. R. O. Simpson, Furman, Ala.
Mr. V. H. Tulane, Montgomery, Ala.
Mr. Belton Gilreath, Birmingham, Ala.
Mr. Charles W. Hare, Tuskegee, Ala.
Dr. Booker T. Washington, Tuskegee Inst., Ala.
Mr. Warren Logan, Tuskegee Inst., Ala.
Mr. A. J. Wilborn, Tuskegee, Ala.
Mr. William J. Schieffelin, New York City, N. Y.
Mr. Charles E. Mason, Boston, Mass.
Mr. Frank Trumbull, New York City, N. Y.
Hon. Theodore Roosevelt, Oyster Bay, N. Y.
Mr. Julius Rosenwald, Chicago, Ill.
Mr. William M. Scott, Philadelphia, Penn.
Mr. Geo. McAneny, New York City, N. Y.
Mr. Edgar A. Bancroft, Chicago, Ill.
Mr. Alexander Mann, D. D., Boston, Mass.
Mr. Emmett J. Scott, Secretary, Tuskegee Inst., Ala

In the earlier chapters of this book it is shown how the warm friendship which he established with President McKinley resulted in his visit to Tuskegee Institute, and how this recognition from the nation's Chief Executive did much to bring the work of the school before the world. In the subsequent years, Dr. Washington was enabled to form other

SYRUP MAKING, TUSKEGEE INSTITUTE.

BOOKER T. WASHINGTON II.

intimate friendships which have had a marked influence upon the advancement of the Institute. Among these might be mentioned ex-President Taft, Hon. Charles W. Fairbanks, former Vice President Mr. Robert C. Ogden, Mr. William J. Schieffelin, ex-Governor Emmet O'Neal of Alabama, former President Roosevelt and a host of others.

The friendship with Mr. Roosevelt began many years before he was even thought of in connection with the presidency of the United States, and remained as a source of much encouragement to Mr. Washington until his death. Particular reference is made to Mr. Roosevelt on account of the now famous dinner which Mr. Washington had at the White House, while Mr. Roosevelt was President. As a result of this incident both Mr. Washington and Mr. Roosevelt were severely criticized, especially by the Southern press. Because no other published statement concerning it was ever made by Mr. Washington, we quote from Mr. Washington's book, "My Larger Education:" "During the fall of 1901, while I was making a tour of Mississippi, I received word to the effect that the President would like to have a conference with me, as soon as it was convenient, concerning some important matters. With a friend, who was traveling with me, I discussed very seriously the question whether, with the responsibilities I already had, I should take on others. After considering the matter carefully we decided that the only policy to pursue was to face the new responsibilities as they arose, because new responsibilities bring new opportunities for usefulness of which I ought to take advantage in the interest of my race. I was the more disposed to feel that this was a duty, because Mr. Roosevelt was proposing to carry out the very policies which I had advocated ever since I began work in Alabama. Immediately after finishing my work in Mississippi I went to Washington. I arrived there in the afternoon and went to the house of a friend, Mr. Whitefield McKinlay, with whom I was expected to stop during my stay in Washington.

"This trip to Washington brings me to a matter which I have hitherto constantly refused to discuss in print or in public, though I have had a great many requests to do so. At the time I did not care to add fuel to the controversy which it aroused, and I speak of it now only because it seems to me that an explanation will show the incident in its true light and in its proper proportions.

"When I reached Mr. McKinlay's house I found an invitation from President Roosevelt asking me to dine with him at the White House that evening at eight o'clock. At the hour appointed I went to the White House and dined with the President and members of his family and a gentleman from Colorado. After dinner we talked at considerable length concerning plans about the South which the President had in mind. I left the White House almost immediately and took the train the same night for New York. When I reached New York the next morning I noticed that the New York Tribune had about two lines stating that I had dined with the President the previous night. That was the only New York paper, so far as I saw, that mentioned the matter. Within a few hours the whole incident completely passed from my mind. I mentioned the matter casually, during the day to a friend—Mr. William H. Baldwin, Jr., then president of the Long Island Railroad—but spoke of it to no one else, and had no intention of doing so. There was, in fact, no reason why I should discuss it or mention it to any one.

"My surprise can be imagined when, two or three days afterward, the whole press, North and South, was filled with despatches and editorials relating to my dinner with the President. For days and weeks I was pursued by reporters in quest of interviews. I was deluged with telegrams and letters asking for some expression of opinion or an explanation; but during the whole of this period of agitation and excitement I did not give out a single interview and did not discuss the matter in any way. Some newspapers attempted to weave into this incident a deliberate and well-planned scheme on the part of President Roosevelt to lead the day in bringing about the social intermingling of the two races. I am sure that nothing was farther from the President's mind than this; certainly it was not in my mind. Mr. Roosevelt simply found that he could spare the time best during and after the dinner hour for the discussion of the matters which both of us were interested in.

"The public interest aroused by this dinner seemed all the more extraordinary and uncalled for because, on previous occasions, I had taken tea with Queen Victoria at Windsor Castle; I had dined with the governors of nearly every state in the North; I had dined in the same room with President McKinley at the peace-jubilee dinner; and I had dined with ex-President Harrison in Paris, and with many other prominent public men."

Another man who contributed greatly to the success of Tuskegee was the late William H. Baldwin, Jr., who died in 1905. Mr. Baldwin came into the life of Tuskegee when it was growing rapidly and needed the wise and steadying influence of an experienced business man. Mr. Baldwin also brought with him a host of strong and sympathetic friends whose generosity aided materially in assuring permanence and expansion for the work of the school.

CHAPTER XXVII.
STATE EDUCATIONAL TOURS.

With a keen appreciation of the needs and disadvantages of his people, Dr. Washington never overlooked an opportunity to serve and help them with his wide experience and knowledge of the fundamentals of living. It was therefore a great privilege and pleasure to him to receive in 1905 an invitation from Hon. J. E. Bush, of Little Rock, Arkansas, to join him and a party of others on a tour of Arkansas and Oklahoma. Here was an opportunity for service and a chance to see the actual conditions of the members of his race; to meet the actual workers and stimulate them with the magic of his personality.

Accordingly the details of the trip were worked out and meetings arranged all along the line of the proposed pilgrimage. The itinerary included speeches at Little Rock and Pine Bluff, in Arkansas: and at Boley, Oklahoma City, Guthrie, Muskogee and South McAlester, in Oklahoma. The results of this educational and speaking tour were so helpful to the communities reached and afforded

Dr. Washington such an opportunity for intimate study into the problems affecting his race that similar tours were arranged for other states. Since 1905 tours have been made covering the states of Mississippi, Tennessee, South Carolina, Delaware, Virginia, Florida, New Jersey and Louisiana.

It is impossible to estimate the good that has been accomplished by reason of the educator's helpful contact with both races in those states through which he has traveled.

Before undertaking any of these tours it was always his rule to fortify himself with all available information concerning the progress of his race in the particular states he was about to visit. With this knowledge he could frequently startle his hearers by pointing out to them some opportunity for development in business or education which they were overlooking or could mildly rebuke the white people for failing to grant his people the educational advantages to which they were entitled.

The last of these memorable trips were made in April, 1915, and covered the state of Louisiana. Reviewing the trip for the newspapers Mr. William Anthony Aery, of the Hampton Institute Press Service, said.

"In accepting the invitation of prominent colored citizens of Louisiana to tour the state, Dr. Washington had one object in view;

namely, to see what were the conditions of the negroes, to bring about greater progress among the negroes, and to bring about, if possible, more helpful and sensible relations between white men and black men. Meetings were held in New Orleans, St. Bernard parish, New Iberia, Crowley, Lake Charles, Lafayette, Southern University, Baton Rouge, Alexandria, Gibsland, Shreveport and Mansfield, La.

"Everywhere Dr. Washington and his party were enthusiastically received at the railroad station by thousands of healthy, prosperous looking black people. Crowds of white citizens gathered to see Dr. Washington and to hear him expound with force and rare clearness his gospel of opportunity and racial good-will. Within four days Dr. Washington spoke to over 50,000 of his own people; and a number of thousand interested white men and women listened eagerly to his practical gospel. Negroes came on mule-back, in carriages and in wagons, long distances—10, 20, 30 and even 40 miles—to hear Dr. Washington tell them of the remarkable progress which Louisiana negroes have been making. They stood for hours to get a chance to hear the most distinguished member of their race tell them of the opportunities which they have in the Southland."

CHAPTER XXVIII.

RURAL EXTENSION WORK.

In an earlier chapter we referred to Mr. Washington's strong personality and ability to lift up friends for Tuskegee Institute. In that chapter we might have mentioned Mr. Julius Rosenwald, but his relationship with the work has been so important that we could not do justice to the breadth and influence of his generosity without devoting a chapter to him and to the great work he has made possible for Tuskegee Institute.

Mr. Rosenwald, of Chicago, is widely known for his generous aid and support to the cause of bettering humanity and his interest in the advancement of the colored people. Perhaps no single individual has done more to encourage the work of the Young Men's Christian Association among the colored people than has Mr. Rosenwald. When this important work was tottering over the abysmal depths of charitable indifference, Mr. Rosenwald came forward with an offer to give $25,000.00 for every $75,000.00 raised for the erection of a building for a colored Young Men's Christian

Association. His offer received a ready response from among the colored people and has been the means of adding considerable impetus to this work.

This big-hearted man has done an even bigger thing for the race in making a somewhat similar offer to encourage the building of model rural schoolhouses. The distribution of his fund is made through the Extension Department of the Tuskegee Institute, and affords this department an opportunity for more effective work in reaching and helping the rural communities which it touches. Mr. Calloway gives personal attention to this work.

The Rural Schoolhouse Building, which is the most important phase of the Rural Extension work, is under the direct supervision of Mr. Booker T. Washington, Jr. Mr. Washington says regarding this work:

"It is impossible to estimate the far-reaching good that has been made possible through the kindly generosity of Mr. Rosenwald. At any rate I know that this rural school work was a matter very close to my father's heart, and he regarded it as one of the most important achievements in the development of the school when Mr. Rosenwald proposed his offer. Already we have been instrumental in erecting seventy-nine model school buildings during the year 1915, and the outlook is most encouraging for greater work in the near future.

"It is gratifying to mention that Mr. Rosenwald's gift for rural schools has been indirectly responsible for more interest in education on the part of colored people who, in order to secure the aid from the Rosenwald fund, have themselves raised $37,610.32. Then it has tended to cement the races in a helpful and friendly way in the several counties in which we have worked. To help the colored people raise the needed funds, white people of the counties have contributed $3,336.50. But in my mind the most important result has been the increased attendance at the colored schools. The increase in enrollment this year over that of 1914 in the counties in which we operate has been 48 per cent."

Concerning the history of the Rural School Building, as done through the Tuskegee Institute, Mr. Washington says:

"The first person to aid in this work was the late Mr. H. H. Rogers, who left $30,000.00 to assist in building better schoolhouses in the South. With this money forty-one schoolhouses were erected. This was about fifteen years ago. But the greatest stimulus to this work was through Mr. Rosenwald who first gave $2,000.00 about two years ago as an experiment in bettering the schoolhouses. The results were so pleasing to Mr. Rosenwald that he increased the amount, and has promised to aid in erecting two hundred schoolhouses instead of one hundred, as he first promised."

The biggest task the Extension Department has had under way is the building of decent and practical rural schools. In this lies the solution of much farm emigration. While the farmers would improve stock and products, there were still many who, not having education themselves, saw little use of any school at all; and any length of session, any kind of teacher, and any kind of building would do. And so ten years ago the department with the Farmers' Conference threw down the gauntlet to shabby school facilities, which included a defiance of shabby homes, and a shake of the fist at community dissensions. It showed mere book-teaching the door, laying down a schedule for and demanding instruction in courses that gave useful training, as well as mere drilling in books. To carry out the plan called for a change in rural school architecture. There must be a room in which to teach cooking, a dining room in which to teach table setting and a room in which to teach sewing.

Now, prior to 1905, nearly every negro school in Macon County was either a log cabin or a one-room cottage, with one or two wooden windows, one door, a rickety wooden floor or a dirt floor, as chance happened to will it; a leaky roof, decaying logs and blocks of wood, broken backed chairs and benches for seats. These are the things that made up the edifice and surrounding for the children of the ex-slaves to get an education or a training for life. To many this was good enough, far better than they had had certainly; but to others it was wretchedness of the deepest dye.

And so arguments began to circulate. The people throughout the county were poor. Some few of them were just getting to their feet in the matter of land buying, but the masses were "share-croppers" or tenants. In a little while a cry had come up from a community known as Magnolia: "We want a new school! Help us!"

"Help us" means funds to a certain extent, but most of all it meant somebody with initiative, suggestion, encouragement and the welding of factions. This last was especially troublesome. The rural colored man is the stanchest of partisans of his faith. A man of Baptist convictions is unwilling to build a schoolhouse anywhere save face to face with a Baptist Church; so it is with a brother of the Methodist faith or of any faith. The people at Magnolia had raised some money, but how much they needed before they could break ground to build, how to go about discovering all this, they were at a loss to determine.

Clinton J. Calloway went down to see what could be done. About half enough money had been raised to begin the work. An appeal to the people for more brought the response that no more would be raised; the people as a mass had lost interest. Faction troubles, religious and social, were boiling at a high heat. Mr. Calloway returned to Tuskegee, reported to Dr. Washington and awaited instructions. It chanced that a donor had given several hundred dollars to be used in helping the Macon County rural schools. A part of this sum was placed at the disposal of the school's representative, with instructions to return to Magnolia.

With this definite plan made out the teacher returned. Said he to the audience at Magnolia:

"A friend who is interested in you, who wants to see you build a schoolhouse and educate your children, has sent you some money under certain conditions. That is, he will give you $50 for every $50 you raise until a sufficient sum is collected. Will you accept?"

A message from paradise could not have been hailed with greater enthusiasm. That some friend was interested in them, wanted to see them get ahead and had sent them some money personally seemed almost too good to be true.

They forgot their factional grievances. Their courage came back. Barbecues, peanut suppers, concerts of divers kinds were started to raise funds. A central spot was bought for the location of the school, a spot near the highway and as near the railroad as possible. It included not only ground for the school, but two acres for a school farm and garden. This was deeded to the trustees, for another limitation of the gift was that the land had to be bought, paid for and properly deeded, the donor giving the money toward the school building only. Two or three times a week these people were together devising new ways of raising funds. They got to know one another undenominationally, or as men and women.

In two months' time they laid down $100 to be covered by $100 from the donor, and work was begun. In six months from the time the representative went down from Tuskegee the school was finished and dedicated amidst shouts and tears of a people in mass, who had just finished their first lesson in the history of devising and constructing a schoolhouse.

Building the school at Magnolia is typical

of what happened in rapid succession in fifty-odd communities. This being the first of the schools to rebuild it set the county aflame. That community which did not have or was not striving for a new school building, with rooms for classes, rooms for cooking and handicrafts and a good school garden or farm to eke out the school term from six to eight months was dubbed "backward."

The Tuskegee Extension Department is helping to solve the race problem in the South by helping that part of the race which is located in the rural districts to attain that degree of contentment which is the advance agent of progress. Their larders are full; their children are happy in the new meaning of education which comes through clean, attractive and sanitary schoolhouses and the outlook is most promising that the next generation will find the farming class of our race a more intelligent and progressive group.

CHAPTER XXIX.
THE 15th ANNIVERSARY OF THE NATIONAL NEGRO BUSINESS LEAGUE.

Characterizing the Fifteenth Anniversary of the Organization of the National Negro Business League as a "wonderful demonstration of achievement under fifty years of sacrifice, struggle and insult," Governor Walsh, of Massachusetts welcomed the officers and members of the National Negro Business League at the annual session held in Boston, August 18th to 21st, 1915.

The National Negro Business League was organized in 1900, following the decision of Doctor Booker T. Washington and his associates to encourage business progress of the race and to call the business men together annually in order to get an insight into their problems and to find a way to make their business enterprises more potent factors in their respective communities.

The members of the National Negro Business League in Boston worked incessantly to make this Fifteenth Anniversary the most glorious in the history of the organization. In response to the numerous calls sent out from headquarters at Tuskegee Institute, delegates

CARNEGIE LIBRARY BUILDING.

THREE BLOODED STALLIONS, TUSKEGEE INSTITUTE.

from twenty-three states, representing every avenue of business enterprise, were present. For three days the discussions dealt with those vital and important topics which make for business progress and advancement of the race's best interests.

Dr. Washington's address to the National Negro Business League on the occasion of the League's Fifteenth Anniversary, Aug. 18th to 21st, 1915:

"This National Negro Business League was organized in the city of Boston fifteen years ago with a mere handful of men. The League during the fifteen years of its life has grown in power, in influence and in usefulness until, either through its local leagues or individual members, it reaches practically every part of the country in which there are any considerable number of colored people. After fifteen years of testing useful service and growth, it is fitting that we should return to Boston, the place which gave us birth.

"From the first this National Negro Business League has clung strictly to the object for which it was founded. It was not founded to take the place of other organizations; nor was this league, as a league, ever intended to go into business as an organization or to become a close, hide-bound concern with grips and signs and passwords. We have such organizations and they are doing their work well, but the central purpose of this National Negro Business League has been, from the first, to foster, to spread, and to create industrial business and commercial enterprises among our people in every part of the country. How well we have succeeded I shall let the facts tell the story later on.

"The founders and promoters of the League fully recognize the fact that it cannot meet all the needs of the race, nor satisfy all its ambition. We fully and frankly recognize the fact that there is need for the particular and distinct work to be done by the religious, the educational, the political, the literary, the secret and the fraternal bodies, as well as those that deal with the civil rights of our people.

"All of these have their place and with none of them would we seek to interfere; but the history of civilization, throughout the world, shows that without economic and commercial success there can be no lasting or commanding success in other fields of endeavor. This League then has for one of its objects, not the tearing down or weakening of other organizations, but rather to give them strength and stability.

"Since our last annual meeting there has been happenings that are of peculiar interest to our race. Among these has been the observance of a National Health Week which was promoted very largely by this Business

League, acting in co-operation with the Virginia Organization Society. Health Week was perhaps more generally observed by all classes of our people in the South and in the North than has ever been true of any similar movement in the history of the race. Until ten years ago the death rate among our people was alarming, but the importance of good health and long life has been called to the attention of the race in so many ways during the last ten years that the death rate has already been reduced by four per cent in certain parts of the country. It is the wish of many that the Health Week be observed again this year.

"Since our last meeting the United States Supreme Court has rendered a decision in the Oklahoma case which is of far-reaching value and importance to our race. The main value of this decision, rendered by a Southern Supreme Court Justice and an ex-Confederate soldier and ex-slaveholder, consists in the fact that it makes plain the idea, once and for all by the Supreme Court of the land, that neither color nor race can debar a man in this country from full citizenship.

* * * * * *

"Since the League met in Boston fifteen years ago, great changes have taken place among our people in property getting and in the promotion of industrial and business enterprises. These changes have taken place not solely because of the work of the League, but this and similar organizations have had much to do with bringing about this progress. Let me be more specific.

"We have not figures covering all the negro's wealth, but the Federal Census Bureau has just released a document which gives the value of the negro's farm property alone as $1,142,000,000. From 1900 to 1910 the negro's farm property increased 128 per cent. In 1863 we had as a race 2,000 small business enterprises of one kind and another. At the present time the negro owns and operates about 43,000 concerns, with an annual turn-over of about one billion dollars. Within fifty years we have made enough progress in business to warrant the operation of over fifty banks. With all I have said, we are still a poor race, as compared with many others; but I have given these figures to indicate the direction in which we are traveling. During the last six years we have experienced, as a race, not a few business failures, including the closing of several banks. We must not let these failures discourage us. We must remember that it is with a race, as it is with an individual, that it is only through seeming failure, as well as success, that we finally gain that experience and confidence which are necessary to permanent success. With all that I have said, we should remember that we have but scratched the surface of industrial and business success.

"Our future is before us, not behind us. We are a new race in a comparatively new country. Let any who may be inclined toward pessimism or discord consider with me for a few moments the opportunities that are before us. It is always of more value to consider our advantages rather than our disadvantages. In considering one's opportunities it is worth while not to overlook the size of our race.

"There are only fourteen nations in the world whose population exceeds the number of negroes in the United States. Norway has a population of only 2,400,000; Denmark, 2,700,000; Bulgaria, 4,000,000; Chile, 4,000,000; Canada, 7,000,000, and Argentine, 9,000,000. When we contemplate these figures and then remember that we, in the United States alone are 10,000,000 negroes, we can get some idea of the opportunities that are right about us.

"Let us be more specific in pointing the way to these opportunities. If you would ask where you are to begin, I would answer begin where you are. As a rule the gold mine which we seek in a far-off country is right at our door.

"Over a million of our people live in the Northern and Western states. In these states at the present time our people operate about 4,000 business enterprises. There are opportunities in the North and West for 8,000 business enterprises, or double the present number. In the Southern states, where the great bulk of our people live, we have about 40,000 business concerns. There should be within the next few years 20,000 more business concerns. In all this we should never forget that the ownership and cultivation of the soil constitute the foundation for great wealth and usefulness among our people. I have already indicated that we operate about 800,000 farms. Within the next decade let us try to double the number. To indicate a little more the direction in which we should seek opportunities: There are now 4,000 truck farms operated by us, we ought to increase this number to 8,000. We ought never to forget that in the ownership and cultivation of the soil in a very large measure we must lay the foundation for one's success.

"A landless race is like a ship without a rudder. Emphasizing again our opportunities, especially as connected with the soil, we now have, for example, 122 poultry raisers. The number should be increased to 1,500. We now have 200 dairymen. The number should be increased to 2,000.

"At present there are far too many of our people living in the cities in a hand-to-mouth way, dependent on some one else for an uncertain job. Aside from what the soil offers, there are other opportunities in business. For example, we now own and operate 75 bakeries. The number can be increased to 500. From 32 brickmakers the number can be increased to 3,000. From 200 sawmills we can increase the number to 1,000. From 50 furniture factories the number can be increased to 300. Where we now have 9,000 dry goods stores and grocery merchants, we should have in the near future 15,000.

"Where we now have 700 drug stores we should have 3,000. Where we now have 1,000 millinery stores we should have 5,000. Where we now have 150 plumbers we should have 600. Where we have 400 tailors we should have 2,000. Where we now have 59 architects we should have 400. We now have 3,000 contractors and builders, we should have 5,000. Where we now have 51 banks we should have 500.

"Few people are aware of the fact that we now have in our race, after only fifty years of freedom, 55 book stores, 18 department stores, 14 five-and-ten-cent stores, 20 jewelry stores, 790 junk dealers, 13 warehouses and cold storage plants, 152 wholesale merchants, 200 laundries, 350 livery stables, 953 undertakers, 400 photographers, 10 opticians, 75 hair goods manufacturers, 111 old rag dealers, 12 buyers and shippers of live stock.

* * * * *

"To accomplish what I have indicated we must have a united race, men who are big enough and broad enough to forget and overlook personal and local differences and each willing to place upon the altar all that he holds for the benefit of the race and our country.

"Some times it is suggested that some of us are over optimistic concerning the present conditions and future of our race. In part answer it might be stated that one on the inside of a house looking out can often see more than the one on the outside looking in. No one enjoys riding in a Pullman car so much as the one who has ridden in a freight car.

"No matter how poor you are, how black you are, or how obscure your present work and position, I want each one to remember that there is a chance for him and the more difficulties he has to overcome, the greater will be his success.

"Everywhere we should be proud of the negro race and loyal to the great human family of whatever color. Whenever we consider what is now going on in Europe, where all the people are of one color, and then compare these conditions with the present conditions and our task for our race, we ought to thank our Creator that conditions are so well with us and that we live beneath the Stars and Stripes."

CHAPTER XXX.

NATIONAL NEGRO HEALTH WEEK.

Early in January, 1915, Dr. Washington sent out an announcement which was published in all the leading colored newspapers, inviting the daily and weekly newspapers, medical journals and the most prominent and influential National Organizations of the colored race, as well as schools and churches and other local organizations to unite with the National Negro Business League in observing a National Health Week. In the announcement Dr. Washington says:

"In Alabama, Louisiana, North Carolina and other states, special Health Days have at one time or another been observed. For some years the Virginia Organization Society, under the leadership of Major R. R. Maton, has observed a Health or Clean-up Week. It is thought to be well to unite all these efforts into a National Movement and join the movement unto the Virginia effort.

"It is thought that the race will welcome this opportunity to unite all these efforts in one great National Health Movement, and thus gain the benefit of the momentum and the enthusiasm that will come from the great United Health Movement. The dates decided upon are March 21 to 27, 1915.

"Without health and until we reduce the high death rate it will be impossible for us to have permanent success in business, in property getting, in acquiring education, to show other evidences of progress. Without health and long life all else fails.

"We must reduce our high death rate, dethrone disease and enthrone health and long life. We may differ on other subjects, but there is no room for difference here. Let us make a strong, long united pull together."

This announcement was followed in quick succession by the publication of certain facts gathered by Director of the Division of Records and Research of the Institution. These facts were essentially as follows:

"Four hundred and fifty thousand negroes in the South seriously sick all the time. The annual cost of the sickness of these 450,000 negroes was $75,000,000.00. Forty-five per cent of the annual deaths among negroes are preventable. This means that forty-five negroes out of every hundred die each year who ought to live. The annual economic loss to the South for sickness and deaths among negroes is $300,000,000.00. One hundred and fifty million dollars of this amount could be saved. This $150,000,000.00 would provide good schoolhouses and six months' teaching for every child, white and black, in the South."

The announcement of these salient facts, together with Dr. Washington's letter, called for co-operation in the observance of National Negro Health Week, caused considerable discussion throughout the country in both white and colored papers. Plans were immediately instituted in all parts of the country to cooperate with Dr. Washington and the National Business League in making this crusade for good health and clean homes effective in every way.

From additional matters sent out from Tuskegee Institute in connection with the National Negro Health Week, we quote the following paragraphs in order to show what a keen appreciation Dr. Washington had of all matters pertaining to the advancement and prosperity of his people:

"Tuskegee Institute, Ala.—In response to numerous calls for suggestions as to how National Negro Health Week may be observed, the following for the first day—Sunday, March 21st—has been issued by the Executive Committee of the National Negro Business League, Dr. Booker T. Washington, President.

"In order that the people may enter heartily into the movement for better health and to the end that the program may be effectively carried out, it is suggested that the ministers of all the colored churches throughout the nation set aside Third Sunday of March as a *Day of Prayer* for better health conditions and that each minister arrange to preach on this day a special health sermon to his congregation.

"In addition to this each minister is requested to arrange, wherever possible, appropriate services which shall include a discussion of local health conditions and any other matters which in his judgment will make the Clean-up Week a success.

"Clean-up Committee.—It is further suggested that each community have a Clean-up Committee which shall investigate the conditions which menace the health of their community, arrange the program to suit these conditions and then see that the program is carried out and that the community is thoroughly and systematically cleaned.

"In cities and communities where there is designated a date other than March 21st to 27th for general cleaning, it may be well for the colored people in such cities and communities to arrange for their cleaning to be done on that date. These suggestions are submitted for cities and communities where no Clean-up Week has been designated."

The following extract from the *New York Age's* report will give some indication of the widespread interest which was aroused by the agitation for better health:

"National Negro Health Week, held March 21 to 27, was another demonstration of the ability of the colored people of the country to co-operate in a movement for their own betterment. This National Negro Health Week also demonstrated how both races, North and South, can get together and work in a movement for the general uplift of the colored people. Never before has there been such a widespread co-operation of the races in a movement for the general good.

"When it was proposed to have a National Negro Health Week, there was some doubt as to whether the colored people would generally co-operate in this effort for their improvement. With the bishops of the several denominations and the ministers taking the lead, there was a general observance by the people throughout the country of Health Week. Several of the bishops wrote special letters to the ministers in their dioceses, urging upon them the importance of their co-operation in this much needed movement for the improvement of the health conditions of the people.

CHAPTER XXXI.

LAST SPEAKING ENGAGEMENTS.

It was a whirlwind finish! With that dogged determination and persistence, which marked Dr. Washington's life, he disregarded the orders of his physicians and the pleadings of his family and friends and spent the last summer of his life in hard work, harder, perhaps, than any summer during the last ten years. In the summer of 1915 he took no vacation. At the close of school, during the last part of May, he immediately left Tuskegee to fill speaking engagements at Meadville, Pennsylvania, and Syracuse, New York, and attended the Fiftieth Anniversary of the Worchester Polytechnic Institute, at Worchester, Massachusetts; he then hurried to New York City to attend meetings of the Trustees of Tuskegee Institute and of Fisk University. Two days later he attended the inauguration of President H. C. Bumpus, of Tuft's College, and returned to Tuskegee in time for the opening of the Summer School for Teachers. During the summer school he delivered a series of lectures to the teachers in attendance. He then returned to New York to meet the Trustees of the Snow Hill Institute, on June 29th, with the Executive Committee of the Anna T. Jeanes Foundation. Immediately at the close of this meeting Dr. Washington left on the New York, New Orleans Limited in order to be in Atlanta upon the evening of July 4th to speak at a meeting which had been arranged by prominent white ministers at the Baptist Tabernacle for four o'clock in the afternoon. At eight o'clock in the same evening he spoke at the Friendship Baptist Church, of which Reverend E. R. Carter is pastor.

On July 10th, in company with Mr. James L. Sibley, the State Supervisor of Negro Rural Schools of Alabama, and a party of other state educators, he motored through the country to the Cottage Grove School, in Coosa County, where Robert W. Taylor, a former student of the Tuskegee Institute, is principal. A week later a series of speaking engagements had to be filled throughout the state of Illinois under the auspices of the Dunbar Chautauqua Association. The first of August found him unusually busy, as he had another series of speaking engagements under the Chautauqua Managers' Association which carried him through Iowa, Kansas, Nebraska and Missouri. Enroute to Boston he stopped at Wocester, Ohio, to deliver an address before the Wocester Academy Summer School, reaching Boston the evening of August 10th, where he met Mrs. Washington, and with her, his son Ernest Davidson Washington, and Doctor and Mrs. J. A. Kenney, he went by boat to Nova Scotia where he was the guest of the colored citizens. After spending a day filled with social activities in Halifax he returned to Boston in time to complete his address for the Negro Business League.

Everyone who has attended any meeting of the National Negro Business League can understand what a large and difficult task it was for Dr. Washington to take charge of all the sessions during the three days and to play his speakers like men in a game of chess in order to get the most effective results in interest and attendance, and then to deliver an important address which must be a message of encouragement to his race for a year to come.

And yet with all the burdens which were thrust upon him in his last summer's work, less than half a dozen persons had any idea that he was so nearly broken down physically as the subsequent events lamentably proved.

At the close of the meeting of the Business League at Boston, Mrs. Washington persuaded him to take a few days' rest in New York City before going to Chicago, where he

Photo Copyrighted by Bedow.
THE BODY OF DR. WASHINGTON LYING IN STATE AT TUSKEGEE INSTITUTE.

FUNERAL PROCESSION ON WAY TO CHAPEL.

was to speak before the annual meeting of the National Baptist Convention. Upon his return to Tuskegee Institute after this meeting arrangements had been made by Mr. Scott, Secretary, for him to take the annual fishing trip at Coden, Alabama, as the guest of Mr. C. W. Allen, Mobile's successful colored undertaker. In company with Mr. Scott, Mr. John A. Kenney, resident physician of the Tuskegee Institute Hospital, Major J. B. Ramsey, Commandant-of-Cadets, Mr. Albert Foster in charge of the Institute Commissary and Mr. Nathan Hunt, traveling secretary, he left Tuskegee on September 18th for Mobile, where he was joined by Dr. George C. Hall, of Chicago, one of his warm personal friends, and a member of the executive committee of the National Negro Business League. From September 18th to October 1st the party fished, hunted and rested, and it was thought that Dr. Washington had regained sufficient strength to take up actively the large amount of work he had outlined for fall. Upon his return to the school after the fishing excursion, he took hold of the work with zest and apparent vigor and handled in his usually effective manner the multitude of details in connection with the opening of the fall term of the Tuskegee Institute.

Invitations from all parts of the country

began to come in as is usual at that time of the year, inviting him to speak at county fairs and various other functions, but in order to conserve his strength and energy he refused to accept any additional invitations. He left Tuskegee on the 23rd of October to deliver the annual address before the American Missionary Association and National Council of Congregational Churches which were to hold a meeting in New Haven, Connecticut, October 25th.

Mrs. Washington during this time was reassured as to the condition of his health on account of the splendid manner in which he had been holding up under the strain of work after his return from Coden, and consented for him to go without her.

When he reached New York on Sunday afternoon, October 24th, he wired Mrs. Washington that he was feeling fine. On Sunday night, the same day, he left for New Haven, Connecticut, where he was to speak the next day, and was to be the house guest of Professor J. E. Schwab of that city. At seven o'clock on the evening of October 25th he was driven in an automobile to Woolsey Hall, where an audience approximating 3,000 were eagerly awaiting his appearance. His speech of that evening was a magnificent effort.

Dr. H. H. Proctor, of Atlanta, Georgia, a

warm friend of Dr. Washington, was on the platform at this meeting, and he said: "Dr. Washington seemed to have summoned every ounce of his latent strength and concentrated it into this eloquent appeal for better educational opportunities for his race." Dr. Washington's speech on this occasion was the last speech of his notable career.

DR. WASHINGTON'S LAST SPEECH.

"A few days ago I visited a little colony of black people near Mobile, Alabama, several of whom were born in Africa and came here on the last slave ship to reach America. Several of the older people still survive and tell interesting stories about their early and varied experiences. A little way from the colony may be seen the hulk of the slave ship on which they were brought to this country.

"This has occurred practically within a single generation. What a transformation has been wrought to my race since the landing of the first slaves at Jamestown and the landing of the last slaves at Mobile. This transformation involves growth in number, mental awakening, self-support, securing of property, moral and religious development, and adjustment of relations between the races. To what in a single generation are we more indebted for this transformation in the direction of a higher civilization than the American Missionary Association?

"I have said we have grown in numbers. Do you realize that today there are as many negroes in the United States as there are persons in the whole of Minnesota, Iowa, Missouri, North Dakota, South Dakota, Nebraska and Kansas? And do you know, as of course you do, that the American Missionary Association was the pioneer factor in the educational work of negroes. Your association established on September 16th, 1861, at Fortress Monroe, Virginia, the first school for freedmen. In this school the first experiment among the freedmen in industrial education was made. Out of this school the Hampton Institute grew. I am, therefore, in a way, the product of your Association.

"No one of the religious organizations which have engaged in the work of educating the negro has done a more useful work than your Association. You are maintaining more schools for the higher and secondary education of the negro than any other board of association. I have had opportunity to visit practically every negro institution in the country. In so doing I have been very favorably impressed with the good work which the educational institutions under the auspices of your Association are doing. I have in mind not only the larger and more prominent schools, such as Fisk and Talladega, but also the smaller and less well known institutions.

"Fifty years ago the education of the negro in the South had just begun. There were less than 100 schools devoted to this purpose. In 1867 there were only 1,938 schools for the freedmen with 2,087 teachers, of whom 699 were colored. There were 111,442 pupils. Eighteen thousand seven hundred and fifty-eight of these pupils were studying the alphabet, 55,163 were in the spelling and easy reading classes, 42,879 were learning to write, 40,454 were studying arithmetic, 4,611 were studying the higher branches. Thirty-five industrial schools were reported, in which there were 2,624 students who were taught sewing, knitting, straw-braiding, repairing and making garments. In 1915 there were almost two million negro children enrolled in the public schools of the South, and over 100,000 in the normal schools and colleges. The 699 colored teachers have increased to over 34,000, of whom 3,000 are teachers in colleges and normal and industrial schools.

"When the American Missionary Association began its work among the freedmen there were in the South no institutions for higher and secondary education of the negro. There were only 4 in the entire United States. In

1915 there are in the South 50 colleges devoted to their training. There are 13 institutions for the education of negro women. There are 26 theological schools and departments. There are 3 schools of law, 4 of medicine, 2 of dentistry, 3 of pharmacy, 17 state agricultural and mechanical colleges, and over 200 normal and industrial schools.

"Fifty years ago the value of the school property used in the education of the freedmen was small. The value of the property now owned by institutions for their secondary and higher training is over $17,000,000. Fifty years ago only a few thousand dollars was being expended for the education of the negroes. In 1914 over $4,100,000 was expended for their higher and industrial training, and $9,700,000 in their public schools.

"Although there has been great progress in negro education during the past fifty years, the equipments and facilities in negro schools are, on the whole, far below those in white schools. The majority of the rural schools in the South are still without school buildings, and the average length of their terms is from three to five months. The negroes constitute about 11 per cent of the total population of the country. A little less than two per cent of the expenditures of the over $700,000,000 expended annually for education is spent upon them. Of the $600,000,000 spent on public schools the negroes receive about one and one-half per cent. More money is spent on special schools for Indians, about $4,800,000 annually, than is expended for higher and industrial training for the negro, a little more than $4,100,000.

"I find in some instances that there is a belief that negro education has advanced far enough for the various philanthropic and religious associations to gradually withdraw their support and use their resources in other directions. The truth of the matter, however, is that after fifty years there is still as great a need for the work of the American Missionary Association and similar organizations to assist in negro education as there was immediately following Emancipation.

"There are about 1,800,000 negro children in the South enrolled in the public schools. This is a large number but not as large, however, as the number not in school. According to the United States census reports, fifty-two per cent of the negro children in the South of school age are not attending school. There are yet in the South over 2,000,000 negroes who are unable to read or write. Almost 1,000,000 of these are of school age.

"Although there are perhaps 100,000 negro students enrolled in normal school and colleges, statistics show that only about one-fourth of these are doing work above the elementary grades. And only about one-third are receiving industrial education. In the fifty colleges devoted to negro education there are, according to statistics, less than 3,000 students who are doing work of the collegiate grade.

"In the North the Jew, the Slav, the Italian, many of whom are such recent arrivals that they have not yet become citizens and voters, even under the easy terms granted them by the federal naturalization laws, have all the advantages of education that are granted to every other portion of the population. In several states an effort is now being made to give immigrant people special opportunities for education over and above those given to the average citizen. In some instances night schools are started for their special benefit. Frequently schools which run nine months in the winter are continued throughout the summer, whenever a sufficient number of people can be induced to attend them. Sometimes, for example, as in New York State, where large number of men were employed in digging the Erie Canal and in excavating the Croton Aqueduct, camp schools were started where the men employed on these public works in the day might have an opportunity to learn the English language at night. In some cases a special kind of textbook, written in two or three different languages, was prepared for use in these immigrant schools, and frequently teachers were specially employed who could teach in the native languages if necessary.

"While in the North all this effort is being made to provide education for these foreign peoples, many of whom are sojourners in this country, and will return in a few months to their homes in Europe, the negro in the South has, as is often true in the country districts, no school at all, or one with a term of no more than four or five months, taught in the wreck of a log cabin and by a teacher who is paid about half the price received for the hire of a first-class convict.

"There is sometimes much talk about the inferiority of the negro. In practice, however, the idea appears to be that he is a sort of super-man. He is expected with about one-fifth or one-tenth of what the whites receive for their education to make as much progress as they are making. Taking the Southern states as a whole, about $10.23 per capita is spent in educating the average white boy or girl, and the sum of $2.82 per capita in educating the average black child.

"In order to furnish the negro with education facilities so that the 2,000,000 children of school age now out of school and the 1,000,000 who are unable to read or write can have the proper chance in life, it will be necessary to increase the $9,000,000 now being expended annually for negro public school education in the South to about $25,000,000 or $50,000,000.

"I find that the total value of all the property owned by institutions devoted to the industrial, secondary and higner training of negroes amounts to about $20,000,000, which is less than the combined values of the property owned by two institutions alone—the University of Chicago and Columbia University. The total value of the property owned by institutions for whites in the United States for secondary, higher and industrial training amounts to almost one billion dollars. The value of the manual training and industrial schools for whites is almost fifty million dollars. If the amount of property devoted to negro higher education was at all proportionate to their numbers in the population of the country, they would have for their higher training about one hundred million dollars invested in property instead of the twenty million dollars which they now have.

"In order to give the negro youth in the South adequate facilities for obtaining thorough training in normal and college courses, it will be necessary to increase the little more than $4,000,000 now being expended annually for negro higher and secondary education to $10,000,000 or more. In other words, negro higher and secondary education needs about $6,000,000 more annually than it is now receiving.

"At the present rate it is taking not a few days or a few years, but a century or more to get negro education on a plane at all similar to that on which the education of the whites is. To bring negro education up where it ought to be it will take the combined and increased efforts of all the agencies now engaged in this work. The North, the South, the religious associations, the educational boards, white people and black people, all will have to co-operate in a great effort for this common end."

CHAPTER XXXII.

SICKNESS—DEATH.

An important meeting of the Investment Committee of the Board of Trustees of the Tuskegee Normal and Industrial Institute had been called by Mr. William G. Willcox, a member of the Board of Trustees for October 26th, at 11:00 a. m. in New York City, and in order to be present at this meeting Dr. Washington, accompanied by Mr. Hunt, left New Haven where he had spoken the night before, on the midnight boat and reached New York City on the morning of the 26th at about nine o'clock. During the progress of this meeting Mr. Willcox, the Honorable Seth Low and Mr. Frank Trumbull were present and noted the first serious indication of a probable collapse of Dr. Washington, and they very vigorously protested against the strenuous activities which they knew he had outlined for the fall and winter. Dr. Washington, however, felt that he owed it to himself and to the colored people in Virginia who had planned a big meeting for him at Petersburg, which was scheduled for November 5th, to visit that place. It was two or three days later before he finally consented to go to the Rockefeller Institute in company with Mr. Willcox, where he was to have a physical examination. The result of this examination astonished the specialists in charge of the case and they stated that it was almost unbelievable that a man in his worn out physical condition could have withstood the gruelling pressure to which Dr. Washington had subjected himself in connection with his varied activities. On the evening of the 4th, he left the Herald Square Hotel where he was stopping, in company with Mr. Willcox, thinking he was going to catch the train for Petersburg, where he was to speak the next day, but instead of going to the Pennsylvania station the automobile carried him to St. Luke's Hospital, where he was put under the care of trained nurse and a physician. By this time word had been forwarded to Mrs. Washington and she had left Tuskegee Institute to be present at his bedside. The people at the Tuskegee Institute and the institute community had some slight indication of his illness, but were not aware of its seriousness until on the morning of the 10th of November, the following despatch appeared in the *Montgomery (Alabama) Advertiser:*

"Suffering from a nervous breakdown Dr. Booker T. Washington, principal of Tuskegee Institute, is confined in a private room in St. Luke's Hospital.

" 'Dr. Washington has been suffering from severe headaches for more than a month,' said Dr. Bastedo tonight. 'His condition became serious enough to alarm the trustees, who I understand have no successor in mind for the position as principal. I made an examination of Dr. Washington a few days ago and found him completely worn out. He has been overworking and was in no condition to resume his work at Tuskegee.

" 'There is a noticeable hardening of the arteries and he is extremely nervous.' "

On November 9th the inaugural exercises of Dr. F. A. McKenzie, the newly elected president of Fisk University, were scheduled, but on account of Dr. Washington's condition, who was on the program as one of the speakers, Mr. Emmett J. Scott represented the Tuskegee Institute. Present at this meeting was Mr. Julius Rosenwald, who is also a trustee of Tuskegee Institute. From Nashville Mr. Rosenwald had planned to come to Tuskegee and spend a day, and it had been Dr. Washington's earnest desire to be at Tuskegee Institute when Mr. Rosenwald came. When Mr. Scott and Mr. Rosenwald reached Tuskegee on the morning of the 10th they found the school wrapped in gloom over the press despatch which had been published in the *Montgomery Advertiser*, and on the evening of the same day when Mr. Rosenwald spoke in the chapel, expressions of regret over Principal Washington's absence and condition were mentioned by Mr. Rosenwald, Mr. Warren Logan, treasurer, and Mr. C. W. Hare of Tuskegee, Alabama, a trustee of the school. During the afternoon Mr. Scott had received a telegram from New York City which seemed to indicate that the condition of Dr. Washington was not quite as serious as was indicated in the press despatch, and in the course of his remarks he read this telegram which seemed to relieve the tension of the hour.

The next day Mr. Rosenwald spent in visiting the various trades and industries of the school, and also attended the Annual Chrysanthemum Show which is under the general direction of a committee of ladies of which Mrs. Emmett J. Scott is chairman. Dr. Washington always took great pride and interest in these chrysanthemum shows, and whenever it was possible always managed to be present.

The following telegram, sent to Mrs. Scott on the morning of the 11th, indicated Dr. Washington's interest in the success of this event:

"It pains me very greatly that I cannot be present at the Chrysanthemum Show, but I know nothing has been spared to make it a success. You can count on my usual contribution as soon as I get home. I congratulate all of you on what you are doing."

The next day Mr. Scott received a telegram referring to some business matters in connection with his office and Dr. Washington's plans for the fall campaign work, and everywhere there seemed to be a feeling of encouragement over the principal's condition. Late on the afternoon of the 12th, Mrs. Scott had a telegram from Mrs. Washington stating that Dr. Washington would leave New York the next day for Tuskegee and would reach Tuskegee late Saturday night. There was nothing further to cause serious alarm over the situation until Saturday morning when a telegram was sent from Charlotte, N. C., by Mrs. Washington to Mr. Scott instructing him to have the ambulance to meet the train which was due to pass Chehaw at nine oclock in the evening, and to inform Booker T. Washington, Jr., and Dr. Washington's brother, Mr. John H. Washington, to be at the station and to notify his daughter, Mrs. W. Sydney Pittman of Dallas, Texas, to come to Tuskegee at once.

Dr. Washington's passing was as simple as the life which he had lived. Realizing that the end was near, he asked that he be brought from New York to the South—the South in which he had been born, in and for which he had labored, and where he had always declared his intention to die and be buried. And so, with his wife, Dr. J. A. Kenny of the Tuskegee Institute, and his stenographer, Nathan Hunt, the long trip was begun.

All day Saturday as the train sped Southward Dr. Washington lay in a comatose condition and was apparently unaware of his surroundings; when the train reached Chehaw Mrs. Washington aroused him and said, "Father, this is Chehaw"; the word "Chehaw" seemed to arouse him briefly and when his son Booker T. Washington, Jr., appeared he asked him "How is Booker?" meaning Booker T. Washington III, the infant son of Booker T. Washington, Jr. Carefully his cot was lifted from the train by tender and loving hands and placed in the ambulance where warm blankets had been prepared and kept waiting to place around his body. Then began

THE BURIAL. DR. WASHINGTON BEING LAID TO REST AMID THE SCENES HE LOVED BEST.

DR. WASHINGTON'S GRAVE A PYRAMID OF FLOWERS.

the slow drive to Tuskegee Institute. The ambulance reached the principal's residence, "The Oaks," about ten minutes past twelve o'clock, and he was at once carried to his room and placed under the care of a trained nurse and an effort made to arouse him from his semi-unconscious condition. He never regained consciousness and at 4:15 o'clock Sunday morning, November 14th, surrounded by those members of his family who were present, Dr. Booker T. Washington breathed his last, and thus carried out his oft-expressed wish when he said: "I was born in the South; I have lived in the South and I expect to die and be buried in the South."

Thus ended the career of a man whose notable achievements and energy, lifted his race from the depths of ignorance and placed it upon the plane of intelligence and industrial efficiency where mankind may see more and more its good qualities and regard it with more tolerant spirit.

On the morning of November 14th, Associated Press despatches were sent out from Tuskegee Institute and immediately long distance telephone calls and telegrams began to pour into Tuskegee bearing words of sympathy and condolence to the grief-stricken family and relatives.

452 THE STORY OF MY LIFE AND WORK,

The Sunday morning sermon by Chaplain Whittaker was in behalf of "Bleeding Armenia," because it was what the late Dr. Washington had wanted done. But the sweetness was gone from the songs of the students; and when the choir sang, "Still, Still with Thee," hearts broke.

Booker Washington's life was dedicated to the education and uplift of his race and the promotion of better relations between negroes and whites throughout the country.

In season and out he carried the message of economic fitness for the negro and of peace between the races. In particular he hoped, he believed, that in the South the negro would at last find his greatest opportunity; and he was, to the end, a friend of the South. With his passing this section and the whole country has lost a great friend.

The Tuskegee educator's life was replete with many unselfish activities in behalf of his race. Possessing rare executive and constructive ability, he devoted himself with much self-sacrifice to the upbuilding and regeneration of his race along moral, material and educational lines. The National Negro Business League, composed of negro business men and women, is the product of his creative genius and has come to a place of commanding influence in the life of the negro people.

He is survived by his wife, a brother, John H. Washington, superintendent of industries, three children and four grandchildren.

The funeral exercises were held on the Institute grounds, Wednesday morning at 10 o'clock, and the body was buried on the grounds of the school to build which his life had been given. The remains lay in state in the Institute chapel from 12 o'clock mid-day, Tuesday, until Wednesday, November 17th.

CHAPTER XXXIII.

THE FUNERAL.

Dr. Booker T. Washington, most famous negro in the world, the man who climbed "Up from Slavery," until he stood before kings and nobles in Europe had received more distinguished honors in America than have ever been accorded to any other negro, was buried at Tuskegee Wednesday with the same simplicity and lack of studied pomp and ceremony with which God's own hand buried Moses in the land of Moab.

No labored eulogies; no boastings of his great work; no gorgeous trappings of horses; no streaming banners; no mysterious ceremonies of lodges—just the usual line of teachers, trustees, graduates, students and visitors which so often marched to the chapel just as it did Wednesday, and the simple and impressive service for the dead, said for the humblest, said so often for those who die in all walks of life.

If there was aught out of the ordinary it was the great crowd of negro leaders from all parts of the continent, the hosts of whites, the multitudes of the simple country folk whom Dr. Washington loved so well, the flowers and plants sent in offering to the dead, a casket before which student guards changed watch every few minutes during the entire service and the tears which fell from all faces.

But any other kind of service less simple would have mocked the kind of life that Dr. Washington had lived.

At high noon Tuesday the remains of the distinguished negro leader were placed into a hearse driven by students and escorted from "The Oaks" by Vice Principal Warren Logan and Secretary Emmett J. Scott, and a guard of forty-four officers of the student batallions to the Institute chapel where it lay in state until Wednesday. Thousands gazed into the casket where the dead chieftain lay.

At twenty minutes after ten Wednesday morning a procession line, composed of trustees, faculty, alumni, visitors, honorary and active pall-bearers and students, began to move slowly from "The Oaks" toward the chapel. The line was long and moved to the beat of muffled drums.

Inside the building was packed to suffocation. Chaplain John W. Whittaker and Dean G. L. Imes of the Phelp's Hall Bible School, conducted the services.

Softly the choir began singing a negro melody: "We Shall Walk Through the Valley and Shadow of Death in Peace." No songs were so sweet to Dr. Washington as these melodies of his race. Before the sweetness of the song had died away the chaplain was intoning the simple words of the most simple burial service. A pause, and the school was singing "How Firm a Foundation." More reading of the burial service and the choir rendered Cardinal Newman's deathless classic —"Lead Kindly Light Amid the Encircling Gloom."

Here prayer was made by Dr. H. B. Fissell, president of Hampton Institute and one of Dr. Washington's former teachers. The choir then sang a melody, "Tell All My Father's Children Don't You Grieve for Me," and "Swing Low, Sweet Chariot."

At this point Secretary Scott read a telegram of consolation from Seth Low of New York, president of the board of trustees, in which the support of that body was unqualifiedly promised to the school. Trustee Wm. G. Willcox of New York next brought a strong message of encouragement.

"Still, Still with Thee" was rendered, the benediction pronounced and the casket and audience moved to a vault, just outside of the chapel.

Briefly the last words of the burial service were said, the Institute bandmaster stood at the head of the vault and sounded "taps" and a heavy-hearted crowd turned slowly and sadly away from the tomb of their prophet.

An unusual honor was accorded this leader of his people by Mayor E. W. Thompson of the town of Tuskegee. Mayor Thompson personally carried a petition to all the business houses of the town and asked them to agree to close their stores during the funeral services. All were glad to do so.

Throughout the town there was general sadness and there were none who had aught but the kindest words about Dr. Washington's life.

But most pathetic of all was the sight of the humble and unlettered colored people of the cotton fields who literally packed the school grounds. They had sustained a loss which they did not know how to voice. You could see them looking into every face near them for encouragement to say how much they were hurt and would miss their devoted friend.

Unless the visitors Wednesday had been with Dr. Washington through a quarter of a century and observed how much he loved these simple poor of his race, how anxiously he worked to help them, he could not understand how broken-hearted these older colored people were. In the past, when they had come to Tuskegee, Dr. Washington had treated them as if they were princes. They were thinking of this when they gazed for the last time upon his silent form.

One old couple, themselves near the sunset of life, walked a long, long distance to be here. Piteously the man approached one of the instructors and, with trembling lips and eyes that overflowed, asked: "Do you reckon they will let us see Booker?" and he hurried to explain: "We have come so fur jes' to see him de las' time. Do you reckon they will mind us looking at him?" They were escorted to the casket and given their heart's desire; for Dr. Washington's love for them when he was here cannot be described.

Mr. Scott in his brief remarks said: "In obedience to Mr. Washington's wishes, and in response to his specific request, we have kept these exercises absolutely simple—just as he would have us keep them. We here have felt that this day is a day too sacred to have even an eulogy imposed upon it. We here have felt as was said of Sir Christopher Wren, one of the earliest and greatest of English architects: 'If you would find his monument, look about you'—at these buildings and grounds at this outpouring of love, this tribute of affection and respect.

"Literally from the ends of the continent there have come to cheer the wife and the children and those of us who have labored here with him, hundreds of messages testifying to a nation's loss, to the loss which has befallen a race.

"His wife and Mr. Logan, vice president of the institution, and others of us have felt that from the great sheaf of messages which have come here, the one from the chairman of the Board of Trustees, Mr. Low, who is prevented from being here today, should at least be read. We will then have a message from the Board of Trustees brought by Mr. William G. Willcox, of New York City, who with Dr. Schieffelin has journeyed all the long way from New York City to mourn with us today."

Mr. Low's telegram was as follows: "On behalf of the Board of Trustees I send to you and through you to the officers, teachers and students to the Tuskegee Institute our warmest sympathy in the death of the school's great founder, Booker T. Washington. In his death the country has lost a great patriot and the negro race an inspiring leader. It is now the hour to show, without his magnetic presence, by loyalty to the school and to his high ideals, how truly you have caught the inspiration of his spirit and of his devoted life of service. The Trustees will not fail you in your hour of need and in keeping Tuskegee a worthy memorial of the great man with whom you have worked so long and well.

"(Signed) SETH LOW, Chairman,
"Board of Trustees."

CHAPTER XXXIV.

THE TUSKEGEE ORGANIZATION AND THE TUSKEGEE SPIRIT.

The heads of the different departments and divisions at Tuskegee Institute are men of vision and stalwart character whose abilities and careful training have been broadened by experience and an intimate personal contact with the greatest character their race has yet produced. These are the men who constituted the "Old Guard" for Dr. Washington and who have stood at his back and been his prop during the pioneering days and early struggles of Tuskegee Institute. And now with his passing and the widespread speculation as to the future of Tuskegee Institute, it is not the voice of an optimist who says the future of Tuskegee Institute is hopeful, but rather a just conclusion based upon the merits and capabilities of the men who must bear the future burdens.

In addition to their own individual abilities and experiences, those who come after Dr. Washington have the sustaining help and encouragement of the Board of Trustees who, through their chairman, Honorable Seth Low, said: "The Trustees will not fail you in your hour of need," and the sympathetic interest of the most cordial sentiment throughout the South reflected in the expression of a Southern white man who said: "The South will do its part." Then there is "The Tuskegee Spirit," the tie which binds them closer than brothers and knits together their interests and ambitions into a common bond of co-operation for the ultimate good of Tuskegee Institute. "The Tuskegee Spirit" is bigger than Tuskegee and gives to those who possess it a bigger and broader conception of life and the fullness of its duties and responsibilities. It is the reflected personality of the man who came "Up from Slavery" and immortalized his name by giving his own life in the full bloom of manhood in order that his race might be exalted and humanity made happier.

The Tuskegee spirit pervades the atmosphere at Tuskegee Institute and students and teachers alike feel the beneficent influence of its mighty power. Graduates leave and carry it with them into their respective communities and there it helps them live more useful lives and to make happier and better those with whom they come in contact. Without "The Tuskegee Spirit" neither student nor teacher can long survive at Tuskegee Institute. It is the mighty force which will carry the work of Tuskegee Institute on to higher and nobler achievements.

---

*Forty-eight pages are here added to the folios to include full page illustrations not before numbered, making a total of 510 pages.

Credit is due Mr. Isaac Fisher and *The Montgomery Advertiser* for the chapter relating to the funeral of Mr. Washington, and Mr. Clement Richardson for material used in chapter relating to Rural Extension Work.